THE LORD OF THE RINGS

THE FILMS, THE BOOKS, THE RADIO SERIES

Jim Smith and
J Clive Matthews

Dedicated to the memory of Professor Michael Mason, a great critic, editor and tutor, who taught me so much and who should be teaching still
JES

For my Grandmother, Mrs DM Clive-Matthews, for going on about the pixies at the bottom of the garden and so probably getting me interested in all this in the first place
JCM

First published in Great Britain in 2004
by Virgin Books Ltd
Thames Wharf Studios
Rainville Road
London
W6 9HA

A catalogue record for this book is available from the British Library.

ISBN 0 7535 0874 5

Typeset by TW Typesetting, Plymouth, Devon
Printed and bound in Great Britain by
Mackays of Chatham PLC

ACKNOWLEDGEMENTS

The authors are indebted to the following for their assistance, patience, time and other contributions, both small and large, knowing and unknowing, to the writing of this book.

Kirstie Addis, Danielle Askew, Scott Bassett, Steve Bassett, www.b3ta.com, Mark Clapham, NP Clive-Matthews, Robin Clive-Matthews, David Collings, Jason Douglas, Stephen Lavington, Christopher Lee, Eri Miyazaki, Dr Richard North, Kirk O'Connor, Dr Henry Potts, Tasha Robinson at The Onion AV Club, Eddie Robson, everyone at Romsey Publishing, Martin Rynja, Matt Symonds, Tehanu at www.TheOneRing.net, Stephen Thompson at The Onion AV Club, Ben Williams and the office of Saul Zaentz.

Special thanks to our respective parental units, the staffs of the BFI Library and The British Library, especially the Rare Books room of the latter institution.

Material taken from The Onion AV club (www.theonion.com) is © The Onion AV Club and used with permission.

CONTENTS

INTRODUCTION

Let us start out by stating what this book is not. This is not a biography of the late JRR Tolkien. Neither is it an attempt at a study (or deconstruction) of the vast written output of his imagination; a mind called by one critic 'the creative equivalent of a people'. There are many such books available, the best of them produced by, or under the supervision of, his son Christopher – the distinguished academic – and available from the Tolkiens' publisher, HarperCollins. We would point you to any, or all, of those for a full and exhaustive discussion of the ferociously imagined world in which most of JRR Tolkien's work (including *The Lord of the Rings*, his best known piece) take place. However, it is worth remembering that when it comes to understanding, and appreciating, any work there is simply no substitute for experiencing it. To those who are fans of Peter Jackson's film trilogy rather than the books it draws upon, we've only one thing to say: go and read Tolkien now. This book doesn't really deal in synopses or summaries and assumes a fair, though not exhaustive, knowledge of the two books printed during JRR Tolkien's lifetime and set in Middle-earth: *The Hobbit* and *The Lord of the Rings*.

So, rather than any of those things above, this book is an attempt to examine the process(es) whereby Tolkien's books have been adapted into performed drama. This means principally, in Tolkien's case, 'adapted for the screen', but we are also taking in another significant adaptation – the 1981 BBC radio serial.

The best known adaptation of Tolkien is undoubtedly the Peter Jackson produced/directed film 'trilogy' as produced and released through New Line Cinema in 2001–2003. This brought the professor's work to the attention of more readers and admirers than ever before, but there are other productions besides, including television specials and cartoons, and all are discussed, debated and compared within. All are, we hope, examined in an equal, fair and respectful way, with production facts, critical comparisons and details of how the books found their way on to the screen. The process of adaptation from one medium to another is our primary interest here; how a beloved book becomes a beloved (or not beloved) film. How the strengths of one medium can become the weaknesses of another, how what is acceptable on the page can seem foolish on screen (or vice versa) and how the difficulties of transplanting something designed for one mass medium to another are overcome.

Both of us read Tolkien's books as children, and enjoyed them again as adults; we appreciate the artistry and skill of all the adaptations of them covered here and any criticisms and qualifications we make herein need to be understood in the context of our vast mutual appreciation both of the books and the films as wholes.

Throughout this book, you will find the chapters on the individual projects in roughly chronological sequence broken down into small chunks of a few hundred (occasionally thousand) words. These all have headings in bold capitals. Some headings are used once, or sparingly, and some recur many times. Hopefully this format (and the index) will allow a reader familiar with Tolkien (or Rankin/Bass, or Jackson, for that matter) to locate quickly a particular topic of interest to them, to discover what we have to say about a particular character, place, trait, actor or theme as easily as possible. There are also a few 'boxouts' of the kind typical to books in this series, including our own previous entries, where we attempt to pull together threads that may otherwise be too widely dispersed throughout the wordcount. We both hope, however, that you will approach our book in the traditional manner, beginning at the beginning and going through until reaching the end in due course. It may not be a journey as long as that undertaken by Frodo Baggins to destroy the One Ring and save Middle-earth from Sauron, but we hope it may amuse, enlighten and provoke discussion of all the works that we look at in the following pages. This is ultimately a book of commentary and opinion and, above all, respect is due to the creators of what we are examining here.

J Smith and J Clive Matthews, 30 January 2004

OF THE BEGINNING OF DAYS: JRR TOLKIEN AND THE BOOKS

In 2003, viewers of the BBC's *The Big Read* voted *The Lord of the Rings* 'The Nation's Favourite Novel' of all time. This came hard upon the similar election of it, in 1999, as the country's favourite novel of the twentieth century. Yet it is arguable that *The Lord of the Rings* is not really a 'novel' at all, nor even 'fantasy', as so many newspapers have described it. Tolkien himself always demurred at the term 'fantasy', which had yet to take on fully the 'sword and sorcery' connotations it has now. He preferred the term 'heroic romance' – an old designation recalling the poetry of Edmund Spenser (which he actually disliked) and even pre-Renaissance literature that, in retrospect, had as much chance of becoming accepted nomenclature as HG Wells's own 'scientific romance' had of displacing the (much hated by him) term 'science fiction'.

JRR Tolkien (1892–1973) was not a novelist by trade or profession; he was a university researcher and lecturer with a professional interest in central and northern European mythology. He was not a writer who deliberately set out to create a bestseller, but an academic who came up with one unwittingly, as an offshoot of a combination of a life-long academic pursuit and a story designed to amuse his own children.

Nevertheless, the vast commercial success of *The Lord of the Rings*, and the devoted fanbase it has inspired, means that Tolkien is, in the eyes of many, synonymous with this one part of one single aspect of his academic work – a perception which has only increased in the years since the 2001 release of the initial film in the Peter Jackson-directed triumvirate of motion pictures based on it.

It is important to remember that, partly because of this immense popularity, Tolkien has become as much a mythical figure as those creatures he set out to create, recreate and record. His life has often become, in the reporting, little more than a series of incidents perceived as serving as inspiration for episodes in *The Lord of the Rings*. Thus, an incident where Tolkien was frightened by a spider as a child is identified as the source of Shelob. The fact that arachnophobia is a common, nearly universal psychological defect in Western society (and thus spiders constitute a fairly obvious horror device) is ignored in favour of a single moment, simply because it happened to an author.

Much as the world of Middle-earth is far more complex than can be perceived simply by reading *The Hobbit* or *The Lord of the Rings*, so Tolkien's life was far more complex than such an approach would suggest. Indeed, due to the nature of what he was writing, Tolkien deliberately tried to keep any sense that there was an author at all out of his most famous work. Tolkien was creating a myth; myths do not have mere authors.

THE VOYAGE OF EARENDEL THE EVENING STAR

The Lord of the Rings is just a small part of six decades' work, almost all of which was left unpublished on Tolkien's death at the age of 81 on 2 September 1973. Tolkien's biographer, Humphrey Carpenter, has identified the summer of 1914 as the time that Tolkien wrote the lines that were to evolve into *The Silmarillion*, his dense guidebook to/history of the peoples and language of Middle-earth that was ultimately published in 1977. In a poem entitled *The Voyage of Earendel the Evening Star*, the 22-year-old Tolkien took the first step towards creating his own fictional world. Asked by his close friend, Geoffrey Smith, what the poem was about, Tolkien replied that he didn't know but that he'd attempt to find out.

The name 'Earendel' had come from two lines in the *Crist* of Cynewulf, a group of Anglo-Saxon religious poems Tolkien had come across while studying at Oxford University:

Eala Earendel engla beorhtast
Ofer middangeard monnum sended.

'Hail Earendel brightest of angels/above the middle-earth sent unto men.' (The 'middle earth' was the world of men, the 'lower earth' hell, the 'upper earth' Heaven, so the second line can also be translated as 'by God sent unto men'.)

Tolkien knew Earendel to be a reference to John the Baptist, or perhaps Venus, the morning star, but at the same time, thanks to his study of ancient European languages, felt the name to have something older than Anglo-Saxon about it. The name's lost origins prompted him to explore more fully what may originally have been intended as no more than another of the many poems he had enjoyed writing while at school and university. By the time *The Silmarillion* was published more than sixty years later, 'Earendel' had become 'Eärendil' the half-elven, father of Elrond of Rivendell and distant ancestor (through Elrond's brother Elros) of Aragorn – both important characters in *The Lord of the Rings*.

There were few 22-year-olds familiar with Anglo-Saxon poetry even in 1914, and there are far fewer now. Tolkien's interest largely stemmed from his late discovery of his mother country, which he saw for the first time at the age of four.

JRR Tolkien was born in South Africa on 3 January 1892, in Bloemfontein, the capital of the Orange Free State, to a mother who had travelled there from Birmingham to be with, and marry, a man thirteen years her senior. (Tolkien's father worked in the Bank of Africa there.) Tolkien, referred to by his family by his second given name of Ronald, suffered ill health in the hot climate and his parents decided to return to England not long after the birth of his younger brother Hillary. The boys' father remained in Africa for work-related reasons and was expected to rejoin his family after a short interval. Just after New Year 1896, his family received the news that he had died of a haemorrhage after a severe case of rheumatic fever.

Tolkien, his younger brother Hillary and their mother Mabel went to live with her family, the Suffields, in Ashfield Road, Birmingham. Ronald also came into contact with his father's family, the Tolkiens, for the first time and was introduced to their overly romanticised family history, which included myth-making tales of ancestors escaping from the guillotine during the French Revolution, and others who fought at the Siege of Vienna in 1829. It was there, according to a Tolkien aunt, that the family – until then Von Hohenzollern – gained the new name Tollkuhn, German for 'foolhardy'. In 1896, Tolkien, along with his mother and brother, moved to the hamlet of Sarehole, near Moseley, about a mile from Birmingham. (Moseley is now contained within the urban sprawl of Britain's second largest city, but then it was considered a separate village and was surrounded by considerable countryside.) In 1900, Tolkien passed the entrance examination to King Edward VI Grammar School (Kes) in Birmingham, the highest academically achieving school in the city. A Tolkien uncle with money to spare paid JRR's fees, and initially Tolkien attended Kes, but in that same year his Mother had undergone a dramatic conversion to Roman Catholicism – incurring the wrath, and losing the financial support, of her Baptist/Methodist family in the process.

JRR Tolkien moved to St Philip's – a far less academically distinguished but, crucially, Catholic school on the other side of Birmingham. As is the way of these things, Mabel's children converted to Catholicism too. Mother and sons moved around the Birmingham area for a time, living in both King's Heath and Edgbaston, as Mabel attempted to find a church of which she was sufficiently enamoured to attend permanently. Eventually Tolkien returned to Kes on a scholarship basis after it became clear that, even if it was good for his piety, his education was suffering at St Philip's. It was here that he encountered teacher George Brewerton, who fuelled the boy's already developing interest in languages by introducing him to Greek. Brewerton also introduced Tolkien to Shakespeare, which the student affected to dislike, and Chaucer, whose 'purer' and earlier form of English appealed to him greatly. Brewerton was a staunch, even aggressive, medievalist with a profound dislike for words he regarded as 'imported' into English unnaturally, in particular French spellings and syntax. He would pass these obsessions on to his pupil who, at the Oxford Union, would be the student who tabled the motion – 'The house deplores the success of the Norman Conquest'.

From a very early age, Tolkien had invented his own languages as a hobby, in the way that children often do, but he continued to do so into adolescence and adulthood; he had created more than twenty of them by the time of his death. Even as a teenager Tolkien's method of language construction was more sophisticated than that, employed by children playing such games, of continuing to use English words – and, more importantly, syntax – as a basis and simply substituting made-up terms for expressions from proper English. His first language using something other

7

than English as a basis was Naffah, which was derived from books in Spanish owned by the Tolkien family Priest and confessor – Father Francis Morgan. It was also Morgan who, according to Mabel Tolkien's will, and despite there being many of her family still living, should become her sons' legal guardian in the event of her death before their reaching maturity. This did indeed take place: she died after slipping into a coma, caused by her recently diagnosed diabetes, in November 1904. Tolkien and his brother were now wards of the Roman Catholic Church.

In adolescence, Tolkien's creation of languages became even more complex. He took to creating words to fill holes in languages for which only an incomplete vocabulary was extant. He conjectured common roots for both the words he had discovered in textbooks and his own conjectural vocabulary. This led to the creation of whole languages with their own rules, logic, grammar and syntax. It is in these, which eventually led to the Elvish languages *Quenya* and *Sindarin*, the Black speech of Mordor, Dwarvish and so on, that the essential roots of Middle-earth and thus the story of the One Ring lie.

After studying at Oxford and gaining a First in English, the first step on his road to the professional pursuit of his interests, Tolkien served in the First World War. He managed to survive the Battle of the Somme, but nearly all of his closest friends were killed. After returning from the front, he worked for a time as an assistant lexicographer on the *Oxford English Dictionary*, thanks to his studies of English writing, traditions and philology (the study of the history of words). Later, as his career progressed, he taught at the University of Leeds, and then became a don at Oxford, where his scholarly reputation grew.

Tolkien wrote his fiction in his spare time. A jovial and deeply spiritual man, he was good friends with CS Lewis, and the two discussed their novels while they were writing them. Tolkien was delighted with the popular success of his novels in many ways, but he always fought their interpretation as allegory. To him, they simply were what they were, and the American college campus craze of the late 1960s, with its embrace of his work towards unintended ends, was a source of consternation. In 1972, he was awarded a CBE by Her Majesty the Queen.

Upon Tolkien's death in 1973, his youngest son and literary executor, Christopher Tolkien, an Oxford don in his own right, prepared his father's great cosmology of Middle-earth, *The Silmarillion*, for publication. Christopher later produced a twelve-volume account of the origins, evolution, and writing of his father's epic tales, *The History of Middle-earth*, and collaborated with his father's authorised biographer, Humphrey Carpenter, in publishing a selection of his letters.

EVEN THE VERY WISE CANNOT SEE ALL ENDS

Thanks to Christopher Tolkien's efforts, the vast majority of his father's work on Middle-earth is available for his fans to study in detail. This has only added to what was already within his lifetime a loyal, near-obsessive fanbase, and spawned a vast network of fans and critics devoted to analysing his work – of which the book you hold in your hands is just a small part. Tolkien's work has become at least as discussed and analysed as that of any twentieth-century author although, thanks to the vast extent of his notes and writings, there is as yet little consensus about his intentions and meanings. Aspects of Tolkien's work can still be interpreted in any number of ways: hence the difficulty that has been encountered by those who have been charged with adapting it for other media.

It is hard to miss the 'Englishness' of Tolkien's hobbits. The Shire and its inhabitants were consciously modelled on the idealised version of England that Tolkien remembered from his first arrival in the country. This hobbit-equals-English concept has, however, led to many attempts to read more into *The Lord of the Rings* than is actually there, something that people have seen as especially compounded by the simple fact that the books that relate the tale of the War of the Ring were written during and after the Second World War. Is Frodo's reluctant undertaking to destroy the Ring analogous to Britain's reluctant undertaking to go to war in 1939? Is Mordor Nazi Germany? Is Sauron Hitler? Is the Ring the atomic bomb? The answer to all of these is an emphatic 'No'. Throughout his life, Tolkien denied any attempt to create an elaborate or extensive analogy in his books with the events of the 30s and 40s. In fact, he vigorously denied the presence of any overarching allegorical or analogical element in any part of his work.

Comparisons between the Second World War and the War of the Ring are of no more value than comparisons between the events of the books and the US-led 'War on Terror', which followed the 11 September 2001 attacks in New York and Washington. Viggo Mortensen, the actor who plays Aragorn in Peter Jackson's film trilogy, found himself hotly debating this topic while ostensibly promoting *The Lord of the Rings: The Two Towers* in 2002 – 'I don't think that . . . Tolkien's writing, or our work, has anything to do with the United States' foreign "ventures",' he told more than one reporter. The simple fact that the title of the second published volume of *The Lord of the Rings* has led to comparisons with the twin towers of the World Trade Center in New York, destroyed in the September 2001 terrorist attacks (and the interpretation of more than one American critic that the film of *The Lord of the Rings: The Two Towers* endorsed the American-led invasion of Iraq in 2003), should make clear how wary any commentator should be when perceiving anterior references to the 'real world' in a work of 'heroic romance' founded in the mythology of an age two millennia removed from commentator's own. (It should be noted, incidentally, that the cast and crew of the Jackson trilogy debated among themselves, and came to no agreement, on how *The Lord of the Rings* could and should be applied to events contemporaneous to the release of the movies. Andy Serkis (Gollum) noted that 'There are big disagreements within the cast about this, but I think [September 11/the War on Terror] changed people's viewing [experiences] of the films hugely. The world has changed . . . Fran [Walsh, Jackson's wife and principal co-writer] and Peter are sensitive people who know what's going on in the world. You can't deny, you can't help it. It certainly affected the way I played Gollum.')

That is not to say, of course, that at no point in *The Lord of the Rings* does reality intrude incidentally. It is rather more likely, for example, that Tolkien's experiences on the Western Front during the First World War, during which many of his close friends (including Geoffrey Smith) were killed, played a part in his vivid depiction of the mud, brutality, terror and senselessness of combat. It is equally likely that the fate of Frodo Baggins, who is so ruined by the experience of fighting to save the world that he can no longer live in it, could be a reference to the experience of many soldiers returning from war who have been forever changed by their experience – be it the ostracising of Vietnam vets in the 1970s, or 'Gulf War Syndrome' in the 1990s.

However, acknowledgment of such parallels does not demand acceptance of the wider analogy suggested by some. Acknowledgement of the archetypal officer/batman relationship as expressed, perhaps unknowingly, through the shared adversity of the 'Master of Bag End' Frodo Baggins (who is nearly crushed by responsibility) and his humbler gardener Samwise Gamgee (who is uncomplaining and loyal), does not require a reader to construct elaborate parallels between the War of the Ring and the Western Front.

Despite being a major part of Tolkien's personal life, religion, either implicit or explicit, is largely absent from his creation of Middle-earth. This was something noted with approval by, among others, the actor Sir Ian McKellen, who plays Gandalf in the Jackson trilogy (on his excellent website, www.mckellen.com). Certainly there is no organised religion of any kind referred to at any point. The hobbits, the characters that the audience is most expected to identify with, don't understand when – while eating with the elves – the more ancient, spiritually aware creatures turn their heads so they are looking westwards in a form of saying Grace in thanks for their food. The more earthly hobbits are simply confused by this action, which makes no sense in their understanding of the world. Although it is possible to identify religious subtexts and allegories within the text, these are no more prominent than any of the other many ideas that run throughout and, again, Tolkien himself largely denied them.

There are naturally other central aspects to *The Lord of the Rings*. For Tolkien it was openly about the preservation of 'that Noble Northern spirit' which he found in the central European mythologies he studied. A rescuing of, even redemption of, the stories and archetypes that had been put to the service of the Nazis, Nietzsche, Wagner and the Prussian military tradition. During the composition of *The Lord of the Rings* and its antecedents these traditions were being co-opted by National Socialism into the creation of a society which would commit worse crimes than any conceived of even by Tolkien's vilest inhuman creations. All these are aggressive, condemnatory, exclusive interpretations of that mythology to which Tolkien was personally opposed.

Is *The Lord of the Rings* actually any good? While millions have enjoyed the films *and* the book, many who have discovered the book through its adaptations would secretly admit to finding them rather harder to read than they expected. It is very long, with large passages where not a lot actually happens; this can tend to dissuade the unfamiliar from persevering with it. Others simply find the idea of reading about elves and dwarves rather silly. This tension was something the poet WH Auden felt when, writing two years later, he conceded that the battle over Tolkien's literary prowess would be as hard fought as the War of the Ring itself had been: 'people find it a masterpiece ... or they cannot abide it ... among the hostile are some ... for whose literary judgement I have great respect.' This succinctly sums up a conflict that has been repeated *ad nauseum* ever since, something Tolkien himself acknowledged in the Foreword to the second edition. He, however, noted that, for all those who disliked the book or found it or certain passages strange or dull, there were others who genuinely did like it.

In the same year that Auden wrote the words above, Edmund Wilson summed up the book's popularity as the result of a simple impulse: 'certain people have a life-long appetite for juvenile trash.' Less than a decade later Philip Toynbee could confidently write in a British Sunday newspaper that 'today these books have passed into merciful oblivion'. He was, inevitably, unaware of the huge bolstering of Tolkien's popularity that was about to occur courtesy of the counter-culture generation. Watch the film of Woodstock today and you can see more than one reveller with a home-made 'Gandalf Lives!' T-shirt flitting across the screen. Toynbee's comment could be seen as the low-point of chronic under-appreciation of Tolkien. The diametrically opposed, yet equally inappropriate, extreme could be said to be represented by the comment in the *Sunday Times* that 'The English-speaking world is divided into those who have read *The Lord of the Rings* and *The Hobbit* and those who are going to read them.' This has the disadvantage, equal to that of Toynbee's own words, of not being literally true, merely opinion presented as though it is incontrovertible, disinterested fact.

Those for whom *The Lord of the Rings* is the ultimate book may, perhaps, be divided into two distinct groups: those who are unaware of the traditions in which Tolkien was (consciously) working, and those who are intimately familiar with it. For the former group a lack of familiarity with *Beowulf*, Nordic sagas, Edmund Spenser's *The Faerie Queen*, the music of Wagner (whose influence is controversial) and Anglo-Saxon poetry makes Tolkien's creation all the more dizzyingly diverse, unexpected and vast in its plenitude. For those as immersed in Tolkien's sources as the author himself, the pleasure, and the value, of the work comes in the recognition of auxiliary literary and cultural codes, and appreciation of the use to which Tolkien put his sources.

For a third group, those aware of much of what Tolkien was working from but without an interest in devoting a life to the study of its minutiae and its interrelation with the professor's own work, there is only a lengthy, occasionally stumblingly written piece that is clearly the product of a vast intellect, albeit one with little interest in prose fiction. As noted critic, author and reserved Tolkien fan AN Wilson has put it, 'You might ask what is the point of reading the etymologies of a fake language when you might be learning Old Norse, Old English or Greek. The same sensible habit of mind might ask why one should read ersatz mythology by Tolkien rather than reading Homer.'

Tolkien was, in the words of one prominent study of his work, 'barely able to use the word literature at all without putting inverted commas around it' and had no interest in notions of literary canonicity or literary theory. His interest was in the 'Language' half of the study of 'English Language and Literature' (as the more old-fashioned English University courses like to refer to it to this day).

Tolkien described himself more than once as a 'pure philologist' – one for whom the study of books, of history, of human beings themselves, was ultimately most interesting when it threw 'light on words and names!' The more abstract practitioners of philology hold that it is possible to reconstruct, via linguistic analysis, extrapolation, links and comparisons, lost legends, history, even languages. What *The Lord of the Rings* seems to have been to Tolkien, or at least what he held it to be, was a reflection of this. He created languages based upon his research and findings and then, in what we would now call 'reverse engineering', he created the mythologies linked to them by 'pulling' them out of his created forms of speech. He called *The Lord of the Rings* 'largely an exercise in linguistic esthetic' and maintained in the Foreword to the second edition that his inspiration had been mostly linguistic, designed at first as a background to the Elvish languages that he was developing. Others have found this argument less than compelling, one critic arguing that 'Tolkien's own off-hand remarks about the importance of philology to the creative conception [of *The Lord of the Rings*] need not be taken too seriously.'

What is of course attractive about viewing of *The Lord of the Rings* in such a manner is that it makes it a more distinct, impressive, intellectual exercise. It prevents it being simply a long, often exciting, book about a magical object, an exiled king and several 'Everyman' characters involved in a vast ground war. While this may explain the enthusiasm with which some of Tolkien's admirers have taken up this view (it is very difficult for virtually anyone to accept that they may simply *like* something, after all), the fact that it was the author's own stated motivation, interest and pursuit in the composition of his hugely popular book means that it must be taken seriously.

The writing of *The Lord of the Rings* – and all Tolkien's other books about Middle-earth – was a lengthy exercise that was, in and of itself, primarily philological (to do with the study of language) rather than narratological in nature. Tolkien's primary area of expertise and interest was, as noted, the study of ancient languages and their interrelation with mythologies, not literature. *The Lord of the Rings* really needs to be understood in this context of academic study, rather than that of straightforward narrative cohesion – or indeed literary merit.

What was of primary interest to Tolkien was not, as with most writers of fiction, the broad plot and individual characters, but the wider world within which his characters' plots began to unfold. In fact, he admitted to his publisher that he had written most of the first ten chapters without any idea where the story was going, or what was going to happen next. This is not how most novelists tend to work.

When looking at *The Lord of the Rings*, it is important not to get carried away in terms of appreciation (as the British public arguably have) and yet it is equally important not to criticise the piece for not being something that it has no intention of being. While millions have enjoyed *The Lord of the Rings* since its initial publication in 1954–55, it is surely difficult for any discerning, well-read reader to disagree entirely with poet John Bayley's earnest assessment of the book (thanks to its shifting-tense prose style, overuse of exclamation marks and somewhat effete sentence construction) as 'fantastically badly written'. But it is equally difficult for someone with any regard for the literary tradition to dismiss outright the words of an unquestionably great poet, WH Auden, who wrote of the first volume of the book: 'No fiction I have read in the last five years has given me more joy'. Although

Bayley's wife, the late – indeed great – novelist Dame Iris Murdoch, was herself a huge fan of Tolkien's imaginary creatures and languages, she could nevertheless see the merit in her husband's viewpoint.

Essentially, though, this argument about the 'merit' of Tolkien's works and his 'right' to his vast popularity really need not be given at all. For if Tolkien's work has any power at all over the reader it is surely the power of Tolkien's imagination, and the sheer scale of his creation, rather than that of his particular power with words.

The first BBC radio version (1956)

This was a 'Painful . . . sillification' according to Tolkien himself. Today, there is little evidence of the first attempt to adapt *The Lord of the Rings* for a different medium other than a couple of mentions in Tolkien's letters, as collected by Humphrey Carpenter. No recording of it exists; indeed, it is unlikely that it was recorded at all, as little of the live radio (or indeed television) of the era was committed to tape for posterity – the BBC did not regard such things as within their responsibilities. For the BBC to maintain an archive was not made a condition or clause of their public operating charter until 1979 and much of the corporation's output before that date is now lost to the public, which paid for it to be produced.

This first version of *The Lord of the Rings* was written and produced by poet Terrence Tiller, who had joined the BBC in 1946, and was a close friend and drinking companion of the likes of George Orwell, Laurie Lee and WH Auden. By the mid-1950s he was one of the leading producers of the 'Third Programme', a precursor of modern-day BBC radio stations Radio Three and Radio Four, intended to be the more intellectual channel. Though founded the year Tiller joined the BBC, it was only in 1954 that it really had made its name, with the dramatisation of Tiller's friend Dylan Thomas's *Under Milk Wood* – still regarded as one of the finest radio plays ever made.

The fact that Tolkien's work (which, on its publication the previous year, had been written off by many as a simple children's book along the lines of *The Hobbit*) was earmarked for the Third Programme when it went into production in 1956 must initially have seemed a very good sign. It suggested a certain amount of respect for the book, and a perception of it as a more serious work than certain reviewers had given it credit for being.

The work was adapted into a twelve-part series, which, though necessitating much cutting to fit the running time, was hardly unreasonable, and it was broadcast during the autumn of 1956. Unfortunately, the result was not what Tolkien had hoped for, and he was left annoyed and perplexed, asking Tiller in a letter dated 6 November 1956 about why the book had received the treatment it had and querying the value of the changes that he felt 'reduced [it] to such simple, even simple-minded terms'.

Details of the precise nature of the adaptation have since been lost, and it is difficult to work out from the records precisely why Tolkien felt that it had failed so badly. One thing is certain: by the end of 1956 he had determined, as he informed Tiller in the same letter, that his book was 'very unsuitable for dramatic or semi-dramatic representation'. Had anyone asked Tolkien at the end of that year whether his book would ever successfully be adapted for another medium, he would almost certainly have said no.

The book that brought Middle-earth and its creator to the world's attention, however, was not *The Lord of the Rings*. It was *The Hobbit* (1937), the story of the hobbit Bilbo Baggins's journey to the Lonely Mountain, during which the One Ring was found – a story originally written for, and read to, Tolkien's children.

THE HOBBIT (1977)

(TVM, 77 minutes)

Rankin/Bass Presents
The Hobbit
Based on the Original Version of 'The Hobbit' Written by
  JRR Tolkien
'The Greatest Adventure', The Ballad of the Hobbit, Sung By
  Glenn Yarbrough
Music Composed, Arranged and Conducted by Maury Laws
Lyrics Written and Adapted by Jules Bass
Production Designed by Arthur Rankin Jr
Adapted for the Screen by Romeo Muller
Produced & Directed by Arthur Rankin Jr and Jules Bass
© MCMLXXVII Rankin/Bass Productions, Inc.

First Transmitted: 27 November 1977 (NBC)

PRINCIPAL CAST: Orson Bean (*Bilbo Baggins*), Richard Boone (*Smaug*), Hans Conried (*Thorin*), John Huston (*Gandalf the Grey*), Otto Preminger (*Elvenking*), Cyril Richard (*Elrond*), Theodore (*Gollum*) with the talents of Paul Fries and Jack De Leon, Don Messick, John Stephenson

THE DIRECTOR: Arthur Rankin (producer/director) started his professional life in television in 1948, as a graphic designer at ABC television. The expansion of television services, and his ambition to direct, saw him move up to being an Art Director (in modern cinematic terms, Production Designer) on live television shows including *Tales of Tomorrow* (1951–53) and *Schlitz Playhouse* (1951–59). Popular and hardworking, he won several awards in his field.

In 1952 Rankin left ABC to set up his own company and pursue animation opportunities. Through a mutual acquaintance he met Jules Bass, who rapidly became the business side of a successful partnership (Rankin would handle the more artistic chores, as befitted his design background; Bass was the entrepreneur). Working mostly in television, the pair's ventures include many holiday specials which constitute national institutions in the

17

United States, but which are almost entirely unseen outside North America. These include *Rudolph the Red-Nosed Reindeer* (1964) and *Jack Frost* (1979). Television cartoon series produced by the duo, less beloved in America but with some international recognition, include *The Jackson Five* (1971) and *ThunderCats* (1985). A recent production for the company was the 1999 full-length animated feature film *The King and I* – the third film based on the popular Margaret Landon novel *Anna and the King of Siam* (1943), itself based upon the heavily fictionalised, historically dubious and self-aggrandising memoirs of Anna Leonowens, first published in 1870.

Jules Bass is no longer as heavily involved in the production company that bears his name as he once was, and now spends much of his time in France. As a proselytising vegetarian, he is the author of the series of children's books concerning *Herb, the Vegetarian Dragon*. He also teaches vegetarian cookery to children and has moved into writing fiction for adults.

Aside from his business acumen, Bass' most significant contribution to the Rankin/Bass canon appears to be as a musician. Together with regular Rankin/Bass composer Maury Laws he wrote songs and music for the company's productions, including *The Hobbit* and *The Return of the King*. To American audiences his most famous tune is probably 'Put One Foot in Frost of the Other' from *Jack Frost*. What is less well known is that Bass also directed some of the Rankin/Bass productions, including *Mad Monster Party* (1967) – a curious stop-motion affair in which Dr Frankenstein invites his 'friends' Dracula, the Hunchback of Notre Dame, a Mummy and a Werewolf to his castle so he can demonstrate his latest inventions to them. What the original authors, such as Mary Shelley or Bram Stoker, would have made of this peculiarly American reinterpreting of their works is unknown.

It is unclear from available information whether the rights' holders United Artists licensed the television production rights to Rankin/Bass while the property was in their possession, creating a contract that Zaentz was bound by once he gained control of the property, or whether Saul Zaentz himself licensed the TV production (see **Journey to the Crossroads** for more information on the rights situation). The latter seems unlikely as there would be probable conflict between them and the Bakshi project, which was the reason behind Zaentz's acquisition of the rights (see **JRR Tolkien's The Lord of the Rings**).

ANIMATION: Although Rankin/Bass is an American company principally connected in the popular imagination with Americana, it turned to a Japanese animation studio to provide artwork for *The Hobbit* – a common practice for it and most other American animation production companies at the time. The company selected the Toru Hara studio, which went on to produce two of Oscar winner Hayao (*Spirited Away*) Miyazaki's films. There, working to a reported $3 million budget and from noted Tolkien illustrator Arthur Rackham's work, 40,000 individual frames of character artwork were produced under the supervision of Tsuguyuki Kubo, who had worked on the Rankin/Bass effort *Frosty's Winter Wonderland* (1976). Hara employees Hidetoshi Kaneko and Kazuko Ito created the background plates for the animation, and further details and designs, working under industry veteran Minoru Nishida. The Japanese director of the piece (uncredited on the US DVD and credits) was Katsuhisa Yamada, famed in certain circles for his animated cult hits *Oz* (1994) and *Urusei Yatsura 6* (1991).

While 40,000 frames (110,000 including backgrounds) and $3 million was less than a first-rank Walt Disney film at the time, it was enough to ensure smooth, detailed animation of a higher standard than was normal for contemporary television productions. (And anyway, there had been no first-rank Walt Disney films since *The Jungle Book* in 1967 – a decade before – which had been the last production initiated by the company's late founder.)

The character designs are simple and – perhaps – errantly childish. The dwarves resemble those of Disney, specifically the work of Vladamir William (Will) Tytla, the principal character designer on *Snow White and the Seven Dwarfs*, responsible for all of the Seven Dwarfs.

When asked about the Disney-like nature of the dwarf design in *The Hobbit*, character designer Lester Abrams reported that in fact he and Tytla had been working from the same Arthur Rackham drawings of dwarfs. Their visuals have a common root: 'I found the source for Grumpy [which was then] used for Thorin.'

In terms of hobbits, Bilbo is more like a squat child than the properly proportioned, yet small, person described by Tolkien. According to Abrams, his character design was done while the artist was still at college as a hypothetical spec drawing, entirely out of the artist's affection for the character. The only change from this old drawing to the design used in the finished film was the Japanese animation team's decision to make his eyes bigger because, in Abrams words, 'All Japanese cartoon characters have big eyes.' Abrams used a Leonardo da Vinci self-portrait as the basis for Gandalf's design. Oddly, there seems to have been no desire to base Gandalf on the painting *Der Berggeist* by the artist Josef Madlener (1881–1967), despite the fact that Tolkien had declared this pastoral picture of an old man in a field to be a prime influence on his visual conception of the character.

Abrams initially used biology textbook drawings of frog anatomy as the basis for Gollum's physicality, but Rankin encouraged him to make the character more horrific and less benign. The decidedly amphibian, greenish look of the character, though arguably based on the orc Shagrat's comment that Gollum is similar in looks to a frog, albeit a starved one (Book IV, Chapter X), would come as a bit of a shock to anyone who has had their vision of him shaped by the more 'human' versions in either the Bakshi or the Jackson films.

The Elvenking was apparently based upon photographs of Yul Brynner in *The Ten Commandments* (Cecil B de Mille, 1956), although the reasoning behind making the wood elves greyish, gangly-legged, pot-bellied and snub-nosed remains unclear. One missing element that was never even considered was the man-bear Beorn, as Abrams was told that the budget would stretch only to Beorn or the giant spiders. Spiders were chosen as they were more visually arresting.

While some of the background plates are more impressive than the character designs, the sky is often unnaturally still, thanks to the clouds being simple static images. It is, on the whole, less gloomy than the Bakshi take on Middle-earth, though it is in its use of shadows that *The Hobbit* is most effective, with real atmosphere generated when the characters are underground.

BOOK AND SCREENPLAY: Based on the recall of Tolkien's own family, it seems likely that the story that became *The Hobbit* originated as a doodle in the 1920s. The word 'hobbit' was one jotted by a bored Tolkien as part of a phrase in the margins of an exam paper he was marking: 'In a hole in the ground there lived a hobbit'. In those ten words lies the start, not of Middle-earth, which had already begun to exist in Tolkien's mind and notes, but of the story that would lead to the tale of the One Ring. Returning to this unconscious scribble some years later, Tolkien determined to 'find out' precisely what a hobbit was.

Tolkien's own children recall *The Hobbit*, or a version of it, as a bedtime story told to them at some point in the late 1920s. An abortive attempt was made, at around the same time, to turn this into written prose fiction, but this got no further than the first chapter and a self-drawn map. A few years later the story had become more or less complete – Tolkien showed a version of it to his friend and colleague CS Lewis, as a neatly typed manuscript, in 1932. Lewis wrote to Arthur Greaves in a letter dated 4 February to say that he had 'had a delightful time reading a children's story which Tolkien has just written . . . whether it is really good or not (I think it is . . .) is another question'. This is high praise indeed coming from one of the twentieth century's most beloved and respected children's authors.

This typescript was, however, unfinished and, with the original audience for Tolkien's story now (theoretically) too old for it, it seems the intention was for it to remain so. It was the intervention of Elaine Griffiths and Susan Dagnell, two young women working in publishing and who were both graduates of Oxford and former students of Tolkien, which led to the story being completed for publication. It reached UK bookshops on 21 September 1937.

Lewis went on to champion the book further, reviewing it glowingly (albeit anonymously) in the highly respectable *Times Literary Supplement* on 2 October 1937, and again in *The Times* newspaper proper six days later. There is no suggestion that Lewis's praise was anything other than genuine.

It is the considered opinion of the more eminent Tolkien scholars, such as Humphrey Carpenter and TA Shippey, that *The Hobbit* was not originally designed to be a part of Tolkien's Middle-earth mythology as it appears in *The Silmarillion*. Tolkien had, as early as the 1920s, begun writing, creating and editing the materials that would later be published after his death as *The Silmarillion*. Largely regarded by the writer as a private fascination, and an attempt to recreate and define 'a mythology for England' (although why this should be considered necessary in a country overburdened with national myths, heroes and mythic figures is unclear), *The Silmarillion* does not seem to have been intended for wider consumption at that time.

There was, on *The Hobbit's* first publication, no hint of anything darker or more significant in the story than the simple tale of a plump hobbit's journey to the Lonely Mountain, and his confrontation with a dragon. Elves, so important in the later books, hardly feature, and there is little indication of a wider mythology beyond that immediately relevant to Bilbo's quest. Just as a particular children's book set in, say, twentieth century Europe would not necessarily feel compelled to explain Communism, Nazism, capitalism and socialism (never mind the history of Europe since the Enlightenment), Tolkien's tale of Bilbo Baggins rarely moves beyond the hobbit's own immediate world. When it eventually does so, it only moves as far as he does, and the prose still does not extensively reference or explain aspects of life outside the protagonist's immediate concerns. This is despite the fact that Middle-earth was already becoming quite well shaped in the author's notes, and that Tolkien always claimed to favour fairy stories that hinted at wider worlds beyond the immediate tale.

Nevertheless, elements of Tolkien's uncovered and recreated mythology found their way into the children's story which he found himself writing in the 1930s. From the presence of mere dwarves and elves to that of the important figures of Gandalf the Grey and Elrond, Tolkien was consciously working if not within the same world then at least in the same *kind* of world as he had been experimenting with in his other, unpublished writings. Even so, no one, not even the author himself, could have guessed what Bilbo's journey with the dwarves would lead to.

It was only in 1951, with the publication of the revised second edition of *The Hobbit*, that something darker, and broader, seemed to be hinted at. This something can, in all honesty, only be discerned by those who already know the story of *The Lord of the Rings* – and the first volume of that was not published for another three years. The change, though minor, made Bilbo's (revised) journey the true start of the saga of the Ring and the return of Sauron (see boxout: **Plot-significant textual changes**, page 32).

Unlike later attempts to film Tolkien, Rankin/Bass' *The Hobbit* (the first successfully completed on-screen adaptation of Tolkien of any kind) doesn't alter much of the author's story and instead presents it largely intact. This is primarily, of course, due to how much shorter *The Hobbit* is than *The Lord of the Rings* and how much more simply, and linearly, it is structured. Romeo Muller's screenplay removes the interlude with Beorn and the squabble over the Arkenstone, as well as the more minor character of the Town Master who appears in Chapter X ('A Warm Welcome'). It also transposes some of the events of Chapters XIII ('Not at Home') and XIV ('Fire and Water') for dramatic effect. But, these changes apart, the alterations are minor, with much of Tolkien's dialogue and even description (thanks to the narrator) surviving intact.

The animated feature begins with a picture of a book, on the verso of which (nearly out of sight) can be seen the words 'The Hobbit, There and Back Again by JRR Tolkien'. The implication is clearly that this is a copy of Tolkien's novel, although the book the audience is looking at is itself in a setting more reminiscent of the film's own representation of Middle-earth than any reality contemporary to the feature's manufacture. On the visible recto there is a drawing of Bilbo's house and the words 'In a hole in the ground, there lived a hobbit'. While these are the opening lines of the novel, the following wording – which is a scene-setting paragraph beginning 'Many ages ago, when this ancient planet was not quite so ancient . . .' – is not from any page of any edition of *The Hobbit*. John Huston as Gandalf/the Narrator then reads out these words, and they then segue into a reading of much of the first few paragraphs of the actual book.

Gandalf introduces the concept of hiring Bilbo for a spot of burglary earlier on screen than he does on the page, before he has introduced himself, in fact, which somehow helps to create a more sinister impression about the character than most would associate with him. The dwarves are then introduced over a short burst of song. This song's words are sourced in the novel, although in Tolkien it is introduced a little later, while Thorin and his crew are eating in Bilbo's house. The whole episode, unlike in the book, seems rather more cruel than comic, although arguably this could be taken as being how Bilbo himself would have interpreted his sudden inundation of dwarves and wizard.

Bilbo's dreams, referred to in passing in the book, become the centrepiece of a lengthy sequence in the cartoon. In this, the hobbit is given all sorts of earthly glories (including being seated on a throne and given a crown and sceptre). Over this out-of-character sequence the special's credits are run (as above). The cartoon makes little of Bilbo's reluctance to leave with the dwarves. In the novel he is practically tricked into following them hurriedly out of the door by Gandalf, almost before he knows what he's doing, leaving behind his stick and his hat to meet the dwarves at the Green Dragon. What is, in the book, a note left behind by the departed dwarves as a *fait accompli* (it details Bilbo's remuneration for helping them with their 'burglary') is presented to him on screen as a firm on-paper offer for his services by Thorin during dinner the night before. It is an offer that Bilbo reluctantly but decisively accepts.

One interesting final addition is that at the end of the cartoon feature Bilbo is seen to keep his magic ring in a glass case on the mantelpiece at Bag End. The book, of course, has him keeping the ring secret and only using it if he wanted to avoid people; it is difficult to see how any adaptation could reconcile public display of the One Ring with the events of *The Lord of the Rings*. The contrast is even more marked when one considers the differing implications of the literary *Hobbit* and its animated adaptation. Tolkien ends his most engagingly written book on a comic note, with Bilbo reaching for his pipe. The decision of certain later editions to print the first chapter of *The Lord of the Rings* ('A Long Expected Party') as an epilogue to *The Hobbit* allows the volume to end on a marvellous note of suspended enigma – Gandalf leaves on urgent business and we are told that he isn't seen back in Bag End again for a long time. In contrast, the Rankin/Bass version seeks closure – unsurprising given that the rights to adapt Tolkien's other works lay elsewhere than with the producers of this cartoon.

CAST NOTES: John Huston, whose instantly recognisable voice doubles for both Gandalf the Grey and the narrator of this cartoon, is one of the most significant figures in Hollywood history. Although a legendary drinker and gambler, he was principally known as a film director, but he did make appearances in both his own pictures and other people's, and turned to acting to raise funds when his directorial career seemed in decline. He was Oscar-nominated fifteen times in the course of 25 years. Born in 1906, the son of the actor Walter Huston, he became a screenwriter at Universal in the 1930s and moved to Warner Brothers before the end of the decade.

Success, including an Oscar nomination for *Dr Ehlrich's Magic Bullet* (William Dieterle, 1940), led to his requests to direct being taken seriously by Jack L Warner. He was given Dashiell Hammet's novel *The Maltese Falcon* to adapt and shoot and, after George Raft turned the film down, secured Humphrey Bogart as a leading man. An enormous success on its 1941 release, the picture was the first in a series of collaborations with Bogart that would continue until the actor's premature death from cancer in 1957. Despite an interruption for wartime service (he left the army with the rank of Major, having produced several propaganda films for the Allies), Huston's career continued unabated.

His pictures as director include *Across The Pacific* (1942), *The Treasure of the Sierra Madre* (1948) and *Key Largo* (1948), all with Bogart. Huston won two Oscars, one for his script and the other for directing, for *Treasure*. His father, Walter, cast in a bit part, picked up a Best Supporting Actor Oscar as well. A leaner period followed, with *The Asphalt Jungle* (1950) and his adaptation of Stephen Crane's American Civil War novella *The Red Badge of Courage* (1951) flopping financially (the former gained Oscar nods despite this). *The African Queen* (1952), again with Bogart, restored Huston's flagging reputation (and featured Theodore Bikel, who would go on to feature as the voice of Aragorn in the Rankin/Bass version of *The Return of the King*). *Moulin Rouge* (1952) starring Jose Ferrer was another success, but there were years ahead where Huston, though prolific, would not score a hit commercially or critically.

Moby Dick (1956) with Gregory Peck, was a moody box office flop. *Heaven Knows, Mr. Allison* (1957), *The Barbarian and the Geisha* (1958), *Freud* (1962), *The List of Adrian Messenger* (1963) and *The Bible* (1966) were all failures, and they were not the only ones. In 1967 he co-directed the dire James Bond spoof *Casino Royale*, openly admitting he was doing so because producer Charles K Feldman was going to clear Huston's gambling debts in exchange. Of his directorial features in this period only *The Misfits* (1961) with Clark Gable and Marilyn Monroe stands out, but that too was unsuccessful at the time and has only achieved prominence *ex post facto* as both Monroe and Gable's last film.

As an actor, Huston was outstanding in *The Cardinal* (Otto Preminger, 1963) and he also appeared in *De Sade* (Cy Endfield, Roger Corman, 1969, a dire biopic of the writer) and *Battle for the Planet of the Apes* (J Lee Thompson, 1973, as one of the Simian contingent), among others. He was most impressive in *Chinatown* (Roman Polanksi, 1974) as an abusive father. His

25

1975 directorial effort, an adaptation of Kipling's *The Man Who Would Be King* (with Michael Caine and Sean Connery filling in roles Huston had wanted Bogart and Clark Gable for twenty years before) restored his reputation in the eyes of many. A lessening of personal problems meant an upswing in the quality of his work and he garnered yet another Oscar nomination for *Wise Blood* (1979) before the pendulum swung back down again. *Phobia* (1980), *Victory* (1981) and (particularly) *Annie* (1982) were the largest creative and fiscal failures of his chequered career.

After a couple of years away from film-making he returned with *Under the Volcano* (1984). Another literary adaptation, this time of Malcolm Lowry's 'difficult', heavily allegorical novel about an alcoholic British diplomat struggling with his personal demons against the backdrop of the Mexican Day of the Dead, it was – to most people's complete surprise – an unabashed triumph. *Prizzi's Honor* (1985), about hitmen working for the mob, was another success, as was his adaptation of James Joyce's *The Dead* (1987), on which he worked with two of his children, actor Anjelica and screenwriter James. John Huston succumbed to emphysema later that year. He was married five times, and he is the only Oscar winner to have both a parent and a child who have also won an Academy Award – a feat given especial distinction by the fact that both his father and daughter won their Oscars for performances given under his direction.

Born in Austria in 1906, Otto Preminger was another director who occasionally acted; most of his on-screen appearances are as Nazis in films made during the Second World War, when every available man with a central European accent was seemingly required to conform to stereotypes and work in propaganda pictures. This is doubly ironic and tasteless given Preminger's Judaism. (He later directed the film *Exodus*, 1960, a personal project about the foundation of the state of Israel.) After working under celebrated producer/director Max Reinhardt in the Austrian theatre in the 1920s, Preminger came to America at the invitation of Universal Pictures; a talent scout from the studio had seen one of his stage productions and felt he had potential as a feature film director.

Preminger rowed with the studio about projects and methods (he was assigned minor films) almost immediately, and found himself effectively blacklisted and prevented from working. The war, and his career as an actor, then intervened. Preminger became an independent film-maker in the early fifties, working outside the studio system in order to direct again. He made the classic *The Man With The Golden Arm* (1955), which starred Frank Sinatra as a heroin-addicted guitar player, produced a memorable adaptation of George Bernard Shaw's *Saint Joan* (1957), the Best Picture Oscar-nominated James Stewart flick *Anatomy of a Murder* (1959), and the musicals *Porgy and Bess* (1959) and *Carmen Jones* (1954). He died in New York in 1986.

Orson Bean was born on 22 August 1928, a second cousin to the then President of the United States Calvin Coolidge, although this failed to prevent him from being blacklisted in the 1950s during the anti-communist purge led by Senator Joe McCarthy. He was for many years a regular panellist on the game show *To Tell the Truth* and it is for this that he remains best known in America. As an actor he appeared as Loren Bray on the dreary television series *Dr Quinn: Medicine Woman* (1993–98) and as Dr Lester in the indie hit *Being John Malkovich* (Spike Jonze, 1999).

Born in Germany in 1906, Theodore Gottlieb, often credited as 'Brother Theodore' or simply 'Theodore' (as here), was a prolific voiceover artiste often used by Rankin/Bass. Frequent television comic collaborations with Billy Crystal made his face nearly as well known as his voice in his later life. Moviegoers may recognise him as Uncle Reuben in *The 'burbs* (Joe Dante, 1989). He died in 2001.

NAMES AND LANGUAGE: As befits a story written more with children in mind, *The Hobbit* is less rich in verbiage than Tolkien's other works about Middle-earth. Whereas, in other pieces, the nomenclature and its etymology would be, according to the author himself, the main point and interest of the works, this is not the case in *The Hobbit*. For the most part, names are simply descriptive – Lonely Mountain, The Shire and so forth – or even literal, for example Bywater. However, there are still numerous interesting invented words and captivating constructions.

Hobbits, unlike elves, dwarves, trolls, orcs and dragons, do not exist in a dominant form in any folklore. This is why, throughout *The Lord of the Rings*, hardly anyone they meet has ever heard of their race, or of the land in which they live. In *The Two Towers*,

Treebeard the Ent cannot place hobbits in any of the old lists of creatures, despite him being, according to Gandalf, the most ancient thing still living in Middle-earth (Book III, Chapter V).

As the rest of Tolkien's world was based on the old legends of the Germanic tribes of Dark Age northern Europe, many critics have also looked there, and in vain, for answers for the origin of the halflings. The only immediately accessible use of the word 'hobbit' pre-Tolkien is in *The Denham Tracts, Volume 2* (1895), a dictionary of folklore produced by the Folklore Society in London. Within, a 'hobbit' is defined as 'a class of spirit' and it may be that Tolkien had read this definition and subconsciously filed it away. What seems more likely is that the professor's mental processes created the word from the Anglo-Saxon words *hol* (hole) and *byta* (dweller), which would, when combined into a conjectural linguistic reconstruction, be a near homophone for 'hobbit' (although it must also be noted that *Hob* is an archaic English word for 'rustic').

Tolkien was always keen to deny any connection between 'hobbit' and 'rabbit', although both live in holes. This seems, perhaps, a little disingenuous, as at several points in *The Hobbit* other characters compare Bilbo to a rabbit. Gollum and Beorn actually do call him that in Chapters V and VII.

There is no full answer to the creatures' origins. It was arguably simply a verbal doodle influenced by some, maybe all, of the above.

The preface to the novel explains that the word 'orc' as used in the piece is the hobbit word for the English goblin, although both are used in *The Hobbit*, and *The Lord of the Rings* complicates this further. The term orc is taken from *Beowulf*. Smaug's appellation comes from the Germanic verb *Smuagen*, 'to squeeze through a very tight hole'.

Mirkwood is a use of the eleventh-century German *Mirkiwudu*, meaning 'dark wood'. The stems of the word, however, suggest a much older origin. 'Merkw' (dark) is not German in origin at all, but Old English Saxon (and also Norse), suggesting the full word *Mirkiwudu* had survived in the language from a much earlier time. It has a peculiar tone of dread to it, at least partially due to the conjunction of 'Merkw' with 'wudu' – a term which, in German, only refers to dead wood rather than living trees. Tolkien may have been aware of the use of the word as the name for a forest of fear in *The House of the Wolflings*, an 1888 novel by pseudo-Gothic author Lillian Morris.

The Arkenstone, although left out of the Rankin/Bass adaptation, has an interesting derivation, being simply a regularised version of 'eorcanstan', Anglo-Saxon for 'Precious Stone'. The wild wolves that are feared by those on the expedition are called Wargs (an Anglo-Saxon term for dangerously wild wolves) and Beorn's name is, while the literal Anglo-Saxon for 'bear', also a term used in the period to describe a large man, or a warrior. Its use here also has an element of *Beowulf* to it.

Beowulf is a clear influence in other ways also, as would come as no surprise to those who know anything of Tolkien's more academic pursuits. For example, in both *Beowulf* and Tolkien's children's book the dragon featured is killed by a blow to its 'lower regions' and both feature a theft of a cup as a significant event.

Tobacco is mentioned on a number of occasions in *The Hobbit*, despite the word (and the substance) being an American import, so out of place in Tolkien's pre-Europe. In *The Lord of the Rings,* the term pipeweed is often used instead. In a similar vein, the author removed the seventeenth-century word 'tomatoes' from later editions of *The Hobbit*, and (in the revised text of 1966 at least – see the box on **Plot-significant textual revisions** on page 32) opted for the English colloquialism 'taters' over 'potatoes'. Taters is also used in *The Lord of the Rings* when Sam discusses one of his favourite foodstuffs with Gollum (Book IV, Chapter IV, 'Of Herbs and Stewed Rabbit'). This is, of course, due to potatoes being a late sixteenth-century import into the British Isles and thus as out of place as tobacco.

It is also worth noting, considering Tolkien's disavowal of rabbits as being part of the inspiration for hobbits, that these long-eared creatures were also originally not native to the British Isles, but introduced accidentally sometime during the Middle Ages – hence (again in *The Lord of the Rings*) Sam's use of the colloquial term 'coneys'.

After *The Hobbit*, Tolkien made a decision that the plural of dwarf in Middle-earth would be dwarves, not the more correct dwarfs as in modern English. When questioned, he admitted that the original decision to use dwarves had been a simple mistake, which he noted was out of character for such a devoted philologist, but he decided to make use of his mistake rather than correct it (the Old English plural of dwarf is dwarrow, not dwarves, anyway).

SOUND AND MUSIC: The little songs sung by the dwarves during the tea at Bilbo's house early in the cartoon *Hobbit* seem both a little twee and out of place. Additionally, they allow an unfortunate air of Disney's *Snow White and the Seven Dwarfs* (David Hand, 1937) to waft across the proceedings, partially thanks to the design of the dwarves. Yet the words are, almost universally, Tolkien's own, and the tune is not entirely to blame, although it is likely that the author would have preferred a more 'English' sound (whatever that may be). Scenes such as this are reminders of the jollier, more childlike (which is resolutely different from *childish*) nature of *The Hobbit* compared to its more famous sequel.

The tune used over the opening credits, though, is a horrid and entirely contrived piece. Sung by former Limeliters frontman Glenn Yarbrough, it seems to be midway between folk and country and western, and is entirely unsuitable to the production, never mind the unfolding story. It is at moments like this that the cartoon betrays its origins and intended audience most clearly.

FILM REVIEWS: A 'disappointment' was the verdict of Bob Sheridan writing in the British fantasy magazine *Starburst* in 1978. He found it 'pleasantly stylised' but 'totally uninvolving' and wondered 'how such a magical tale could be filmed so unengagingly'. The previous year the *Hollywood Reporter* had been a little kinder, but only just – 'the animation was two dimensional' and while the cartoon got across the essential 'Faith, honor, courage and generosity' of the book, it was a shame that the book hadn't 'conjured more imagination' from its adapters in their transferring of it from one medium to another.

AVAILABILITY: This production is currently available on Region 1 NTSC DVD only, from Warner Bros DVD, both as an individual release and as part of a three-disc set with the Bakshi *The Lord of the Rings* and the Rankin/Bass *The Return of the King* (WB DVD 566/ISBN 0-7907-6259-5).

Prequel?

Often referred to as the 'prequel' to *The Lord of the Rings*,
The Hobbit is no such thing. The word 'prequel' is generally
accepted, including by US dictionaries, as having been coined
in 1973 by either Francis Ford Coppola and/or George Lucas
to describe the sections of the planned *The Godfather – Part
II*, which would occur, chronologically speaking, before any
part of the earlier film *The Godfather*. (Lucas was
Vice-President of Coppola's company American Zoetrope at
the time.) The word was popularised by Lucas and Steven
Spielberg, who used it publicly and repeatedly to describe
their collaboration *Indiana Jones and the Temple of Doom*
(1984) set a year before, in fictional terms, the previous
picture, *Raiders of the Lost Ark* (1981). It later became the
accepted appellation for the three *Star Wars* films Lucas
made between 1999 and 2005, which were set before those
he made between 1977 and 1983.

Of course, the coining of the word after the publication of
The Hobbit in 1937 does not mean that *The Hobbit* is not
one. *The Magician's Nephew* (published 1954), the sixth
published, fifth written and first in terms of actual
chronological sequence of Tolkien's friend CS Lewis's
Narnia books, is inarguably a prequel, despite being
published twenty years before Lucas/Coppola came up with
the term. What makes *The Hobbit* not one is that the term
prequel (which is etymological nonsense, a good enough
reason for Tolkien himself to hate it had he ever heard it)
refers to a work created *after* another work, but set before it
within their mutual fiction. *The Hobbit* was completed, and
published, long before *The Lord of the Rings* was. There
could be a case made that Tolkien's alterations for the 1951
second edition sufficiently altered the book for it to count as
a prequel, but it would be a tough and flimsy one to argue.

The term the Tolkien estate uses to describe the work is the
prelude, a musical description that is entirely appropriate. Just
to confuse matters further, the projected and
much-anticipated New Line Cinema/Peter Jackson adaptation
of *The Hobbit* will, of course, be made long after production
on *The Lord of the Rings* film trilogy is completed.

Therefore, that film adaptation – should it ever happen – will *actually* be a prequel to the film trilogy, which is based on the work to which *The Hobbit* is a prelude, though emphatically not a prequel, to. That is probably all as clear as mud.

Plot-significant textual revisions

In both editions of *The Hobbit*, Bilbo finds the Ring in the tunnel beneath the Misty Mountains; here he comes across Gollum in the dark, and then begins their riddle competition. In the revised version Bilbo's bet is his life and Gollum's to help the hobbit escape the mountains.

As anyone who has read the later books (or indeed come across any of their adaptations) will know, Gollum's attachment to the Ring is so all-consuming and powerful that his desire to regain it is enough for him to leave the safety of his tunnels, venture into the outside world that he hates, and trek right across Middle-earth in an attempt to find the 'thief' that took his 'precious' from him. In the most familiar, revised edition of *The Hobbit*, this is very apparent, as is the fact that he does not intend to honour his bet (which in any case is simply to show Bilbo out, not to give him the Ring), and goes to get the Ring to help him kill Bilbo despite losing. When the hobbit realises and escapes, Gollum screams after him that he has stolen the ring and that Gollum will therefore detest him forever.

In the first edition, however, Gollum bets the ring rather than his assistance and his reaction on finding the ring gone is quite different – he continually apologises for cheating and swears he meant to give it to Bilbo as a present if he won. Gollum, in this first version, was entirely willing to give up the Ring. He is even embarrassed that he cannot give Bilbo that which he has rightfully gained by winning the riddle game and offers, rather sweetly, to catch Bilbo some fish to make up for it. Gollum's murderous pursuit of Bilbo later in the chapter was also added for the 1951 revision.

Tolkien made these changes during and because of the composition of *The Lord of the Rings*. In the preface to the

1951 edition Tolkien refers to the change, claiming that the alteration now means the book contains not Bilbo's story of how he got the ring, but the real tale of the encounter. 'Shadow of the Past' (Book I, Chapter II of *The Lord of the Rings*) also contains reference to the change, with Gandalf noting to Frodo that Bilbo was already under the influence of the Ring at this point, hence his lying about how he had acquired it. This is an intriguing example of Tolkien planning smart metatextual games with his pet universe. However, in the 'Note on the text' (not written by Tolkien) at the front of the 1995 HarperCollins edition of the book, which omits the author's 1951 preface, it is admitted that the changes were made simply 'to bring the storyline of *The Hobbit* more in line with that of its sequel'. It is also worth pointing out that in the original text Gollum uses the term 'precious' to refer only to himself, not the object the lust for which so consumes him in *The Lord of the Rings*.

Most other textual revisions Tolkien made to *The Hobbit* during his lifetime were largely corrective; however, there are others which, while not strictly plot-relevant, have an impact on his world-building exercise. The 1966 US edition, as prepared by Tolkien, makes a number of interesting changes. The implication that one of Bilbo's ancestors may have married into a goblin family is removed – presumably because of what *The Lord of the Rings* says about goblins. The adjective 'little' is removed from an early description of Gandalf, and occasions where hobbits use the word 'man' to colloquially describe themselves or each other are removed. In Chapter II of the original edition, there was the implication that men and elves are all common sights to a hobbit. In Chapter III, there was a mention of kinds of elves that are now known as 'Gnomes'. This undignified correlation of Tolkien's beautiful creatures with garden decorations is disposed of both here and from Chapter VIII.

There are two more changes of real interest. In Chapter XIX, the word 'age' to refer to a very long time is amended, presumably because it conflicted with Tolkien's elaborately designed scheme of 'ages' for Middle-earth. The other is the removal from Chapter II of a reference to 'Lilluputians'. It would not do for a book implicitly 'true', and derived from ancient factual material within the content of Tolkien's fiction (see **The Grey Havens: Conclusion**), to reference a work of fiction, i.e. *Gulliver's Travels* by Dean Jonathan Swift, written in 1726.

JOURNEY TO THE CROSSROADS: THE STORY OF THE FILM RIGHTS

Despite the failure of the 1956 BBC radio adaptation (see the boxout on page 15), *The Lord of the Rings* continued to do well in its original book form, and it was not long before Tolkien's publishers were approached with another offer – for a cartoon version.

In September 1957, Tolkien wrote to his son, and later literary executor, Christopher on the topic of a proposed film of *The Lord of the Rings*. The interest came from a consortium of three, led by Forrest J Ackerman, a B-movie special effects technician best known for his *Famous Monsters of Filmland* magazine. The other two members of the troika were Morton Grady Zimmerman and Al Brodax, the first of whom was an untested writer, the second an executive producer of the *Popeye* (the sailor man) cartoons. The trio provided the author with sample character designs, and Ackerman was granted an option on the film rights for a period of up to six months.

In June 1957, Tolkien wrote to his publishers stating that, as far as he was personally concerned, he would 'welcome the idea of an animated motion picture, with all the risk of vulgarization; and that quite apart from the glint of money, though on the brink of retirement that is not an unpleasant possibility'.

Tolkien had decided on a pragmatic approach towards the proposed movie: he would either have total control or make a great deal of money from his creations. He wanted, as he wrote in another letter to his son, either 'very profitable terms indeed' or 'absolute author's veto on objectionable features or alterations'. Presumably gaining both of these things was not considered an option, as the author clearly presents it as a binary choice in his correspondence. Tolkien put it rather less prosaically in a phrase that would become the name of a chapter of his authorised biography – 'Cash or Kudos'.

Having been approached, Tolkien was happy to play along on the off-chance he might be able to make some money. Morton Grady Zimmerman wrote a synopsis for the proposed film. Upon perusal, Professor Tolkien disliked the treatment intensely. As well as numerous misspellings, the synopsis used the Eagles (which Tolkien utilises sparingly in his book) to transport the characters around. It also had a crass conception of how magic should be used in Middle-earth. It furthermore, in the author's opinion, 'murdered' the book on which he had worked for decades by, most heinously, failing to make the journey of Frodo and Sam, as the bearers of the One Ring, to Mordor, the centre of the tale with the attention fixed on big battles and garish action.

Although some fans of the books have found much to complain about in the adaptations that have been made (be it the cutting of Tom Bombadil, the presence of elves at Helm's Deep, or seeing the Nazgûl on flying horses), it appears that Zimmerman's version would have been far more extreme. According to Tolkien, it introduced a 'fairy castle' and transformed the magic of the books from an understated background presence to flashing blue lights and incantations, and introduced a levitation scene to help Faramir escape from his father's pyre.

This 'vulgarisation' of his tale proved too much to bear. Tolkien wrote to his publishers again the following year, warning that 'I feel very unhappy about the extreme silliness and incompetence of Z[immerman] and his complete lack of respect for the original.'

In short, Tolkien felt, 'He has cut the parts of the story upon which its characteristic and peculiar tone principally depends.' Tolkien was prepared to accept a shortened version of his story; he was prepared to accept a 'vulgarised' version of his story; what he was not prepared to sacrifice was the *tone*.

In June 1958 Tolkien wrote to Forrest J Ackerman concerning this synopsis, and asked that Zimmerman be made aware of 'the irritation [and] resentment' that he felt when reading a treatment in which his work had been 'carelessly' and 'recklessly' altered without 'evident signs of any appreciation of what it is all about'.

Tolkien's complaints were not simply that changes had been made. He was too intelligent a man not to understand that different media have different concerns, strengths and weaknesses. He was more than aware that a film is not a book, that what works on the page may not work on the screen and vice versa, and that these differences are not qualitative but related to technique. He had written to Terence Tiller in a letter dated 6 November 1956 to say as much, observing, 'Can a tale not conceived dramatically . . . be dramatised – unless the dramatiser is given or takes liberties, as an independent person?'

What Tolkien did object to is that Zimmerman's adaptation made changes to the *sense* rather than just the *detail* of his work; it altered 'what it is all about'. Almost as bad were the alterations that seemed to have no purpose, alterations 'without any practical or artistic object (that I can see)'. On another occasion, he labelled Zimmerman's treatment 'willfully wrong without discernible technical reasons'. It is the 'without discernible technical reasons' which is the most important point when considering any and all adaptations of Tolkien's, or any other writer's work. Tolkien felt that the problem was simply that Zimmerman was, personally, 'quite incapable of excerpting or adapting' *The Lord of the Rings*. This does not mean that he considered it impossible. It means that he felt that Zimmerman was not up to the task. That particular proposed adaptation went no further.

Tolkien finally sold the rights for both *The Lord of the Rings* and *The Hobbit* in 1967, to United Artists. By then he was an old man (he would live for only another six years), and had perhaps concluded (correctly, as it turned out) that he was unlikely to live to see whatever production the rights sale resulted in, and equally unlikely to be able to micro-manage the adaptation himself.

The deal gave the filmic adaptation rights to the purchasers *in perpetuity*. If anyone purchased them from UA later on, they would also possess them in perpetuity. Tolkien's heirs would have no control over any film adaptations of either *The Hobbit* or *The Lord of the Rings*. They would, however, retain control and approval over the two books' literary manifestations – in terms of both presentation and editorial. They would also continue to receive income from the books. Tolkien had reached an agreement with his publishers whereby he received a larger than normal share of profits from his writing, and his heirs would continue to receive income under this arrangement after his death. To a degree, the same applies to work of JRR Tolkien that has been published posthumously.

In the end, perhaps cash had won out over kudos but, while his estate would have no legal authority over film adaptations, the popular affection for Tolkien's work had created a powerful legacy of goodwill towards his family. This, deliberately or accidentally (it is impossible to say), has ensured that, in the eyes of Tolkien's most fervent admirers, the Tolkien family continue to have *moral* authority over all manifestations of his work. Future adapters of Tolkien would, in degrees varying from lip service to deferential collaboration, acknowledge the primacy of the Tolkien family's authority – particularly that of Christopher Tolkien – over all works related to Middle-earth even when the Tolkien estate was not involved, directly or otherwise, in the process of adaptation.

This acknowledgement of the Tolkien estate has seemingly often occurred as much to be *seen* to be respecting 'what Tolkien actually wrote' (to use a phrase which crops up time and again on the Internet, in magazines and books and in conversation) as due to actual deference. Elijah Wood (Frodo in the New Line Cinema trilogy) thanked Tolkien, who died eight years before he was born, *first* when picking up an award in 2003. Ralph Bakshi, director of the 1978 film, has called the book 'perfect' and said that 'There isn't a page of *The Rings* that you wouldn't want to re-read a hundred times'. Virtually every reviewer of every production related to Tolkien has been concerned with the adaptation's respect for the integrity of the original work. Certainly no one has ever dared to make the Ringbearer's journey anything other than the 'spine of the story', as writer/director Peter Jackson would later call it, and very minor changes have been debated and discussed in virtually every conceivable forum.

It is difficult to think of another twentieth-century author whose work has become regarded in such a way. Sonia Orwell's stewardship of her late husband's literary inheritance has raised hackles and debate since 1951, but few have sweated and wailed when *Nineteen Eighty-Four* has been altered to fit the screen.

The 1954 BBC adaptation of *Nineteen Eighty-Four* changes the colour of the Anti-Sex League's sashes from vivid red to black and white check because it was broadcast on monochrome television.

This is the kind of alteration for which there is a sufficient 'technical reason'; the kind of change we feel that Tolkien would have understood. The same production clearly states that the world of *Nineteen Eighty-Four* is one that has suffered a limited nuclear war. This is not the case in the book. While indefensible on the grounds of 'remaining true to what Orwell wrote', it is a reflection of a shift in perceptions of the future between 1948 (when the book was written) and the time of the programme's manufacture. The change also enables the collapse of the post-war world and the emergence of Orwell's future to be conveyed visually. This is also a 'technical reason', in that it is a reason related to technique. It is a change that Orwell and/or Tolkien surely would have understood. The sense of the piece remains intact. The alteration to the ending of *Animal Farm* in the 1954 cartoon version, and thus the negation of the entire *point* of the piece, is indefensible. However, it has been condemned publicly by fewer people, and with less fury, than the arguable smaller fact that in Peter Jackson's *The Fellowship of the Ring*, unlike Tolkien's, Aragorn carries around a fully-functioning sword rather than the shards of Narsil in his scabbard.

Tolkien never seemed to consider that an adaptation of his work could achieve both cash and kudos. Yet his reputation, and the long shadow he casts over anyone who attempts to dramatise his work, has ensured that all adaptations have been approached with respect, even reverence, for what the adapter seems to think the author would have wanted. Though less true in his lifetime, the influence of Tolkien's perceived intentions has grown ever stronger since his physical death. It is quite common for critics, and to a greater extent devotees, of Tolkien adaptations to give much of the credit for what they like about the dramatisation to Tolkien and conclude that any problems with the production come from a lack of fidelity to, and respect for, his writings. It may in fact be that Tolkien was wrong, and that the simple choice (cash or kudos) he set out to his son has been circumvented entirely. Both the Tolkien industry's profits and the late author's reputation continue to grow exponentially, and there is no sign of this process even slowing down in the short or medium terms.

The Road Goes Ever On (1969)

Donald Swann (1923–1994) was a musician who became known for his theatre tour ('At the Drop of a Hat') with Michael Flanders. In the 1960s, inspired by *The Lord of the Rings* and hoping to cash in on their growing popularity within the music-mad counterculture, he added music to some of the poems and songs of *The Lord of the Rings*, creating the songcycle 'The Road Goes Ever On'.

The lyrics were taken from Tolkien's book and the songcycle was made up of seven songs: 'The Road Goes Ever On and On', 'Upon the Hearth the Fire is Red', 'In the Willow-Meads of Tasarinan', 'In Western Lands', 'Namarie', 'I Sit Beside the Fire and Think' and 'Errantry'. In addition he produced a version of 'Lúthien Tinúviel' and another, entitled 'Bilbo's Last Song', although these were not released until later. 'Lúthien Tinúviel' is actually sung in Elvish, one of Tolkien's made-up languages, and the author corresponded with Swann, informing him on how to 'correctly' pronounce various words (it's all about rolling the Rs, apparently).

With the songs now complete, Swann was keen to get Tolkien's full approval, and he performed the songs for Tolkien and other guests at the author's Golden Wedding Anniversary party at Merton College, Oxford, in March 1966. Afterwards Tolkien bowed to the musician and claimed, 'The words are unworthy of the music.'

Tolkien granted his consent for the songs to be released. Does this mean that Swann's scores for Tolkien's lyrics are the officially sanctioned ones? Because of the way Tolkien began to regard his creations, does it mean that these are the tunes the characters hear within the fiction? Or is it simply the case that Tolkien was flattered, and happy enough for his poems to be turned into songs as they were meant to be? They are just another adaptation.

Radio Hobbit (1966)

BBC radio broadcast an adaptation, 'The Hobbit', in 1966. In eight half-hour episodes it is an exhaustively faithful version of the book. This is made possible by the shorter length of the book as compared to *The Lord of the Rings* and the use of a narrator (played by Anthony Jackson), who takes much of the book's omniscient narratorial voice. Paul Daneman plays Bilbo effectively, despite usually being associated with authoratative, even sinister, roles. Heron Carvic is an impressive, alternatingly avuncular and powerful, Gandalf. The production exists in its entirety and is on CD as part of the BBC Radio Collection (ISBN 056352880 X).

Leonard Nimoy

Leonard Nimoy (born 1930), the co-star of the TV series *Star Trek* and director of two of the subsequent spin-off theatrical films, also had an unlikely, but equally profitable, career as a singer. It was on his 'difficult' second album 'The Two Sides of Leonard Nimoy' (the follow-up to 'Leonard Nimoy presents Mr Spock's Music From Outer Space') that Nimoy recorded 'The Ballad of Bilbo Baggins'. Co-written with songwriter Charles R Grean, this is a sing-along version of the plot of *The Hobbit* inhibited by its general tunelessness, insipid lyrics and even Nimoy's singing. The plot gets lost pretty quickly anyway, but our Len is convinced that Bilbo is 'the bravest little Hobbit of them all' and proceeds to tell his listeners so; many, many times in fact. This is not Nimoy's best record, but it certainly isn't his worst either – as anyone who has heard his version of the Joni Mitchell classic 'Both Sides' will tell you.

JRR TOLKIEN'S THE LORD OF THE RINGS (1978)

Fantasy Films presents
JRR Tolkien's The Lord of the Rings
Edited by Donald W Ernst, A.C.E
Music Composed and Conducted by Leonard Rosenman
Director of Photography: Timothy Galfas
Screenplay by Chris Conkling and Peter S Beagle
Based on the Novels of JRR Tolkien
Studio Production Supervisor: Jacqueline Roettcher
Animation Production Supervisor: Daniel Pia
Assistants to the Director: Lynne Betner, Leah Bernstein
Assistant to the Producer: Nancy Eichler
Produced by Saul Zaentz
Directed by Ralph Bakshi

Released: 15 November 1978 (USA)

PRINCIPAL CAST: Christopher Guard (Frodo Baggins), William Squire (Gandalf Stormcrow), Michael Scholes (Samwise Gamgee), John Hurt (Aragorn), Simon Chandler (Meriadoc), Dominic Guard (Pippin), Norman Bird (Bilbo Baggins), Michael Graham Cox (Boromir), Anthony Daniels (Legolas), David Buck (Gimli), Peter Woodthorpe (Gollum), Fraser Kerr (Saruman), Phillip Stone (King Théoden), Michael Deacon (Wormtongue), André Morell (Elrond), Alan Tilvern (Innkeeper), Annette Crosbie (Galadriel), John Westbrook (Treebeard).

CAST NOTES: Bakshi's voice-over cast is largely composed of hardworking, if not terribly well-known, British stage actors who have occasional memorable film and television roles to their credit.

William Squire (1916–1989) was a long-standing member of the Royal Shakespeare Company. His credits for that institution include playing The Duke of Buckingham in Peter Hall and John Barton's revered 1963 'The Wars of the Roses', a complete run/adaptation of Shakespeare's cycle of eight history plays. On screen he played Thomas More in *Anne of the Thousand Days*

(Charles Jarrot, 1969), starring Richard Burton, and appeared in many British TV series including *Rumpole of the Bailey* (1988), *Doctor Who* (as a villain in 'The Armageddon Factor', 1977) and *Blake's 7* (1979).

Christopher Guard played Kenneth Hodges for a year in the dreary British hospital soap *Casualty* (1993–94) and has made guest appearances in everything from *The Professionals* to *Agatha Christie's Poirot*. His brother Dominic plays Pippin in this adaptation. Dominic also survived a year on *Casualty* (1995–96). Minor film roles for him include *Ghandi* (Richard Attenborough, 1982) and *Picnic at Hanging Rock* (Peter Weir, 1975). Both have also played guest roles in *Doctor Who*.

John Hurt, who seems sadly underutilised as Aragorn, is rightly one of Britain's most respected and recognised actors. Oscar nominated for his title role in *The Elephant Man* (David Lynch, 1980) and his supporting turn in *Midnight Express* (Alan Parker, 1978), his other outstanding film roles include *Alien* (Ridley Scott, 1979) and as Winston Smith in *Nineteen Eighty Four* (Michael Radford, 1984). Career highlights include the film *Love and Death on Long Island* (Richard Kwietniowski, 1997), his portrayal of Quentin Crisp in *The Naked Civil Servant* (1975) and playing Caligula in *I, Claudius* (1976), both for the BBC. In 2004 he played the rogue Tory MP Alan Clarke in the Corporation's *The Alan Clark Diaries*, based on the late Minister's frank, amusing and sometimes alarming journals.

Anthony Daniels (Legolas) plays C-3PO in all of the *Star Wars* films, the only speaking principal to appear in all six pictures. Other notable roles include the pathologist in *Prime Suspect*, for British Independent TV.

Annette Crosbie's voice is recognisable as that of the long-suffering Margaret Meldrew, wife of Victor, in the BBC's long-running *One Foot in the Grave* (1990 to 2000). She played Catherine of Aragon the first of *The Six Wives of Henry VIII* on British television in 1970, ageing from adolescence to middle age over the course of 90 minutes with minimal make-up. Another Queen, Victoria, provided her with another stand-out role in ITV's *Edward VII* five years later. She played Dorothy in John Mortimor's brilliant *Paradise Postponed* (1986) and has enjoyed roles in several of the BBC's entries in *The Complete Works of William Shakespeare* series (1978–1985), including a fantastic Duchess of York in *Richard III* (1983).

Andre Morrell played O'Brien in the Rudolph Cartier-directed/ Nigel Kneale-scripted production of George Orwell's *Nineteen Eighty-Four* (1954) opposite Peter Cushing and was the hero of their later collaboration *Quatermass and the Pit* (1958), both for BBC television. His film roles include Sextus in *Ben-Hur* (William Wyler, 1959), with Charlton Heston, and the Earl of Wendover in Stanley Kubrick's beautiful William Makepeace Thackeray adaptation *Barry Lyndon* (1975).

It is fair to say that none of the cast delivers a particularly impressive performance and that none of the better-known actors achieves anything like what they are capable of, as demonstrated in other productions in which they have appeared. Michael Scholes's Samwise Gamgee in particular is a profoundly irritating characterisation. The simple fact that he is playing along with, rather than against, the nature of his dialogue will give anyone watching this picture renewed and reinvigorated respect for what Bill Nighy and Sean Astin achieve with almost identical dialogue in the 1981 BBC radio version and the New Line Cinema trilogy respectively.

The principal movement actors (see **ANIMATION**) were Paul Gale (Gandalf), Sharon Baird (Frodo), Trey Wilson (Aragorn) and Billy Barty (Sam and Bilbo), none of whom received credit for their work. Barty later took the matter up with various actors' and performers' rights groups, which agreed that, although no violation of the rules as they stood had been committed, from now on actors who made significant, but dialogue-free, appearances in a motion picture should be entitled to on-screen credit.

THE DIRECTOR: Born 19 October 1938 to Russian émigré parents, Ralph Bakshi was raised in Brooklyn, New York City. He graduated from the High School of Industrial Arts in Manhattan and was quickly recruited by Terrytoons, the company responsible for making the *Mighty Mouse* cartoons. After less than ten years at Terrytoons he was, at the age of 26, running the company. He left Terrytoons for Paramount, where he worked on Marvel Comics properties such as *Spider-Man* and *The Fantastic Four*, on cartoons that remain in syndication to this day. Gulf and Western, which had recently bought Paramount out, closed the animation studio less than a year after Bakshi's arrival.

After forming his own company, Bakshi expressed a desire to produce animated films for adults. He stood by his intentions by producing *Fritz the Cat* (1972), an adaptation of Robert Crumb's underground comic book, which became the first X-rated animated feature. Crumb himself hated it, but it made a lot of money and made Bakshi a cult figure with industry clout. His next picture, *Heavy Traffic* (1973), mixed autobiography with ghetto smarts and while at times profoundly shocking, it remains his best work. *Coonskin* (1975) was a satirical piece that dealt with racism and stereotyping but which was, in tune with the spirit of the times, decried as racist itself. It received only limited release and Bakshi was shattered by its poor reception. He then made *Wizards* (1977), in part influenced by the equally underground comics of Vaughn Bode. Of *Wizards* Bakshi has said that it is 'about the creation of the state of Israel and the Holocaust, about the Jews looking for a homeland, and about the fact that fascism was on the rise again . . . *Wizards* was a very personal film.'

Wizards was in part a show-reel to demonstrate how he would handle an adaptation of Tolkien's three-volume *The Lord of the Rings*, a book he had first read as an 18-year-old animation opaquer at Terrytoons, and the rights for which he had been chasing ever since he had the power to pursue his own projects.

Although Bakshi would later erroneously claim that Disney had held the rights when he first enquired, he was later obligated to withdraw this when the Walt Disney Corporation proved it had never held the rights to any Tolkien-related property at any time. In the mid-1970s the rights to *The Lord of the Rings* were held by United Artists, which had bought them from the writer in 1967.

According to Bakshi, MGM and/or UA intended to make *The Lord of the Rings* as a live-action film with John Boorman attached as writer/director and Mike Medavoy as producer. (MGM was a company with a complicated interconnected legal relationship with UA; the two companies were both involved in the James Bond film series at the time. As of 2004, MGM owns UA outright.) Bakshi had 'heard that Boorman was taking the three books and collapsing them into one screenplay, and I thought that was madness . . . why would you want to tamper with anything Tolkien did?'

Bakshi, who has called his annual attempts to pick up the rights 'like a yearly trek', approached UA and was told that Medavoy was unhappy with Boorman's 700-plus page screenplay. Bakshi's idea was to produce *The Lord of the Rings* as a series of animated films. His reasons were simple. He felt that a sophisticated cartoon, less adult than his earlier animations but 'nevertheless more adult than a Disney film', was the only way to create Tolkien's visual universe convincingly on screen. 'Tolkien asks us to suspend our disbelief, to accept the whole physical universe of Middle Earth [sic], its history and its inhabitants. How can you create the concepts of all of that in live action? Where do you get live action hobbits, elves and orcs? The answer is, of course, you can't.'

At the time, MGM and UA shared office space and so, according to Bakshi, he literally walked across the hall to the office of Dan Melnick, then President of MGM, and then he and Melnick went back to Medavoy's office. Melnick reimbursed UA the development money already spent by them by using MGM funds and turned the project over to Bakshi. Shortly afterwards, Melnick left MGM and the new management thought less favourably of the project.

Bakshi then approached award-winning independent producer Saul Zaentz, who had invested in his own *Fritz the Cat*. 'So now we were back at UA, and Saul and I made the picture', stated Bakshi. What Bakshi misses out of his telling is that Zaentz bought the Tolkien rights outright from UA/MGM and retains them in their entirety to this day.

Despite not being obliged to do so, Zaentz and Bakshi travelled to England to meet with the late writer's children and discuss their planned films with them. During production Bakshi took time out to assure fans that the film would not, despite being animation, be errantly childish and trivialise the source material, insisting to reporters that 'The evil and the violence . . . is what I can relate to . . . I will make it Evil with all intensity.' Ultimately, Bakshi's film would be far from traditional in terms of its animation (see **ANIMATION**).

THE PRODUCER: Zaentz's Fantasy Films company was a subsidiary of Fantasy Records, a small company that Zaentz bought out while still an employee and turned into a recording and financial powerhouse thanks to his signing of the Creedence Clearwater Revival. Zaentz then set up Fantasy Films as a sub-company in order to produce motion pictures independently of the Hollywood system, funding them out of his own capital while being involved in a hands-on manner in the actual production. His first major picture, *One Flew Over The Cuckoo's Nest* (Milos Forman, 1975), won five Academy Awards, including Best Picture (and garnered a Best Supporting Actor nomination for future New Line Cinema *The Lord of the Rings* actor Brad Dourif). It was thanks to this success that Zaentz was able to buy the rights to Tolkien's books from United Artists.

Since the failure of *JRR Tolkien's The Lord of the Rings* (see **BOOK AND SCREENPLAY**) and the non-commissioning of the sequel/second half, Zaentz has continued to produce movies. His infrequent, but prestigious, contributions to American film in the last quarter-century have included *The Mosquito Coast* (Peter Weir, 1988), *The English Patient* (Anthony Minghella, 1997) and *Amadeus* (Milos Forman, 1984). He continues to own studio and production facilities and operates out of Berkeley, California. He stands as one of America's most successful independent film producers of all time.

BOOK AND SCREENPLAY: Bakshi felt the production was under considerable pressure of expectation from the very beginning. Considering the book's vast popularity, he once commented that his production office got 'about fifteen hundred letters a week from the Tolkien freaks ... "You'd better do it right or you're dead".' Hopefully, either the actual death threats were not meant literally, or Bakshi was being hyperbolic.

Bakshi wanted to make three films, closely corresponding to each of the three volumes that Tolkien's book was originally published in. He was persuaded instead to make two films of two and a half hours each, using the divide between the two to take advantage of the point where the narrative of *The Two Towers* doubles back on itself (i.e. between Books III and IV).

The Lord of the Rings by JRR Tolkien is a book that is uniquely ill-suited to being dramatised. This is not for qualitative reasons. Many better books than *The Lord of the Rings* have been successfully and faithfully dramatised, from Dennis Potter's brilliant TV adaptation of Thomas Hardy's *The Mayor of Casterbridge* to Francis Ford Coppola's films based on Mario Puzo's novel *The Godfather*. Neither is it for reasons related to the ferocity of the fanbase, although some (though by no means all) fans of *The Lord of the Rings* can give the very worst excesses of any fan group a run for their money. No, the simple reason is the way that *The Lord of the Rings* is structured.

It is divided into six books, each comprising around ten chapters. Each of these books follows a set of characters (in Book III Merry, Pippin, Aragorn, Legolas and Gimli, in Book VI Frodo and Sam, for example) in a linear and chronological fashion. Within these books the audience only discovers what the characters they are following discover, and learn of it when they learn of it. When characters enter or re-enter the narrative after a long time away they frequently detail, at length, what has happened to them while they have been out of the company of the audience/the characters the audience follow.

Additionally, the six books of *The Lord of the Rings* do not follow one another chronologically but instead some of the books are about events that occur separately, but simultaneously, to different groups of characters. This rambling approach to structure seems to have been a deliberate conceit on the author's part (*The Hobbit* has a more disciplined, obvious structure), an attempt to emulate aspects of the epics that he particularly liked. These, generally written before concepts of plotting had been formalised, seemed to represent, to Tolkien, something purer than the delicate plotting of Shakespeare (whom he despised). It is at least an equally valid viewpoint that *Beowulf* and, say, the Welsh epic *Otherworld* are exciting examples of early literature *despite*, rather than because of, their free-form and erratic nature and that the development of a clear narrative structure, but not restrictive concepts of what constitutes plot development, is a positive thing.

There are no flashbacks or cutaways of any kind in *The Lord of the Rings*; information is always conveyed from one character to another through dialogue. This means that the reader frequently learns of an event long after it happens, chronologically speaking, and only when the character to whom it happened explains the event to another. Here is a simple example. Gandalf's encounter with Radaghast The Brown, of his order, takes place not long after Gandalf leaves Frodo in Book I, Chapter III. However, the audience, and the other characters, do not learn about his encounter until Book II, Chapter II ('The Council of Elrond'). There are many, many other such examples. Performed drama, especially film, uses the 'cut' from one scene to another, from one set of characters to another, as a matter of course. 'Montage' is probably the single most important, and most used, storytelling technique used within the medium of filmed drama.

In short, in *The Lord of the Rings* there is an entirely asynchronous plotline unfolding non-chronologically across hundreds of thousands of words. To make plot matters more confused still, plot-relevant material is occasionally only conveyed to the audience through a character's dreams.

Thus it is a situation where an eccentrically, even meanderingly structured book is having to be adapted to a medium where the chronological conveyance of information is paramount. The first thing anyone adapting *The Lord of the Rings* into drama has to do is to sort its events into narrative order – the order in which they would occur if they were 'real'. This will necessitate all but abandoning much of Tolkien's structure, particularly after the end of Book II, and relying heavily on his explanatory chronology of events presented in the book's 'Appendix B'.

When preparing the first draft, Ralph Bakshi told his writers to 'become "as Tolkien" as they could in remaining faithful to the books'. Primary screenwriter Chris Conkling recalls the process of adapting and drafting the screenplay as laborious: 'We wrote it as three films, and then I [put it together and then] cut it in half and wrote it as two films.' (The second film was, of course, never made – see below.) Conkling says that this approach was attempted because of the difficulties of scripting a 'middle' film from the already difficult-to-adapt Books III and IV. (Conkling has since stated that had he seen *Star Wars: Episode V – The Empire Strikes Back* (Irvin Kershner/George Lucas, 1980) he would have a far clearer idea of how to script a film which is 'all middle'.) Bakshi commented that, when it came to writing the screenplay, 'The structure was a big problem . . . [we] started by constructing the script directly from the book [but] the dramatic balance kept shifting' – presumably due to both the travelogue nature of *The Fellowship of the Ring* and the dog-leg structure of *The Two Towers*.

Conkling's draft (dated 13 September 1976) adopts the entirely un-Tolkien-like structure of beginning with Merry and Pippin fleeing from the orcs (as at Book III, Chapter III) before going into flashbacks to narrate the story up to that point. (This draft, incidentally, does feature Tom Bombadil in one of these flashbacks.) After this version of the screenplay was completed, Steven Beagle was brought in as a co-writer.

The finished screenplay of the (un)finished film rejects Book I, Chapters IV–VIII ('A Short Cut to Mushrooms', 'A Conspiracy

Unmasked', 'The Old Forest', 'In the House of Tom Bombadil' and 'Fog on the Barrow-Downs') and Book II, Chapter IX ('The Great River').

It is easy to see why much of the cut material was lost. Bakshi decided, as Peter Jackson later would, that Tom Bombadil 'didn't push the story along'. It is also true, as Tolkien's own letters show, that much of the material between Book I, Chapter II and Book I, Chapter IX was written without a clear idea of where Frodo and his companions were heading or even that Bilbo's old ring was the One Ring at all. Rewrites, long before publication, cleared and clarified the situation earlier in Book I, but these chapters all have elements of simple travelogue to them; Tolkien was taking his audience on a tour around his world.

Apart from this, the second version of the screenplay proceeds in a straightforward single line until the end of Book III, Chapter II, 'The Riders of Rohan'. After this point Bakshi/Beagle/Conkling considered it necessary, as Jackson and Muller would later (see **The Fellowship of the Ring**), to cut back and forth between the two separate books of *The Two Towers* (Books III and IV), the events of which occur simultaneously but are treated as two separate linear plotlines by Tolkien. Thus, Book III, Chapter III ('The Uruk Hai') is split in two and interlaced with elements of Book IV, Chapter I ('The Taming of Sméagol'). After this Book III, Chapters IV to VI ('Treebeard', 'The White Rider', 'The King of the Golden Hall') are then adapted in an abridged but uninterrupted form. This is followed by Book III, Chapter VII ('Helm's Deep'), which is divided into three chunks, with cutaways to Frodo and Sam experiencing elements of Book IV, Chapter II ('The Passage of the Marshes') and Book IV, Chapter VIII ('The Stairs of Cirith Ungol'). Book III, Chapters VIII–XI ('The Road to Isengard', 'Flotsam and Jestsam', 'The Voice of Saruman' and 'The Palantir') are skipped over, as are Book IV, Chapters III–VII ('The Black Gate is Closed', 'Of Herbs and Stewed Rabbit', 'The Window on the West', 'The Forbidden Pool' and 'Journey to the Cross-Roads'), and IX–X ('Shelob's Lair' and 'The Choices of Master Samwise'). These chapters were presumably intended to be used in the second part of Bakshi's projected duet of films. (At the time, Bakshi commented: 'in the second picture we'll try to pick up on sequences we missed in the first book ... I'm going to backtrack ... Tom Bombadil might make it'.) The shooting draft ends with Frodo and Sam heading towards

Mordor in orc armour with the camera pulling back to reveal Gollum following them, rather than with Gandalf's victory at the Battle of Helm's Deep as in the final film.

Co-scriptwriter Beagle calls the finished film, in a deeply unpleasant phrase, a 'partial birth abortion'. He insists that the preview-screened version of the picture ends, as does the script, with Sam and Frodo heading unknowingly towards Shelob's cave, but that between the preview and the full release Zaentz ordered that the final two reels be switched so that the film ends with Helm's Deep. Zaentz flatly denies this ever happened. Third-party evidence is inconclusive on this point. Alexander Stuart's review in *Films and Filming* (Vol. 25, No. 10, July 1979) is clearly of the film as currently available on DVD, but that in *Screen International* (No. 198, 14 July 1978) describes, if obliquely, the ending as reported by Beagle. If such a switch was made, therefore (and it would make sense given the anti-climactic and abrupt ending of the picture) it must have been during the preview-screening process (i.e. between one showing for journalists and another). This is unlikely and Beagle's assertion must be considered unproven unless further material comes to light.

While Bakshi considers the script 'faithful', it is worth bearing in mind the alterations that are made in addition to the deletions. Not all of these are down to matters of technique or story structure, and some appear to be – quite simply – mistakes. Space prevents us from listing every 'deviation' from the text of the book, or every point of contentious interpretation. We draw attention only to those that seem to demonstrate, to us, either a particular understanding or, conversely, a lack of understanding of the book being adapted.

Conkling and Beagle's script adds a prologue that draws on *The Silmarillion* and *The Hobbit* in order to explain the background of Middle-earth and the One Ring. This contains the assertion that 'the Dark Lord learned the craft of Ring-making' *after* the elves had made the Rings. This has been criticised. However, in Book I, Chapter II it is not at all clear how all the rings came into being. The first three rings are explicitly said to have been made by the elves, but there are implications from Gandalf that Sauron both made and gave away, and sought and acquired some of the other Rings of Power. Gandalf states outright that the One Ring was made by Sauron himself, which also implies that many of the others were not. On balance, that the Ring can only be destroyed at Mount Doom where it was made makes it clear that that Sauron created the One Ring. The screenplay's decision to make the earlier rings the product of elves and the One Ring Sauron's only creation, made after he discovered the art of ring-making, is a sensible straightening out of a situation that is already confused before the end of Chapter II in the book. (It is in *The Silmarillion* that further details are found, and the screenplay does not co-opt these for further explanation.)

One inexplicable change/mistake in this section is the claim that the last alliance of elves and men lost their war with Sauron's forces. 'As the Last Alliance of Men and Elves fell beneath his power,' narrates the voiceover, the direct opposite of what happens on the page. The Bakshi film also tells of how 'Prince' Isildur (Aragorn's ancestor) cut off Sauron's hand by sneaking up behind him rather than attacking the Dark Lord head on. Isildur's decision not to destroy the Ring is not mentioned. He is killed by arrows, but seems to throw the Ring into the river before his death rather than it coming off his finger after he is already swimming.

This prologue also uses elements of Gandalf's tale of Sméagol and Déagol in Book I, Chapter II to create an 'origin story' for Gollum, which is viewed by the audience as an independent observer. After this, the audience sees elements of Chapter V of the revised version of *The Hobbit* ('Riddles in the Dark') including Gollum's protestations of eternal hatred for Bilbo Baggins.

The adaptation of Book I, Chapter I is a largely faithful condensation (which loses much of the middle-class flummery between Bilbo's various inheritors and concentrates on the plot) but has further odd omissions and changes. It does keep the seventeen-year gap between Bilbo's going away party and Gandalf's return with information about the Ring. This is a good example of retained detail (a detail that even close readers of the book may not notice), but it is clumsily achieved as, due to the nature of the medium, portraying the passage of several years in a matter of a few seconds is difficult to pull off well. Despite retaining this time-gap, the film then dispenses with the detail that Gandalf's return is around Frodo's fiftieth birthday and the information that Gandalf has come back to see Frodo occasionally, if infrequently, during those seventeen years. (Tolkien writes that Frodo did not see Gandalf for three years after Bilbo going away, and that he saw him periodically over the next few years but that he did not see him at all for the last nine of that seventeen.)

The script also loses Gandalf's initial worries, before his departure, about the nature of Bilbo's ring and the months between Gandalf's revelation to Frodo about the Ring and Frodo's own departure from Hobbiton. This telescoping of lackadaisical events, which would both lack urgency and be oddly difficult to present on screen, is largely sensible and all other adaptations went on to do something similar (see the screenplay for *Harry Potter and the Philosopher's Stone*, Chris Columbus, 2001, for a simply disastrous attempt to retain casual prose details in a motion picture).

However, what seems less sensible is that, when Gandalf does return to see Frodo and throws the Ring into the fire at Bag End in order to see the writing on it, neither he nor Frodo actually bothers to look at it once it comes out of the fire. They never see the writing and neither does the audience, despite Gandalf having spoken of it as being the ultimate proof of the Ring's identity just moments before. This is not so much a change as a monumental inconsistency *within* the adaptation.

An odd change is that Gandalf and Frodo's discussion of the One Ring and what must be done with it takes place outside, at night, rather than during the day in Bag End. This has the knock-on effect that Samwise's overhearing of their discussion stops making logical sense. In the book, Sam is under the window, doing some gardening (which is, after all, his job) when he overhears the conversation. In this film, he appears to be hiding behind a bush. In the middle of a wood. At night. For no reason. It isn't even made clear that Samwise *is* Frodo's gardener. Gandalf also, here, seems to decide to send Samwise along on Frodo's journey to Rivendell for no reason other than he wants to go and see elves rather than, as in the book, as some kind of punishment inflicted on him by Gandalf for inadvertently eavesdropping. This is especially odd as, on screen, Sam's eavesdropping is less inadvertent/defensible, and Gandalf's 'punishment' would make far more sense in this context than it does on the page.

On the page Merry and Pippin accompany Frodo out of the Shire because they are his cousins and they are helping him in his ostensible purpose (moving house). In this screenplay, they are simply sent with Sam and Frodo by Gandalf. While the necessary deletion of the 'moving house' subplot (which would take up vast amounts of screentime to no gain at all) makes coming up with a new reason essential, this is not a particularly elegant one. Merry's assertion that he once saw Bilbo use the Ring to hide from the Sackville-Bagginses comes from the end of *The Hobbit*.

A particularly irritating alteration is that Saruman is referred to as both Saruman and Aruman in the picture. This seems to be because of the potential confusion between Sauron and Saruman. Unfortunately further confusion, rather than further clarity, is created by this because of the inconsistency. Presumably, the inconsistent pronunciation of Sauron by the actors (some say Sow-Ron, some Soar-Ron) evolves out of a similar logic. It is similarly unsuccessful.

At the Council of Elrond, Aragorn lets it be known that he is a descendant of Elendil, and that he has 'the Sword that was Broken'. Unfortunately, the movie has not yet explained, indeed never does explain, who Elendil was or why this broken sword is relevant. It is also relevant that the re-forging of the sword is omitted. This means that when Aragorn then draws his sword at Moria, and it is no longer broken, this comes across as a continuity error rather than the missing plot-element it actually is.

At the council of Elrond, it is spectacularly unclear that the Ring must be taken to Mount Doom to be destroyed as that Mountain, which is where it was forged in the first place, is the only place with fires hot enough to melt it. This is not a complex concept yet, on screen, Elrond continually trips over the fact that the ring *cannot* be destroyed (meaning except at Mount Doom) and seems to propose sending the Ring to the mountain for no clear purpose. It is possible that this is deliberate, an attempt to hide from the audience what will happen to the Ring until the end of the second movie, but, if so, it is clumsy in both intention and execution.

In fact, much of the film only really makes sense to a viewer already familiar with the ins and outs of Tolkien's plot. It almost seems as if the screenwriters were so familiar with the book thanks to the process of adaptation that they could not step back and see what needed to be explained and what was already clear.

ANIMATION: Bakshi saw his mission as to 'develop another level of animation, realistic animation' that could achieve the same 'level [as] painting'. He later commented that he wanted his films to 'look Dutch [like] Rembrandt in motion' with his particular obsession: 'I want my forests real.'

His solution was to rotoscope the entire film. The Rotoscope was invented by cartoon pioneers Max and David Fleischer (who produced the still wonderful 1940s *Superman* shorts) for their *Out of the Inkwell* Betty Boop short in 1938. In simple terms, the rotoscoping process involves shooting live action on film, printing it, and then tracing over the live action frames in order to provide the basis for animation. The process, as used on *The Lord of the Rings*, would allow Bakshi to achieve a density of action unlike anything ever seen before. Bakshi called his own version of rotoscoping a 'breakthrough' and also said, 'I had done a lot of experimenting over the years with live action and animation in different combinations', eventually arriving at a point where 'I designed a technique' whereby it would be possible to 'shoot an entire movie and then trace every frame'. Defending himself against the allegation that this system wasn't proper animation, Bakshi observed that 'It wasn't a cheat, it was a choice' and pointed out that, while his use of rotoscoping was more extensive than had been attempted on any previous film, it was also true that 'Disney used rotoscoping on [nearly] every film he did, but he kept it a secret'.

Because of this decision, before the animation could begin, the whole film needed to be shot using live action. But before that could happen, Bakshi wanted to record all the voices for the characters so that the actors on set would know what they would/should be interacting with on screen. When shooting began, on Hollywood soundstages utilising full costume but minimal sets and props, Bakshi worked fast. He shot between 75 and 200 set-ups a day, playing back the pre-recorded dialogue to the movement performers. For the Battle of Helm's Deep, Bakshi shot at Belmonte Castle on the plains of La Mancha in Spain – perhaps appropriate for what was seen by many Tolkien fans as a highly quixotic enterprise.

Bakshi was effectively making two films at once: 'I've been shooting a live action picture and the animation studio has been running in parallel.' When asked if this meant that he was exerting less control over the animation than he would like, he responded that 'the direction of the live action sets the direction of the animation' and that the live action as directed by him was 'designed to be expanded' in the animation studio. He told *Screen International* that 'the pressure has been enormous', although he was, nevertheless, 'Very proud and happy' to have done the production.

Bakshi hired animators from the Art Center College of Design at Pasadena and the California Institute of the Arts (CalArts – a long-established Disney feeder school whose alumni include directors Tim Burton and John Lasseter), swelling his normally 100-strong staff to more than 200 by the end of production. It was the 'most devastating and nerve-wracking two and a half years of my life', Bakshi reflected later.

While the level of motion detail demonstrated through much of the film is hugely impressive, there are other less likeable aspects to the technique. The opening prologue is not so much live action film that has been 'animated-over' as live action film that has been tinted red and black. The battle in this sequence is small, confused and horrible, with actors visibly just slapping one another with prop swords. The canvas effect laid on to the film looks odd, rather than suggestive of artwork or fibres, and the small amount of set dressing used for the live action is distressingly noticeable. Without the benefit of the animation the movements of the actors seem horribly exaggerated and ugly, needlessly 'big' and needlessly 'quick', especially the leaping Gollum with his furry feet. It is an inauspicious beginning. There is a single exception – the shot of Ring Wraiths riding along the crest of a hill. This is film shot on location and is far more impressive.

Much of the physical action of the film is unimpressive generally, with ill-co-ordinated physical movements from the performers, suggesting that Bakshi's undoubted expertise in certain areas relating to animation did not then extend to an ability to shoot and choreograph live action.

Other visual incongruities include the striking contrasts of the scene at the Inn at Bree. Here the hobbits (and indeed Strider) are rotoscoped as normal, fully animated based on the exposed live action film, but the background characters are simply crudely coloured in halftones. They look like they belong to a different physical universe entirely than that occupied by the hobbits. That this is an attempt to demonstrate visually the gross nature of men (made much of at the appropriate point in Tolkien, and more so during the same sequence in Jackson's version) is a possibility, but, if so, it is a fumbled one. Logically, Aragorn, or at least the Innkeeper, should be animated in a manner slightly more akin to the background action, surely? As it stands, the glaring difference in animation style detracts from any sense of a believable world, and heightens the audience's growing sense that this film is somewhat flawed.

The battle at Helm's Deep descends into abject visual confusion by its end. Character's faces – notably Théoden's – seemingly do not match what they are supposed to be feeling. (He smiles, casually and warmly, at the realisation that he may lose the fight; in context, it is neither an ironic smile nor a grim one.) This may have resulted from off-cuts of film or moments of the actors 'not acting', i.e. not demonstrably being in character, being used as the basis for rotoscoped pictures. While there is no evidence that this happened, it is certainly what it looks like. The troops' movements at Helm's Deep seem to make little physical sense in relation to one another and it is very difficult to work out what is meant to be going on.

Admittedly Tolkien's own explanation of how and by whom, where and why the battle at Helm's Deep is fought is sketchy (see **The Lord of the Rings: The Two Towers**) but there really is no excuse for, in a visual medium, things falling apart to this extent. Bakshi's version of the battle achieves the rare distinction of being incomprehensible without being complex. The bloodbath that results from Gandalf's attack on the orcs seems out of place, with blood splashing on to the camera in gory animated gallons. The one distinction of this sequence is that this version's decision to have a character who appears to be Éomer come to the aid of the besieged Rohirrim makes a certain amount of sense while not being faithful to the book. It was later also used by Peter Jackson.

FILM REVIEWS: *Films and Filming*'s Alexander Stuart didn't like Bakshi's film very much at all – 'uninvolving, at times even boring', he commented warily and noted that Tolkien's story 'looked pretty simple minded when broken down into its basic line of action'. He felt that the animation's strong point was the 'wealth of detail' but this did not compensate for the picture's frequent 'major visual flaws'. *Screen International*'s Marjorie Bilbow was more positive, feeling that the film was 'an adaptation made with affection and integrity' but found little else to say about it.

Variety, too, saw little to like in the film: 'Bakshi overlooks the uninitiated completely.' The picture was 'confusing . . . boring is an equally good word' and the producers would have to expect 'bad word of mouth' leading to inevitable 'trouble appealing to a broad audience'. Vincent Canby of *The New York Times* was also overwhelmingly negative about the film, saying that it would be 'difficult to recommend this movie to anyone . . . not familiar with

Tolkien's home-made mythology' thanks to 'incomprehensible exposition', most of which he blamed on screenwriters Beagle and Conkling and their clumsy adaptation.

One person who was impressed by Bakshi's film was the young Peter Jackson. He would later take a number of visual and plotting motifs from the Bakshi/Beagle/Conkling adaptation, and carefully examine their mistakes to provide an indication of what to avoid when it came to producing his own film version nearly twenty years later. Despite not having read the book when the film came out in New Zealand, Jackson was immediately taken with the story, and he rushed off to pick up a copy of Tolkien's original to find out how it ended.

PART TWO?: The *New York Times*' Vincent Canby resented the lack of conclusion, protesting he wanted to 'rip up a seat' in frustration at the (non) ending. The lack of a conclusion became even more of a problem when the second movie failed to appear. When Bakshi's picture was released on DVD to coincide with the theatrical exhibition of the first Jackson/Walsh instalment (see **The Lord of the Rings: The Fellowship of the Ring**), this was the primary point of discussion for most reviewers; one British magazine noted in 2001 how the film 'ended just as it's getting interesting'. This aspect of the picture, its deferred ending and the lamentable lack of a second instalment to complete the story, was something over which the director of the picture had no control.

The film concludes part of the way through Tolkien's *The Two Towers* with a voiceover that refers to the film the audience has just watched as 'the first great tale of The Lord of the Rings!' This is despite there being no mention on the opening credits of this being only part of the story. 'It was supposed to be called *The Lord of the Rings: Part One* on the marquee,' said Bakshi years later. According to the director, he was informed late on in the production process, just after the delivery of the film, that the 'Part One' would be dropped as people would not go to see what they would think of as half a film. Bakshi protested the decision: 'I told them they can't drop the Part One, because people are going to come in thinking they'll see the whole film, and it's not there,' but he lost the argument. Years later he was still protesting: 'They screwed me royally, because they never put "Part One" on the screen.'

Just before the revelation that this film is only 'the first part' comes the summary that 'The forces of darkness were driven from

Middle-earth forever by the valiant friends of Frodo', as we see Aragorn leading a troop of horsemen away from Helm's Deep. Does this mean that it is not thanks to Frodo's journey across Mordor and the destruction of the Ring that Sauron is defeated? Does this mean that the whole emphasis (which Tolkien placed at the very heart of his book) that it is the actions of a single brave individual that can change the world has been lost? As the story was never finished, and the proposed second part never made, yes.

What would have been simply a rather poor attempt at an adaptation had Bakshi been able to complete the story, instead, through this truncated ending and ill-considered summary of the rest of the story, becomes a travesty. The fact that this was not entirely Bakshi's fault does excuse him to an extent, but even had he been able to complete the second part, his version of *The Lord of the Rings* would never have been the faithful one he claims to have envisaged. Nonetheless, it is hard not to feel sorry for a film-maker who received such little support. The major lesson to be learned from Bakshi's experience was the importance of having understanding backers. 'People keep telling me I never finished the film,' said Bakshi decades later, 'and I keep saying, "That's right!" That's what they cost me, United Artists and probably the producer; I'm not sure who made the final decision. I was screaming, and it was like screaming into the wind.'

Jackanory: The Hobbit (1979)

One of the most satisfying Tolkien on-screen versions can be found as part of the BBC's long-running, now sadly defunct, children's strand *Jackanory*. Running from 1965 to 1995, with nearly 700 books featured in that time, *Jackanory* featured actors and celebrities reading, to camera, books for children. Occasionally myths, legends and folk tales were related instead. During these tellings, the camera would often also show illustrations taken directly from the book (if possible) as an aid to the imaginations of the children watching.

It was hugely popular in the middle years of its existence and readers included Kenneth Williams, Tom Baker, Billie Whitelaw, Judi Dench, Alan Bennett, Joyce Grenfell, Rik Mayall, Clement Freud, Jon Pertwee and HRH Charles,

Prince of Wales. The most prolific reader, however, was Bernard Cribbins, who made 111 appearances on the programme between 1966 and 1992. It was Cribbins who narrated *The Hobbit*, unabridged, between 1 and 12 October 1979 (there were no episodes of *Jackanory* on Saturdays or Sundays) in ten fourteen-minute instalments, backed by illustrations taken from the author's own contributions to the various editions. Engagingly read by the vocally dexterous Cribbins, the finished production is a delight. Cribbins's Bilbo stands easy comparison with those of John Le Mesurier and Ian Holm, and towers over Orson Bean's performance in the Rankin features. The episode titles (all taken from one of the chapters contained within the episode) are given here for completeness' sake. The production was directed by Roger Singleton-Turner. It has never been released commercially, but off-air VHS copies do exist in private hands. The episode titles were as follows:

1 An Unexpected Party
2 Over Hill and Under Hill
3 Riddles in the Dark
4 Out of the Frying Pan, Into the Fire
5 Flies and Spiders
6 Barrels out of Bond
7 Inside Information
8 Fire and Water
9 The Cloud Burst
10 The Return Journey

The Mind's Eye (1979)

While the BBC's radio adaptation is the primary audio version of Tolkien's work (indeed, until the Jackson films it could have been argued to be the primary adaptation of Tolkien full stop), there are other sound-only versions of Tolkien that have been attempted over the years.

Most of these are in the form of readings, abridged and unabridged, usually by a single actor. These vary in quality (probably the best is Martin Shaw's reading of the unabridged *Silmarillion*) but arguably do not constitute 'adaptations'. The unabridged readings certainly do not, and to abridge a book is a different process from adaptation. Losing words from a text, especially a long, even over-written, one is not the same as transferring the essence of said text to another medium, one with different concerns, strengths and weakness entirely.

The most significant other adaptation is that produced in 1979 by a company called The Mind's Eye (later Soundelux). This is now available in the USA on cassette tape (ISBN 1-56511-549-X) and CD (ISBN 1-56511-550-3) from audiobook publishers Highbridge Audio, a large company that has titles ranging from Jane Austen to *Star Wars*.

The Mind's Eye version was adapted by Bernard Mayes (who also cast himself as Gandalf and Tom Bombadil and served as director on the project) and utilises a narrator as a means of keeping as much of Tolkien's description intact as possible (within the scenes that are directly adapted). In this sense, the Mind's Eye version is more like a multiple-person reading (albeit a massively abridged one) than a dramatisation per se. The retention of Tom Bombadil, while it would delight Tolkien purists, is largely possible because the Bombadil scene isn't *adapted* – it is just transferred directly as it would be in a reading; the only difference is that the 'saids' are deleted and there's more than one voice involved. It still makes little narrative contribution to the piece, naturally.

The rest of the cast are local theatre actors from in and around Pittsburgh, where the production was recorded. Reportedly a one-microphone recording (it certainly sounds like one) and dominated by on-microphone real-time sound effects, it stands no comparison, sound-wise, with the BBC's lavish effort.

The performances are also variable: Mayes is a fine Gandalf, and Gale Chugg's narration is effective, but Frodo's descent into twitchy ring obsession isn't conveyed by James Arrington's one-note performances. He sounds like someone who has something tedious to whinge about, rather than an

Everyman crushed by the weight of his responsibility, and Lou Bliss's Sam is too obviously a New Yorker for his pastoralisms to be effective. (In the Jackson films the American Sean Astin makes a fair stab at a British West Country accent for the duration.)

PRINCIPAL CAST: Ray Reinhardt (Bilbo), James Arrington (Frodo), Pat Franklyn (Merry), Mac McCaddon (Pippin), Lou Bliss (Sam), Bernard Mayes (Gandalf), Gale Chugg (Narrator), Bernard Mayes (Tom Bombadil), Time Luce (Aragorn), Pat Franklyn, Mac McCaddon, Bob Lewis, Gail Chugg, John Vickery, Erik Bauersfeld, Ray Reinhardt, Carl Hague (Additional Voices).

JRR TOLKIEN'S THE RETURN OF THE KING – A TALE OF HOBBITS (1980)

(TVM 97 minutes)

A Tale of Hobbits
An Arthur Rankin Jr, Jules Bass Film
© RANKIN/BASS PRODUCTIONS, INC. MCMLXXIX
Based on the Original Versions of 'The Hobbit' and 'The
    Return of the King' by JRR Tolkien
Adapted for the screen by Romeo Muller
Production Designed by Arthur Rankin Jr
Music: Maury Laws
Lyrics: Jules Bass
Music Arranged and Conducted by Maury Laws and Bernard
    Hoffer
Associate Producer: Masaki Tizuka
Produced and Directed by Arthur Rankin Jr and Jules Bass
Animation Coordinator: Toru Hara
Continuity Design: Tsugyuki Kubo
Character Design: Lester Abrams, Tsugyuki Kubo
Background Design: Minoru Nishda
Animation Director: Katsuhisa Yamada, Koichi Sasaki
Animators: Kazuyuki Kobayashi, Tadakatsu Yoshida, Hidemi
    Kubo

First Transmitted: 11 May 1980 (NBC)

PRINCIPAL CAST: Orson Bean (Frodo Baggins/Bilbo Baggins), Theodore Bikel (Aragorn), William Conrad (Denethor), John Huston (Gandalf), Roddy McDowall (Samwise Gamgee), Theodore (Gollum), with the talents of Paul Frees, Casey Kasem, Don Messick, John Stephenson, Sonny Melendrez, Nellie Bellflower, and Glenn Yarbrough as the Minstrel.

CAST NOTES: Born in Vienna and raised in Palestine, Theodore Bikel is a distinguished stage performer and best-selling folk singer. He was nominated for a Best Supporting Actor Oscar for his performance in *The Defiant Ones* (Stanley Kramer, 1958) in which he played the Sheriff pursuing Sidney Poitier and Tony Curtis. He was the German boat captain in fellow cast-member John Huston's *The African Queen* (1951) and was memorable as 'that awful Hungarian!' in *My Fair Lady* (George Cukor, 1964). He was second choice for the title role in *Goldfinger* (Guy Hamilton, 1963), the James Bond adventure. His screen test is included on the DVD issue of that film.

Roddy McDowall started acting as a child, first becoming noticed at the age of twelve in John Ford's multiple-Oscar-winning *How Green Was My Valley* (1941). He went on to play Malcolm in Orson Welles's Macbeth (1948), Caesar in *Cleopatra* (Joseph L Mankiewicz, 1963), for which he was nominated for a Golden Globe, and innumerable parts – great and small – in countless films and television shows. However, despite a career spanning seven decades, he will forever be most associated with the various iterations of *Planet of the Apes*. He appeared in four of the six films and starred in the spin-off TV series – primarily under a rubber mask and furry monkey suit. He died in 1998, having just completed recording his part for the Disney/Pixar flick *A Bug's Life* (1998).

Casey Kasem is one of America's most prolific voiceover artists. He has played Shaggy in every version of *Scooby-Doo* for over thirty years, is the voice of *Hong Kong Phooey* (1974) and played Dick Grayson/Robin in *Super-Friends* (1973) and various other *Batman* and DC Comics-related cartoon series. He was also the DJ in Martin Scorsese's much-underrated *New York, New York* (1977), and Bluestreak/Cliffjumper in the original English-language *Transformers* series, as well as in the 1986 Orson Welles-starring movie.

Don Messick (1926–1997), who provides additional voices, was the voices of Boo Boo and Ranger Smith in every *Yogi Bear* cartoon made between 1958 and 1994. In 1969 he was cast as a cowardly cartoon dog called *Scooby-Doo*. He would play the character in more than a dozen iterations of the cartoon series for 25 years, only retiring after a stroke made it impossible for him to continue working. Other credits include the narrator of *Hong Kong Phooey* (1974), playing Bam Bam Rubble in later series of *The Flintstones* and featuring as heroic Autobots Gears and Ratchet in both *The Transformers* cartoon series (1984 to 1987) and the movie spin-off *Transformers: The Movie* (Nelson Shin, 1986).

While the on-screen credits do not specify roles for many of the supporting cast, Paul Frees plays the orcs and Elrond, Casey Kasem plays Meriadoc Brandybuck (Merry), Sonny Melendrez voices Peregrin Took (Pippin), and Nellie Bellflower plays Éowyn. Although not credited at all, it is audibly voice-over artiste Alan Oppenheimer playing the Witch King of Angmar; the chief Nazgûl sounds exactly like Oppenheimer's second most famous role (after his turn as *Mighty Mouse* in the mid-1940s) – that of Skeletor in *He-Man and the Masters of the Universe* (1983).

PRODUCTION NOTES: The production of the Rankin/Bass *JRR Tolkien's The Return of the King* was announced in the *Hollywood Reporter* on 7 April 1977 (Vol. 245, No. 2). This was *during* production of Bakshi's film and *before* the transmission of *The Hobbit*. This fact contradicts both Rankin's assertion that 'we did that [*The Return of the King*] only because *The Hobbit* was so successful' and the widespread assumption on Tolkien Internet fansites that the second Rankin/Bass special only came into existence as a project because of the widely perceived failure of the Bakshi/Zaentz project.

It seems likely, based on the available information, that even if Bakshi *had* successfully produced and released his second film, completing the story in the process, Rankin/Bass would have produced *The Return of the King* and had it available for showing on television before Bakshi's *The Lord of the Rings: Part Two* (or whatever it would have wound up being called) was showing in cinemas. The apparent conflict is presumably down to the television and theatrical rights to the plot/property being subtly different legal entities. (Ralph Bakshi has stated, when objecting to the New Line Cinema trilogy, that his original contract for the 1978 film gives him 'all sequel rights'. This raises interesting legal possibilities.)

BOOK AND SCREENPLAY: Romeo Muller's script misses out Book V, Chapters II ('The Passing of the Grey Company') and VIII ('The Houses of Healing'), and Chapters VII ('Homeward Bound') and VIII ('The Scouring of the Shire') from Book VI. Because the book doubles back on itself, telling the story in two separate continuous sections (i.e. Books V and VI), the script is also forced to adapt much of the novel out of sequence, cutting from one storyline to another in standard televisual/filmic technique. The addition of an opening framing sequence, drawn largely from Book VI, Chapter VI ('Many Partings'), further disrupts Tolkien's own design for the story. While this may sound drastic, Muller should be commended for successfully condensing not only *The Return of the King*, but also elements from the whole of *The Lord of the Rings* and *The Hobbit* into a mere 97 minutes and finding, for the most part, useful and convenient reasons/explanations for things that are explained in other books of *The Lord of the Rings*.

The cartoon begins with Sam and Frodo heading back towards Rivendell, having completed their mission (Book VI, Chapter VI), and then moves into a sequence from the same chapter, Bilbo's 129th birthday party. In the books, this takes up just two paragraphs, and the attendees and details are not specified, but here Bilbo is joined by Frodo, Gandalf, Elrond, Sam, Merry and Pippin – all logical guesses. Some of the dialogue between Frodo and Bilbo is also taken from Book VI, Chapter VI. Then Bilbo notices that Frodo is missing one of the fingers on his right hand. He asks for an explanation and, as a result, Gandalf introduces a minstrel who has written a ballad about Frodo's adventures. The minstrel begins to sing, narrating elements from *The Hobbit* (chiefly from Chapter V, 'Riddles in the Dark') and *The Fellowship of the Ring* (chiefly from Book I, Chapter I, 'A Long Expected Party') and this succinctly brings the story up to Book VI, Chapter I ('The Tower of Cirith Ungol') at 07.43 minutes into the adaptation.

The structure of the rest of the cartoon is quite intricate and the breakdown of the chapters from the two books that comprise *The Return of the King* is noted below for interest's sake. When chapters are divided into several pieces and the action cuts back and forth from one to the other, then each time part of a particular chapter is used, the chapter title is noted. Times are from the US DVD version and are in minutes and seconds. (Please note that a DVD player converting from NTSC to PAL playback may alter the timing by a few seconds; these timings are as accurate as they can be – they will never be universal.)

Book VI	Chapter I	'The Tower of Cirith Ungol'	07:43
Book V	Chapter I	'Minas Tirith'	21:11
Book V	Chapter IV	'The Siege of Gondor'	22:07
Book V	Chapter VII	'The Pyre of Denethor'	23:16
Book V	Chapter III	'The Muster of Rohan'	23:55

At 72:31 the audience is told that Sam and Frodo have been walking for 'days' since it last saw them; when the story returns to the Battle of the Pelennor Fields at 74:27 the voiceover informs the viewer, in the past tense, that the battle has turned in favour of Rohan and Gondor. While an eccentric choice of technique (to jump forward and then flashback to the point just before the move forward), this does make sense on screen, and is an attempt to create a single unified structure for the plot that does not exist in the book.

Within this structure, which is not inelegant, there are other changes to the essence and sense of Tolkien's plot. In Muller's version, the Steward of Gondor orders his own execution rather than live under the tyranny of Sauron. In Tolkien (in Book V, Chapter VII, 'The Pyre of Denethor') he takes his own life, yes, but is immolated while attempting to burn his own son alive. He is partially doing this because, in his derangement, he believes that his second (still living, but unconscious) son, Faramir, is as dead as his first son, Boromir. In his grief-induced madness, he has mentally conflated the two.

In both Tolkien and Muller's versions, Denethor has looked into a Palantir, a large globe with magical powers, which is being bent to the will of Sauron. Denethor believes that a black fleet of warships, which is coming up the river Anduin towards Minas

Tirith, will bring about the end of Gondor. They will not. The ships contain Aragorn and his army, who will guarantee victory for the men of the west. It is implied that the Palantir told Denethor that the ships would guarantee the end of Gondor *as Denethor saw it* (i.e. as ruled by the Stewards). As the ships will bring the King, Aragorn, to his ancestral capital, this is, in a sense, true. It is a deceit without being a lie. In Tolkien, Denethor climbs on to the funeral pyre he has lit, clasping the Palantir. Gandalf and Pippin rescue Faramir from his insane parent. In Muller, we do not see exactly how Denethor dies (not unexpected in something intended for children), and Faramir does not feature at all.

Muller states that Gandalf despatched Merry to Rohan, from Minas Tirith, to ask King Théoden's army to come to the assistance of Gondor. In the book, Merry is already with the Rohirrim, having been simply left there by Gandalf when he took Pippin to Minas Tirith. (In the book, Pippin looks in the Palantir belonging to Saruman the White and is seen by Sauron, who then believes Pippin is the Ring Bearer. This places him in great danger and this is why he is at Gandalf's side.) The screenplay's explanation is a neat inversion, one that has its own internal logic.

There are some less successful changes. Muller's version sees Aragorn march on Minis Tirith in a genuine attempt to destroy Sauron by force of arms, which Gandalf blankly tells him is impossible. Aragorn goes ahead with this plan anyway. In the books, he goes expressly for the purpose of distracting Sauron to buy Frodo time to destroy the Ring, even though Aragorn knows that to attack Mordor means almost certain death. It would be too emotive to call this a 'betrayal' of the character, but it does miss more or less the entire point of him. The ghost army that fights for Aragorn is removed and Aragorn himself does not arrive on the ships until after the battle outside Minas Tirith. It is also hinted that he cannot return to claim his crown until after the Ring is destroyed, reducing him to little more than a weak exile who, when the time finally comes to reclaim his throne, is prepared to throw away his entire military in a futile attempt to destroy a far superior force. The characters of Gimli, Legolas and Arwen are completely absent, although it is worth noting that all three are barely in the book version and that Legolas, as presented in Books V and VI of *The Lord of the Rings*, is largely irreconcilable with elves as set up in the earlier Rankin/Bass animation.

An odd notion contained within the Muller screenplay is that hobbits *become* humans; over time, the halflings will evolve to the point whereby they are indistinguishable from humans. Gandalf points out that the younger hobbits are taller than the older ones and says that in the future humans will not know if they have 'a little hobbit in them'. He then virtually winks at the camera. While cute, and obviously designed to reassure children watching that the hobbits will not all die out in some hideous cataclysm before the modern day, this has no basis in Tolkien's many writings.

What makes this change necessary in the eyes of the screenwriter is that he retains Tolkien's conceit of the story being true. This version features the book that Bilbo, Frodo and Sam have all written part of – the book that will, according to Tolkien, one day be found, translated into Old English and lost again, with the Old English translation, *The Red Book of Westmarch*, coming into the hands of Tolkien himself and providing the basis for all of his writings on Middle-earth.

'It was a big challenge to take material from that book and turn it into an animatable [sic] script and production,' said Rankin, looking back twenty years later: 'I think we bit off a little more than was necessary.' This is arguably, despite the obvious problems of the screenplay, a harsh self-judgement. This version has elements of *The Lord of the Rings* presented solely for the audience of *The Hobbit*; and not the literary *Hobbit* at that, but the even simpler version that Rankin/Bass had already made as a cartoon. This is Tolkien for the audience of *Super-Friends*, as the cast list really makes clear. The abandonment of the ghost army makes sense in this context. It is a concept too horrific for the under-fives (and the finished cartoon was criticised for its nightmare-causing potential anyway).

The additional subtitle makes clear that the producers are linking this production as much as they can to their earlier success with *The Hobbit* and while this cartoon resolutely ignores much of Tolkien's work, it at least does not stray from making the actions and burdens of the Ringbearer the story's essential core.

ANIMATION: The humans' armour is of an essentially Norman design, which is absolutely wrong for Middle-earth as envisaged by Tolkien.

When the eagles arrive at 86:43, the footage is visibly that of a similar moment in the Rankin/Bass *The Hobbit*, although the actual animation has been flipped to make it less immediately obvious.

SOUND AND MUSIC: The orcs' marching song 'Where There's a Whip There's a Way' is, with its sub-disco production and trite rhymes, rather horrible yet strangely catchy. It must be the 'phat' sounds of the analogue synthesizers. Although he was not credited for this, it is quite clear that one of the voices singing the song is that of Theodore Bikel.

The linking ballad, 'Frodo of the Nine Fingers', is truly, mind-numbingly awful. Its only redeeming feature is that it is, very loosely, based on an idea in the book. Lying on the side of Mount Doom, thinking that they will both shortly be dead, Sam turns to Frodo and tries to cheer him up, asking if Frodo thinks they'll write a story about the pair's exploits, 'Frodo's nine fingers and the Ring of Doom', and desiring to hear it (Book VI, Chapter IV). It is unlikely that Sam would have wished to hear *this* version.

NAMES AND LANGUAGES: 'Orcs. Old Bilbo called them Goblins,' ponders Samwise out loud – an attempt to paper over the differences in nomenclature between *The Hobbit* and *The Return of the King* that was a fault of the original author. This explanation is, however, one of which Tolkien approved – he had used it himself on occasion.

FILM REVIEWS: Gail Williams reviewed this production in the *Hollywood Reporter*. She called the animation 'magnificently intricate and powerfully fluid' but found that the script had a 'bewildering structure' that forced the audience to 'expend too much energy just trying to figure out what's happening'. She disliked the songs for the way they 'clutter up' the story and felt that the whole production 'should not be seen by children given to nightmares'.

AN UNEXPECTED PARTY: THE LORD OF THE RINGS (BBC RADIO SERIAL 1981)

Prepared for Radio in 13 episodes by Brian Sibley
Adapted by Brian Sibley and Michael Bakwell
Music composed and conducted by Stephen Oliver and played
  by members of the New Chamber Soloists with Susan
  Bradshaw
Singers: David James, Matthew Vine and Oz Clarke with the
  Ambrosia Singers and members of the cast
Radiophonic Sound: Elizabeth Parker
Technical Presentation: Peter Novis and David Greenwood
  assisted by Richard Beadsmoore, Tim Sturgeon, Diana
  Barkham and Paul Pearson
Produced and Directed by Jane Morgan and Penny Leicester

First Transmitted: 8 March–6 June 1981 (BBC Radio 4)

PRINCIPAL CAST: Ian Holm (Frodo), Michael Hordern (Gandalf), Robert Stephens (Aragorn), Peter Woodthrope (Gollum), John Le Mesurier (Bilbo), William Nighy (Sam), Richard O'Callaghan (Merry), John McAndrew (Pippin), David Collings (Legolas), Douglas Livingstone (Gimli), Michael Graham Cox (Boromir), Peter Vaughn (Denethor), Andrew Seear (Faramir), Jack May (Théoden), Anthony Hyde (Éomer), Elin Jenkins (Éowyn), Peter Howell (Saruman), Paul Brooke (Grima Wormtongue), Hugh Dickson (Eldron), Marian Diamond (Galadriel), Simon Cadell (Celeborn), Stephen Thorne (Treebeard), James Grout (Butterbur), John Bott (Farmer Maggot), Philip Voss (Lord of the Nazgûl), John Rye (Mouth of Sauron), Gerard Murphy (Narrator).

CAST NOTES: Sir Michael Hordern (1911–1995) had a career on stage, film and television that it is impossible to do justice to in summary. Small roles in films such as *Passport to Pimlico* (TEB Clarke, 1948) helped revive a promising career that had been interrupted by the Second World War. More films followed, with

Hordern playing the Commander of HMS *Prince of Wales* in *Sink the Bismarck!* (Lewis Gilbert, 1961) and the Governor of Gibraltar in *I Was Monty's Double* (John Guillermin, 1958) but for the most part Hordern's career was in the theatre. On stage or on screen his persona varied between confused, frightened men and reliable, crusty authority figures. Examples of the former include the terrified lead of *Oh, Whistle and I'll Come to You*, Jonathan Miller's brilliant 1968 TV adaptation of the MR James' short story. Examples of the latter would include the narrator of the children's series *Paddington* or as Prime Minister Gladstone in *Edward VII* (1975) for ITV. Hordern's most enduring roles were where he was called upon to combine both aspects of his public person; when he played confused old men who had once been great authority figures or frightened men who had to find a certain courage. He was *King Lear* twice, once for the BBC and the performance was thankfully recorded. He also preserved his performance as Prospero in *The Tempest* by recreating it for television. Hordern's alternately confused, avuncular, magnificent and powerful Gandalf is very much in the spirit of these performances and is a highlight of both this production and his career.

Another theatrical actor with an impressive career on the legitimate stage is Ian Holm, who has made enough films to be a household name. Born in 1931, he spent fourteen years at the Royal Shakespeare Company playing both Henry V and Richard III under the direction of Peter Hall and John Barton. To take on two such vastly different Shakespearean roles while not out of his thirties is a testament to his enormous versatility. On film too, Holm has played a wide variety of parts from the sinister android Ash in *Alien* (Ridley Scott, 1979) to inspirational track trainer Sam Mussabine in *Chariots of Fire* (Hugh Hudson, 1981). His performance as Frodo here draws on his gentility and the sonorousness of his voice; what is interesting is that when called upon to play Bilbo in the Jackson trilogy (on the strength of his performance here) he chose to take a completely different tactic much of the time (see **The Lord of the Rings: The Fellowship of the Ring**).

Sir Robert Stephens (1931–1995) is one of the all-time great actors of the British stage. His career came in three phases: epic promise in the sixties, a sad decline exacerbated by heavy drinking in much of the seventies and eighties and a spectacular late flowering of his talent which saw him tackle both *King Lear* and

Falstaff in *Henry IV* in single year for the Royal Shakespeare Company. He essayed both roles with awe-inspiring conviction, dignity and depth, drawing ecstatic reviews and regular standing ovations. His major film roles include those in *A Taste of Honey* (Tony Richardson, 1963), *The Prime of Miss Jean Brodie* (Ronald Neame, 1969) and, most perfectly, as the Great Detective in *The Private Life of Sherlock Holmes* (Billy Wilder, 1970). British audiences may know him best from memorable turns on television including the villainous Abner Brown/Reverend Bottledale in John Masefield's *The Box of Delights* (1983) and as John Dryden in *England, My England* (1995). He was knighted shortly before his death in 1995, also the same year he married his long-time companion, actor Patricia Quinn.

John Le Mesurier (1912–1983) was the long-suffering Sergeant Wilson in every episode of *Dad's Army* (1968–1977) and the spin-off film (Norman Cohen, 1971). As a veteran of BBC Radio he had made a memorable appearance as the Wise Old Bird in the second series of Douglas Adams's *The Hitchhiker's Guide to the Galaxy*. He narrated the legendarily psychedelic children's TV series *Bod* (1975) and his films include *The Italian Job* (Peter Collinson, 1969) and *The Pink Panther* (Blake Edwards, 1963). Playing Bilbo in this series was among his last work, alongside playing Father Mowbray in the tremendous *Brideshead Revisited* for BBC television. Le Mesurier plays Bilbo's confusion over the ring as precisely that. There is little threat in his portrayal of an old, yet brave, man who now lives in a nastier, darker and more complex world than the one in which he had his own adventures.

William Nighy is these days more usually credited as Bill Nighy. As a star of British television, his roles include the editor in Paul Abbott's *State of Play* (2003) and a corrupt government minister in the third season of *Auf Wiedersehen, Pet*. In 2004 he received a Best Supporting Actor BAFTA for his turn as an ageing rock star in Richard Curtis's successful romantic comedy *Love Actually*.

Peter Vaughn is the kind of actor who has been in everything. He was 'genial' Harry Grout in *Porridge* (1974–77) and Robert Lindsay's conventional father-in-law in the first half of *Citizen Smith* (1977–78), both for BBC television; he later played the ruthless Thomas Franklyn in *Chancer* (1989–90), ITV's definitive statement on the eighties as the decade of greed. Guest appearances in just about any British TV series you can think of round out a CV that also includes films such as *Time Bandits* (Terry Gilliam,

1984) and *The Remains of the Day* (James Ivory, 1993). Denethor is an excellent role for Vaughn's ability to combine being authoritative with elements of cruelty and confusion.

Jack May (1922–1997) was a staple of BBC Radio drama. His credits include *The Hitchhiker's Guide to the Galaxy* (1977) and he played Nelson Gabriel on daily soap *The Archers* for decades. Small but memorable film roles include playing the cook in *A Canterbury Tale* (Michael Powell, Emeric Pressberger, 1943), the boatman in *Brief Encounter* (Noel Coward, 1945) and the District Commissioner in *The Man Who Would Be King* (John Huston, 1975).

TECHNICAL: For the most part the sound is 'clean', with the actors clearly gathered around one large microphone – the sound is flat and even – rather than having the feel gained by giving individual actors their own microphone and getting them to move around the studio in a attempt to create the feel of people standing in three-dimensional space.

An echo that emphasises the sibilants in dialogue is added to many of the more supernatural of 'evil' creatures in order to distinguish them; unfortunately it sounds rather more 'electronic' than 'organic' much of the time. There is much multiple layering of tape in order to achieve, for example, the sound of Elvish chanting and Frodo remembering Gandalf's warning to him when he is hiding from the Ring Wraith who is hunting him in Episode Two.

Elizabeth Parker of the Radiophonic Workshop (who later created memorable music for *Doctor Who*) seems to have had her work restricted to the application of pre-existing effects and layering of sound rather than sound creation. The sound effects used are largely on-mic, performed in studio by effects people present during recording and those other effects that are used are largely from analogue tapes. Most of them are familiar to the ears of anyone who has listened to much BBC Radio drama of the period. For example, the sound effect of a horse neighing used prominently in several episodes has been heard in programmes from *Rentaghost* to *I, Claudius*. Before use of synthesisers and portable sound recording equipment became commonplace there were only a limited number of sound effects in existence. Pay enough attention to film, television and radio and some particular repeated noises become as familiar as the voices of favourite actors.

BOOK AND SCRIPTS: Like the earlier Bakshi and later Jackson/ Walsh versions, the BBC Radio adaptation begins with a scene-setting prologue that fills the audience in on the background of the One Ring's creation – here said to have been made by the Dark Lord Sauron after the elves had made the other rings, and describing the war between the alliance of elves and men and Sauron's forces as mentioned in *The Lord of the Rings* and demonstrated in *The Silmarillion*.

While Brian Sibley and Michael Bakewell's scripts retain more of Tolkien's dialogue than any other adaptation discussed in this book (chiefly because of the dialogue-heavy nature of the radio medium), Sibley does, as a matter of absolute necessity, trim a lot of it down. In *The Lord of the Rings*, characters do not so much converse as declaim at one another, often for nearly a page at a time. This is entirely acceptable on the printed page but would tax even the greatest of actors, and this production is fortunate in having a great many great actors in it. Trims mostly take the form of extra details removed from the middle of long paragraphs of speech, especially genealogical detail. Strangely, the words of the narrator (voiced by Gerard Murphy) are very rarely those of Tolkien and the warm persona that comes across from Murphy's performance is little, if anything, like the omniscient narrating tone of the book itself.

It is also worth noting that the script for this serial often turns events that are merely reported in Tolkien into scenes in their own right (such as the Ring Wraiths interrogating the miller); but on other occasions (such as when the Black Riders attack the bed they believe Frodo will be sleeping in at the Inn at Bree) it leaves the sequences to be reported by one character to another. This, when it happens, is usually to get around the unforgivable radio sin of having characters talk out loud to themselves, which would be the only way of putting across the details of a scene in which there is only one character.

It is worth noting that as with all BBC Radio, and indeed television, adaptations of the era, it is the writer of the original book being adapted that is credited first, not the scriptwriter. The opening credits as read out are: 'The Lord of the Rings by JRR Tolkien, prepared for radio in thirteen instalments by Brian Sibley'.

EPISODE ONE: THE SHADOW OF THE PAST: The first actually dramatised scene is of Gollum being captured by identified henchmen of Sauron and then taken to Barad Dur and tortured for information about the One Ring. This is drawn from information relayed to Frodo in Book I, Chapter II from which Episode One takes its title. Gollum (after some horrific punishment at the hands of a torturer, audibly played by 'additional voices' actor Michael Spice) reveals that 'Baggins!' of the Shire has the One Ring now. An odd thing about this scene is that its structure and much of its dialogue seems to imply that Sauron's forces have only come across Gollum (their only clue to the whereabouts of the One Ring) by accident. Indeed, it seems that they only take him into custody because of his insolence.

After this awkward and somewhat unpromising start, the narrator invites the audience go back in time seventeen years in order to learn more about this 'Baggins'. The next scene is Tolkien's own; set in a tavern, it introduces lots of minor hobbits and again informs the audience, occasionally clumsily, of background details of the Shire and Bilbo and Frodo's family. Not all of the dialogue is Tolkien's own, but the additions are small. The next scene introduces a few more small changes to the book, mostly related to radio technique. Frodo is heard packing cases and unpacking presents with his Uncle Bilbo before Gandalf calls. This is entirely sensible as it gives Bilbo someone to talk to before Gandalf arrives and it also successfully brings Frodo, who is the story's protagonist, in slightly earlier. The warm conversation (both Holm and Le Mesurier are excellent) is a perfect 'radio' way of introducing the character of Frodo to the audience even if it has no basis in Tolkien (see **The Lord of the Rings: The Fellowship of the Ring** for an equally excellent, and equally Tolkien-free, visual introduction of Frodo Baggins).

This is then followed by a straight dramatisation of the Gandalf/Bilbo conversation from Book I, Chapter I ('A Long Expected Party') and an equally straight, if subtly trimmed, version of the party scene from the same chapter. Bilbo returns to Bag End, invisible, for a conversation with Gandalf, during which there is a lengthy flashback to *The Hobbit*, Chapter V, and Bilbo's acquisition of the Ring from Gollum. The script for this flashback follows Tolkien's revised version of this scene rather than as originally published in 1937 (See boxout: **Plot-significant textual revisions** on page 32).

Interestingly, this scene keeps the concept of Bilbo lying to Gandalf and his friends about how he acquired the Ring, made much of in Book I, Chapter I, and Tolkien's preface to *The Fellowship of the Ring*, but it changes what the lie is. After Bilbo goes and Frodo comes in to talk to Gandalf, Frodo mentions that Bilbo (unbeknownst to Frodo, like Gollum) has claimed that the Ring was a 'birthday present'. This, although superficially an alteration, is an intelligent way of staying true to Tolkien's (revised) intentions without going through the impossible process of attempting to incorporate elements from prefaces and footnotes into performed drama. The script for Episode One also misses out Frodo's confrontation with the Sackville-Bagginses but retains the song that Bilbo begins to sing as he leaves Bag End for the last time.

There is then a break in the episode (on the cassette release this is the division between sides one and two), which is used to retain the gap of seventeen years between Bilbo's departure from Bag End and Gandalf's return with information about the One Ring. Although Frodo's implication in this scene that he has not seen Gandalf for seventeen years is a simplification of Tolkien's complex pattern of comings and goings (as related in 'A Long Expected Party'), the essence of Gandalf's leaving in order to discover information about the Ring and not returning in any significant way for more than a decade is maintained.

Much of the remainder of the episode follows Book I, Chapter II faithfully, including Gandalf's telling of the tale of how Isildur took the Ring from Sauron during the battle between the Alliance and Sauron's forces and with a short dramatised flashback of Sméagol and Déagol's fight over the Ring on the day that they found it. Gandalf's dialogue to Frodo copies that from the book exactly, except that it adds the explanation that Sauron took the Rings, which he later gave to dwarves and men, from the elves who had made them. This is Sibley's attempt to clear up an area where there is much confusion in Tolkien. Jackson and Bakshi's solutions are different again (see **JRR Tolkien's The Return of the King** and **The Lord of the Rings: The Fellowship of the Ring**).

The episode covers some of Chapter III as well, including various scenes involving gossiping hobbits and a conversation between Gandalf and Frodo over the urgency of Frodo's departure to Rivendell.

Gandalf's meeting with Radagast the Brown, of his order, which Gandalf relates in Book II, Chapter II ('The Council of

Elrond') is included here. It is presented as a scene in its own right, one which is cut away to, and at the point where it happens to the character rather than related through Gandalf telling the others of its occurrence much later on, as happens in the book. It is followed by the confrontation between Saruman and Gandalf at Orthanc, which also comes from Book II, Chapter II.

EPISODE TWO: THE BLACK RIDERS: Episode Two begins with further dramatised extracts from Book II, Chapter II, with Gandalf's rescue from Orthanc by the Wind Lord Gwaihir – the Lord of the Eagles – as related by Gandalf at the Council of Elrond. Here it is presented as a scene in its own right, with the reported speech being turned into direct speech. This scene retains Tolkien's interval of two months during which Gandalf is trapped at Orthanc. It also dramatises Gandalf's brief visit to Rohan and his acquisition of a horse there, including his brief quarrel with King Théoden, again as related by Gandalf at the Council. Although present in Tolkien, this is not adapted in any other performed version. The script here uses dialogue from Gandalf's return to Rohan later in Book III, Chapter VI ('The King of the Golden Hall'), and furnishes additional details from Book III, Chapter II ('The Riders of Rohan'), when Éomer tells Aragorn and company about that meeting from the perspective of Rohan. The scene is an elegant combination of many elements. It also introduces the character of Wormtongue (Théoden's evil counsellor) to the story, earlier than in the books.

The script then adds scenes of Saruman consulting with the Nazgûl, them departing to find Gandalf, Wormtongue being found by the Wraiths and informing them of Gandalf's intention to return to the Shire, as well as Gandalf's acquisition of a horse from Rohan.

This episode then returns to Book I and Chapters III–V for details relating to Frodo's pretended permanent move from Bag End to Buckland, when he is actually setting out with the intention of eventually making for Rivendell. There is an additional scene where a Nazgûl bullies Gaffer Gamgee while looking for 'Baggins!' This is another scene which implicitly happens in the book but which is not presented as a scene in its own right. Tolkien purists may object to this, but they are likely to delight in the retention of Tolkien's own walking songs as sung by the journeying hobbits. Chapters VI and VII, which mostly concern Tom Bombadil and his house, are omitted entirely and the episode skips to Chapter IX and the Inn at Bree, where again the sense and thrust of the proceedings are adapted faithfully and almost entirely right up to the end of Chapter X ('Strider').

Tolkien's songs are retained, as is Frodo's accidental use of the Ring and his annoying of the staff of The Prancing Pony. Gandalf's delayed letter to Frodo, which the innkeeper Butterburr (brilliantly played by James Grout) presents to the younger Baggins, is also kept in. Robert Stephens successfully makes Strider a sinister figure and a potential enemy, softening only when the dialogue does. The broken sword of Aragorn's ancestors is introduced here as Strider shows it to Sam and notes its damaged status. The script creates an impressive cliffhanger by making more than Tolkien does of Merry's horror at his sight of the Riders while outside the Inn: 'I've seen them! Frodo! I have seen them here in the village! The Black Riders!'

EPISODE THREE: A KNIFE IN THE DARK: This begins with a straightforward telling of Book I, Chapter XI (from which it takes its title), although it makes a point of incorporating elements of Chapter X not included in the previous episode and then continues into Chapter XII. Notably, this is the only adaptation to incorporate the elf Glorfindel – Frodo's rescuer in the book (in Bakshi, the role is given to Legolas; in Jackson, it is Arwen – both films choosing to expand more prominent characters at the expense of a walk-on).

Exactly halfway through the episode we move between Books I and II. Book II, Chapter I ('Many Meetings') is trimmed heavily in the process of adaptation, with details from Gandalf and Frodo's conversation (which takes up most of the first half of the chapter) removed. Mostly, the removed dialogue refers to the specifics of the amount of time since Frodo and company left Bag End, but also gone are some of the more laborious passages relating to the defeat of the Nazgûl in the previous chapter/earlier in the episode. This is perhaps because the events are mere minutes previously in the timescale of the audio script.

Some of the feasting from the episode (a visual scene that would work well on screen or in prose but not in audio) has been removed and a comment by the dwarf Gloin about how Frodo was very fond of Bilbo is given to Gandalf to act as a cap to their long conversation. (This means that Frodo's comment that he would rather see Bilbo than 'all the towers and palaces in the world' comes before, not after, the feast and him being shown around Rivendell, but the overall effect on the sense of these scenes is minor.)

Frodo and Bilbo's meeting has some backstory related to Aragorn and Arwen's romance added into it, and the character of the elf Lindir is removed in order to concentrate the dialogue on Bilbo and Frodo. A large-ish but ultimately insignificant alteration then follows when the Council of Elrond takes place immediately after Bilbo and Frodo's conversation, rather than on the morning after it.

EPISODE FOUR: THE RING GOES SOUTH: This is a trimmed version of elements of Book II, Chapters II–V with the more simple words of the narrator replacing Tolkien's own prose but with most of the dialogue intact. The slow, dread drumbeat that accompanies the build-up to Gandalf's fight with, and apparent death at the hands of, the Balrog is enormously atmospheric and an effective radio interpretation of Tolkien's prose's repeated 'doom' in this passage. The episode ends with Gandalf's 'Fly you fools!' but it is unfortunately unclear *exactly* what has happened to him, and the scene lacks the emotional impact it has in Jackson (and indeed Bakshi) as a result.

EPISODE FIVE: THE MIRROR OF GALADRIEL: This is redeemed slightly in episode five, where Tolkien's mourning dialogue for Gandalf is used in full. This episode uses the end of Chapter V as well as Chapters VI–X. The script (which is by Sibley's collaborator Michael Bakewell) adds in a scene in which Gollum appears and attempts to climb the tree that Frodo and Sam are sleeping in. This is something that Frodo talks about in Chapter IX but here it is dramatised in its proper chronological place. Though clearly intended to introduce the character to the audience in preparation for what comes later, this is perhaps too brief to be truly effective.

Chapter X, 'The Breaking of the Fellowship', is the one most satisfyingly condensed: two conversations about where and why the Fellowship should head are condensed into one. The episode ends with Sam and Frodo in the boat headed towards Mordor and an artificial (though impressive) cliffhanger as Boromir charges into battle to save Merry and Pippin from being killed by orcs. Incidentally, Michael Hordern is still billed second on this episode despite only appearing in the reprise from the previous one (much as Sean Bean is credited at the end of Peter Jackson's *The Return of the King*). Nice work if you can get it.

EPISODE SIX: THE BREAKING OF THE FELLOWSHIP: Despite adapting scenes from six chapters, Episode Six takes no material from the chapter of the book from which it takes its title. It begins with Book III, Chapter I ('The Departure of Boromir') and then follows Aragorn and his party in Chapters II and IV according to Tolkien's own design. Scriptwriter Sibley's treatment of Boromir's death is interesting (as Jackson's would later be). He splits Boromir's not-particularly-long, but single and uninterrupted, death speech into two and in fact places the first half after the second half once he has done so. This has the effect of making Boromir's last thoughts of the halflings he has betrayed and then died protecting rather than of his home city.

When Boromir's body is placed in a boat and floated downstream, the audience hears perhaps the longest stretch of uninterrupted (albeit edited) Tolkien prose up to this point. Gerard Murphy's reading allows the audience to appreciate how evocative Tolkien's prose can be in the right hands. In keeping with condensation and simplicity, two conversations about what the remainder of the fellowship (Aragorn, Gimli, Legolas) should do are combined into one, retaining the salient points, and most memorable phrases, of each. These scenes allow David Collings as Legolas, an actor and character who has been kept in the background for the most part, a chance to shine.

Eventually Chapter II is interrupted by scenes from Chapter III (which features Merry and Pippin) before Chapter II is revisited and completed. It is then that we move on to Chapter IV, Merry and Pippin's meeting with Treebeard and the Ent Moot. These scenes are some of the least effective in the series. Merry and Pippin's voices are equally faux-childlike and slightly camp, and are almost indistinguishable from one another. Stephen Thorne, an actor with a long history of playing megalomaniacs, mafia dons, renegade Time Lords and the like, is noisy but not particularly emotive as Treebeard. The episode then jumps the rest of Book III and goes to Book IV, Chapter I ('The Taming of

Sméagol') in which Peter Woodthorpe's sinister but not terribly varied Gollum shows a tendency to ad-lib.

The climax of the episode comes with a much-shortened version of Chapter V of Book III where Legolas, Aragorn and Gimli encounter a resurrected Gandalf. It is unclear exactly how and why Gandalf returns from the dead here, but he explicitly was physically dead (something that is perhaps not the case in the Jackson film) and Legolas calls him 'Mithrandir', another name for the spiritual entity of which Gandalf's both Grey and White are merely two iterations. Microphone effects do not hide the fact that it is Michael Hordern playing the titular 'White Rider' despite the suspicions of the company that he is Saruman. As in Bakshi earlier and Jackson later, the return of Gandalf is slightly incoherent and unsurprising in dramatised execution. While this is partially a shame, as the written chapter contains some of Tolkien's most evocative and dramatic writing, the scene is based upon the perceptions and false assumptions of a group of people. This is a sequence created for prose fiction and it does not really translate to other media; it does not lend itself to a medium where an objective reality is often, even usually, paramount. (The disorientation achieved here is more impressive, and the character-led confusion makes more 'sense', than the second Jackson film's decision to have Christopher Lee (Saruman) speak some of Gandalf's dialogue when the audience cannot see his face; for which there is no real justification within the film outside the aim of confusing/'deceiving' its audience for a few moments longer.) It is worth noting that, having spent five hours on *The Fellowship of the Ring*, the radio adaptation deals with more than a third of *The Two Towers* in a single hour.

EPISODE SEVEN: THE KING OF THE GOLDEN HALL: This episode returns to Book III, Chapter IV for the (singing) March of the Ents before moving on to Book III, Chapter VI from which it takes its title. Roughly halfway through this chapter the narrative returns to Book IV, Chapter II ('The Passage of the Marshes') and Frodo, Sam and Gollum. Halfway through this chapter the episode returns to the point of Book III, Chapter VI that it left and follows it to its end before returning to and completing Book IV, Chapter II. Book III, Chapter VII ('Helm's Deep') is then adapted, although a scene of Gandalf reaching the wrecked Isengard and asking Treebeard for help is created rather than have the Ents simply appear as a *deus ex machina* at the end of the siege of Helm's Deep. This would, in any event, be too visual an event to present on the radio without foreshadowing in dialogue. While it is unclear how the battle at Helm's Deep is fought, at times the atmosphere of dread and doom is all-pervasive and hugely impressive, with choral chanting and unnaturally loud sound effects.

EPISODE EIGHT: THE VOICE OF SAURON: Chapter VIII of Book III opens Episode Eight ('The Road to Isengard'). Much of Chapter IX is missing, but it is mere description of comings and goings and its absence is no real loss. Peter Howell is brilliantly ambiguous as Saruman in the adaptation of Chapter X ('The Voice of Saruman'), drifting from mellifluous to almost bestially savage from moment to moment without either mood seeming to contradict the other.

Chapter XI ('The Palantir') is much simplified. Pippin is looking into the eponymous crystal ball more accidental and thus less prompted by curiosity than on the page and is less in contradiction of Gandalf's direct instructions too, presumably to remove unnecessary rancour between the heroic principles, which would slow the drama down at this point. Gandalf relates the history of the many palantiri to Pippin as they ride for Minas Tirith, rather than explain it to most of the company at the camp. This is another sensible act of economy, combining a visual, and largely wordless, scene (which needs to take place but which would be impossible on audio) with information that the audience will find interesting and of use in understanding Middle-earth.

With Book III now completely related, the episode now turns to Book IV, Chapter III ('The Black Gate is Closed') and then jumps on to Book V, Chapters I ('Minas Tirith'), II ('The Passing of the Grey Company') and III ('The Muster of Rohan'), cutting from one to another in accordance with the chronology of Appendix B of the book. The episode ends with Book IV, Chapter IV ('Of Herbs and Stewed Rabbit'), creating a cliffhanger out of the moment where Faramir's party from Gondor chances on the hobbits.

EPISODE NINE: THE TWO TOWERS: Picking up where the previous episode left off, Episode Nine then adapts Chapter V of Book IV and the conclusion of Book V, Chapter II (with Aragorn at Dunharrow gaining the services of the army of the dead). It then returns to Book IV for Chapters VI ('The Forbidden Pool') and VII ('Journey to the Cross-Roads') for Frodo and Sam taking their leave of Faramir and Book V, Chapter I for the meeting between Denethor, Steward of Minas Tirith, and Gandalf and Pippin. After a sequence from Book V, Chapter III where Théoden confirms that Rohan will ride to Gondor's aid, the episode returns to Book IV to finish off Chapter VII and the titular 'Muster of Rohan'.

EPISODE TEN: THE CHOICES OF MASTER SAMWISE: This episode takes its title from Book IV, Chapter X. The bulk of its running time is taken up with Book IV, Chapters VII–X, which run directly into Book VI (yes, VI), Chapter I. This strand (Frodo and Sam, Gollum's betrayal and the battle with Shelob) is intercut with material from Book V, Chapter IV (scenes with Gandalf and Pippin at Minas Tirith and Denethor and Faramir's arguments about tactics) and Book V, Chapter X ('The Last Debate') for the scenes of Aragorn allowing the army of the dead to rest in peace after fulfilling their oath to him. Shelob, like many creatures in this production, sounds oddly electronic due to the nature of the microphone effects used to produce her noises.

Towards the end of the episode there is a long scene of Sam mourning the apparently dead Frodo, lamenting that he is (to his knowledge) the last survivor of the Fellowship and taking the task of destroying the Ring upon himself. Bill Nighy really shines in this sequence. Forced to talk to himself at some length, his performance is so strong that you fail to notice the collapse of normal radio technique and the absence of anything resembling standard radio 'realism'. The episode ends with Book VI, Chapter IV (Denethor's advancing mental collapse) and Book VI, Chapter I (Frodo and Sam). Here is a *superb* cliffhanger, created by stopping the episode as the newly awakened Frodo loudly and aggressively accuses Sam (who has saved Frodo, and indeed the whole world, by taking the Ring from what he perceived to be Frodo's dead body) of being a 'Thief!' in hideous tones reminiscent of Gollum at his most bestial.

EPISODE ELEVEN: THE BATTLE OF THE PELENNOR FIELDS: Starting with a reprise/conclusion of the cliffhanger of Episode Ten, this episode then adapts Book VI, Chapters II–III and cuts back and forth from here to Book V, Chapters IV–IX (although the first half of Chapter IX, a tale of the recent past told by Aragorn, has already been used in the previous episode).

The bulk of Episode Eleven is concentrated on the battle from which the episode takes its title. The success of the musical presentation (as a sort of ballad) of the Battle of Pelennor Fields is debateable. It is the kind of dramatic conceit that individual audience members either do or do not buy into. It is either alarming and movingly odd or just the wrong side of bathetic, depending on your point of view.

It is worth pointing out here that Éowyn's killing of the Witch King – which cannot be killed by any man living and is thus killed by a woman – is an obvious lift from the end of Shakespeare's *Macbeth* (1608, probably) wherein the anti-heroic lead character cannot be killed by man of woman born. He is killed by a rival 'from his mother's womb untimely ripped', i.e. delivered by Caesarean.

When Aragorn heals several injured soldiers just by touching them the concept of the hands of a king being 'the hands of a healer' is raised. The rightful monarch has a de facto supernatural ability to make the gravely ill well again. This is an old tradition in England, Scotland and France, among others, believed to be literally true for centuries. Although the scenes featuring it are adapted faithfully here, they seem odd to our more egalitarian, and less superstitious, era. They are not included in the New Line Cinema film. Robert Stephens decision to play Aragorn's reprimand of Merry for losing his pack and wanting a smoke in the aftermath of his recovery from his injuries 'straight', i.e. as a genuine complaint rather than a joke, is very strange indeed and makes a nonsense of his next line. The episode ends with Gandalf, in a line not from Tolkien, reminding his preparing-for-war comrades that all their 'hopes and fears' ultimately lie not with armies, but with Frodo and Sam.

EPISODE TWELVE: MOUNT DOOM: Beginning at the very end of Book VI, Chapter II ('The Land of Shadow'), the penultimate episode improvises some inspired comic orc dialogue before moving almost immediately on to the chapter (III) from which its title comes. Ian Holm excels at portraying Frodo's physical and mental collapse using only his voice. It is an enormously difficult task and Holm always stays the right side of melodrama. It is a loud, aggressive, occasionally ranting performance but it never crosses the line. His quiet delivery of the line 'There is no veil between me and the wheel of fire' is chilling.

Halfway through Book VI, Chapter III the action cuts back to Book V, Chapter X ('The Black Gate Opens') and finishes off Book V at last. This sequence includes the Herald of Sauron's attempt to parlay with Gandalf by showing him Frodo's possessions and claiming that Frodo is the Dark Lord's prisoner. The other major adaptations leave this out. (In the cinematic cut of Jackson film it is replaced with more on-screen fighting.) Unfortunately, the voice of the Herald is oddly uncompelling.

After the end of Book V we return to Frodo and Sam and find them being attacked by Gollum. Sam sees him off and a brilliantly played adaptation of the final moments of the chapter follows. While additional, not terribly subtle, dialogue is needed for the purely visual action of Gollum biting off Frodo's finger and falling into the pit, the atmosphere of dread created by Elizabeth Parker's oppressive effects, the performances and some brilliant incidental music courtesy of Stephen Oliver's chamber orchestra ensure that this is a moment of pure catharsis for the listener. The script removes the beginning of Book VI, Chapter IV so that the audience stays with Frodo and Sam for longer without interruption.

There is no sequence of Gandalf and company outside Mordor realising that the Ring has been destroyed. Oddly, this means that after nearly twelve hours of their scripts adding cuts back and forth to Tolkien's structure, Brian Sibley and Michael Bakewell ignore virtually the only time the author himself used this technique for dramatic effect. (This may well be a colossal in-joke on the writers' parts.) This episode then follows the book and goes straight into Chapter VI with a final cliffhanger created (not easy when the whole point of the story has now been dealt with) by having Gandalf worry about what he will find if he visits Isengard and the imprisoned Saruman while accompanying the hobbits back to the Shire.

EPISODE THIRTEEN: THE GREY HAVENS: Adapting as it does Chapters IV to IX of Book VI, the final episode of the BBC Radio version does include 'The Scouring of the Shire', in which the hobbits return to their home and discover it under the control of Saruman. But before this the episode is very slow, with characters bidding one another farewell and cameos by earlier characters such as Treebeard (the title 'Many Partings' is, like a lot of Tolkien's chapter titles, simply literal). Although seeming initially very much a coda, these scenes do give characters such as Legolas and Gimli final scenes which, while not dramatically necessary, are emotionally satisfying. The scene of Gandalf discovering Saruman and Wormtongue when they are, unbeknownst to him, heading towards the Shire is skipped over.

The 'Scouring', rendered just in Tolkien's words and the actors' performances, is part environmentalist, Romantic paean and part neo-Luddite fretting at the very possibility of change. The distressing fate of Lobelia Sackville-Baggins, who dies after being imprisoned by Saruman and leaves all her money for the helping of the poor, is missed out. While understandable, this is a shame. It is one final example of Christian redemption in the story with a vindictive old woman becoming the model of charity shortly before death.

Despite Tolkien's protestations to the contrary, when the 'Scouring' sequence is dramatised it is very difficult to see this sequence as anything other than a 'spirit of the blitz'/'resistance in occupied Europe' thriller. While this is in part down to the performances, it does seem to come from the material. This is not to say that Tolkien lied when he said it wasn't a deliberate allegory, merely that the writing was ultimately of its own time and reflected, despite its pseudo-mythic nature and being set in an imagined past, contemporary concerns.

Given the last line of Tolkien's book, it is entirely fitting that Bill Nighy virtually picks up and walks away with the final episode, with Samwise becoming totally the audience's identification figure due to Frodo's increasing vagueness and dislocation – which is superbly portrayed by Ian Holm. Because there is virtually no dialogue in the final parting on the shore in the book, it is carried solely through the prose, and because the actors deserve farewells, some dialogue from just before Sam and Frodo ride there is co-opted for use on the shore. The effect is sensitively done and deeply moving. Gandalf's last words in Middle-earth are 'Not all tears are evil'. Some other words of Frodo's are moved so that the audience first hears them as Sam remembers them as he heads back into Bag End to his wife and children. Saying 'Well, I'm back' carries a weight of expectation for any actor, but Nighy more than pulls it off.

* * *

AVAILABILITY: The series was repeated in 1986, divided into 26 half-hour episodes (a process which seems to have been anticipated during production as there are clean scene and recording breaks at about the 29-minute mark in every single episode). However, when the production was on tape it was in its original thirteen instalments (with each one an individual one-hour cassette). This release came courtesy of BBC Enterprises, as part of the BBC Radio Collection in 1987. It was available for several years and there was more than one 'run' (later copies credit BBC Worldwide, the company that BBC Enterprises metamorphosed into in the early 1990s) but it has long since been made unavailable for sale by its producers and can no longer be ordered. It can still occasionally be found second hand or covered in dust in larger bookshops or record retailers that carry audiobooks and pay little attention to their stock.

There was also a CD issue of the production in this format, this time on fourteen compact discs with the fourteenth disc being an uninterrupted suite of the incidental music for the series (this is, incidentally, fantastic). This too has been withdrawn.

In 2001, about the time of the release of the first of the New Line Cinema movies, BBC Worldwide issued three quadruple CD releases, using the titles 'The Fellowship of the Ring', 'The Two Towers' and 'The Return of the King'. This release abandoned Brain Sibley and Michael Bakewell's obviously painstakingly worked out chronological restructuring, and reorders the recorded scenes back into Tolkien's own character-led, out of chronistic sequence structure. While this can be said to be a 'return' to what the author intended, it isn't what the scriptwriters intended and there are moments when there are a succession of very short scenes for no apparent reason, or where characters disappear for a very long time. Again, this is the kind of thing that can work in prose but seems odd in drama. In order to cover the gaps, new narration was written and recorded by Ian Holm in character as Frodo. These three releases are available individually, but are cheaper if bought as a box set of all three (ISBN 0563528885). It is recommended only if you cannot find a copy of the serial in its original form.

The Lord of the Rings Symphony

Symphony Number 1: The Lord of the Rings was written by Dutch composer Johan de Menj in 1988. As the title suggests, it is a symphonic interpretation of the plot of Tolkien's story. It has no lyrics or book of any kind and is written for a wind and woodwind band rather than a full orchestra. Menj, a graduate of the Royal Dutch Conservatory in The Hague, entered it into the Sudler International Wind Band Composition Competition in Chicago in the year in which he wrote it and was awarded the competition's highest prize.

The symphony lasts for 45 minutes and is divided into five movements:

1 Gandalf (the Wizard)
2 Lothlorien (the Elvenwood)
3 Gollum (Sméagol)
4 Journey in the Dark
5 Hobbits

While it is obviously impossible to judge the 'changes' made to a narrative as presented in symphonic form, especially when a musical layman, Menj's expressive soaring music does express much of the character of Middle-earth and its inhabitants for some Tolkien aficionados in, perhaps, a similar manner to how Vaughn Williams's 'Lark Ascending' (1914) is often said to express much of the character of pre-First World War England. More than one recording of the piece is available on CD.

A LONG EXPECTED PARTY: PETER JACKSON AND PRE-PRODUCTION ON THE NEW LINE CINEMA TRILOGY

Peter Jackson's life has become, alongside that of former video store clerk Quentin Tarantino, the epitome of every movie geek's fantasies. It is the classic story of a life-long film buff going from making 8mm movies in his parents' back yard to major critical and commercial success, taking in low-budget weekend shoots with a cast and crew of friends along the way. It is an almost clichéd rags-to-riches tale that, had the information about his path into film-making only become available after he started to make *The Lord of the Rings*, would sound like PR-company myth-making. He now commands a salary of $20 million per film (his pay for his 2005 release, a remake of *King Kong*), placing him in the first rank of Directors-for-hire. It is easy to forget that, until 2000, he was hardly known.

Before the hype and anticipation for *The Lord of the Rings* really got under way with the release of stills from the movies during late 1999, those who had heard of Jackson were more likely to have done so due to his least-typical but Oscar-nominated film, *Heavenly Creatures* (1994) than his earlier cult hits *Meet the Feebles* (1989), *Bad Taste* (1988), or *Braindead* (1992). He was best known for the latter two – both gore-laden and crude low-budget horror comedies – and his biggest-budget (and most recent) film to date, *The Frighteners* (1996) starring Michael J Fox, which cost $30 million but failed to make that back at the box office. None of these movies, at least on the surface, could inspire much hope among Tolkien fans that Jackson was really the man for the job.

The decision to allow Jackson to direct such a massive-budget movie that, due to the immense popularity of the books, was certain to attract much media and fan attention, was incomprehensible when it was first announced in a New Line Cinema press release in August 1998. If anyone was going to bridge the chasm between 'cash' and 'kudos', the two mutually incompatible potential outcomes of a *The Lord of the Rings* feature film as identified by Tolkien himself, it seemed unlikely to be a relative unknown with a patchy track record whose films were mostly liked by self-conscious film buffs and found their audience on video cassette.

Jackson was born on 31 October 1961 in the small town of Pukerua Bay, New Zealand, the only child of English immigrants Bill and Joan. Growing up watching TV programmes such as Gerry Anderson's puppet sci-fi *Thunderbirds* and fantasy films such as *King Kong* and the Ray Harryhausen stop-motion Greek epics, the young Jackson had already been inspired to start building his own monsters and spaceships by the time he got his first opportunity to try his hand at filming. He was only eight years old when his parents bought themselves a Super8 camera for Christmas, but had soon appropriated it for himself, filming his models in an attempt to replicate the kind of movies he loved to watch but, in those pre-video days, could not see nearly as often as he would have liked.

In 1971, at the age of ten, Jackson embarked upon his first short film, a First World War piece entitled *The Dwarf Patrol*. Starring him and some schoolfriends, including *Bad Taste*'s Pete O'Herne, his low-tech approach to effects came into play for the first time as he punched holes in the film to simulate gunshots, and his parents' dug-up garden acted as the Western Front. His modest success inspired him to make a follow-up in 1973, *World War Two*, where he again starred, and over the next decade more were to follow. Mostly inspired by films he had liked, these ranged from the James Bond spoof *Coldfinger* (1977), with Jackson himself playing the spy, to *The Curse of the Grave Walker* (1981), a Roger Corman meets George Romero-style zombie flick shot in a primitive form of cinemascope. However, the most recognition he managed to receive for these shorts was the NZ$100 runner-up prize he got for 1978's *The Valley* (a homage to Ray Harryhausen, complete with low-rent stop-motion animation) when he entered it into a local television competition.

After leaving school, Jackson applied for an apprenticeship at New Zealand's National Film Unit, but was turned down (only to get his revenge in 1998 when he bought the NFU for NZ$1–3 million). Instead, he ended up taking on an apprenticeship in the photo-engraving department of the Wellington *Evening Post*, dashing home after work to sit up into the small hours creating props and effects for his numerous planned films. The most ambitious of these evolved from a short entitled *Roast of the Day* that began shooting in October 1983, with old school mates and work colleagues helping out both in front of and behind the camera. Almost every weekend for the next four years, Jackson and friends laboured away, materials and film paid for out of Jackson's salary and his mother paying the helpers in food, while he spent his evenings building all the props, prosthetics and effects from scratch.

The result was *Bad Taste*, an aptly titled comic gorefest about a rag-tag group of alien-hunters trying to stop an extra-terrestrial fast-food chain from turning humans into burgers. As slightly mad scientist Derek (played by Jackson) puts it, 'There's no glowing fingers on these bastards – we've got a bunch of extra-terrestrial psychopaths on our hands!' Packed full of oozing brains, severed arms, cannibalism, exploding sheep, vomit, slime and blood, it is not recommended for those with weak stomachs.

This four-year project ended up costing around NZ$20,000 of Jackson's own money and, midway through the shoot, the realisation dawned on him that he needed more cash to make it to the screen. Terrified that his film might falter in the final stages, Jackson got his old schoolfriend (and part-time alien) Ken Hammon to make the call that might help their dedication pay off – to New Zealand Film Commission executive director Jim Booth. In March 1985 the answer came: 'Neither the film nor the effects as shot are up to the standard which would see the Commission obtain a return on its investment.'

For the next year and a half, Jackson ensured he kept in contact with the Film Commission and Booth on the off-chance that he might be able to persuade them differently. It was during this time that he met Costa Botes, who was working as an Assistant Director on the Jon (*Doctor Who*) Pertwee TV series *Worzel Gummidge Down Under*, a revival to the 1979–81 Willis Hall children's programme about the adventures of a somewhat absent-minded scarecrow. Jackson had landed himself a freelance job producing effects for the series, and ended up showing Botes his film. In return he got some professional advice, another extra as Botes joined the cast, and a long-term film-making partner, most notably on their superb 1996 fake documentary *Forgotten Silver*.

Whether the advice of Costa Botes made any real impact is hard to determine, but by late 1986 the New Zealand Film Commission had changed its mind about *Bad Taste*, funding it to the tune of an initial NZ$30,000 and appointing a consultant producer to oversee the project.

As the fine-tuning of *Bad Taste* continued, Costa Botes began introducing Jackson to various friends he felt might be of use; the most significant of these were to be writer/comedian Danny Mulheron and the theatre and TV writers Stephen Sinclair and girlfriend, Fran Walsh. These three would end up writing Jackson's second feature, *Meet the Feebles*, with him. Sinclair also devised and co-wrote *Braindead* (with Jackson and Walsh), as well as helping out on the script for *The Lord of the Rings: The Two Towers*. Fran Walsh has worked on all of Jackson's subsequent films and, most significantly, later became his wife. Although their two children, Katie and Billy, can be seen in cameos in *The Lord of the Rings*, Walsh prefers to remain behind the scenes and away from the cameras – bar her contributions to DVD commentary tracks and a brief appearance as the 'Mother at Park' in *Braindead*.

MEET THE FEEBLES (1989)

Produced with money (budget: $75,000) made from *Bad Taste* and the New Zealand Film Commission and described by *Halliwell's* as 'A semi-pornographic horror with Muppet-like creatures that is determined to offend', *Meet The Feebles* is a very odd film. The concept could be said to be 'Backstage at *The Muppet Show*', the only problem with this being that *The Muppet Show* itself often demonstrates what happens backstage. Many of the jokes are simply making explicit what is implicit in Henson's productions anyway. A big hit at Fantasy Film festivals, the picture – although amusing – is nowhere near as subversive or striking as it appears to think it is. The songs, however (particularly 'Sodomy!'), are brilliant.

BRAINDEAD (1992)

Known as *Dead Alive* in the US, Jackson's comedy gore-fest and thematic sequel to *Bad Taste* is cheerily dumb and cheap, yet strangely stylish. Featuring arguably the bloodiest sequence in film history as the male lead, armed with a rotary lawnmower, takes on a houseful of zombies, it is firmly in the tradition of Sam Raimi's *Evil Dead* series of tongue-in-cheek horror movies. Though lacking a character as immediately engaging as Bruce Campbell's chainsaw and shotgun-wielding 'Ash' in the Raimi films, the kung-fu Catholic priest and the zombie baby alone make this a worthy addition to the genre. Add to that the utterly evil Sumatran rat-monkey, the knowing nods to Hitchcock's *Psycho*, the faux-serious pre-credits intro and a delightfully disgusting dinner sequence, and you have the film that ensured that even without Jackson's subsequent success he would have earned a mention on any thorough list of top cult movie directors.

HEAVENLY CREATURES (1994)

Made by Jackson's production company, WingNut films, for $5m, *Heavenly Creatures* is based on the true story of two teenage New Zealanders, Pauline Parker and Juliet Hume, who embarked upon a matricide. It is a handsome, intelligent film with strong performances from Kate Winslet and Melanie Mynsky as the two girls. While the film flirts with suggestions of a lesbian, or at least homoerotically charged relationship between the two girls (some readers of the actual case had suggested this), it is never explicit about this. Instead the picture prefers to present the girls' obsessive friendship within the boundaries of often alarmingly deep-seeming adolescent same-sex friendships and tries to understand the, in many ways, childish nature of the girls' shared fantasy life.

The screenplay was nominated for both an Oscar and a Writers' Guild of America Award, while the film picked up a Silver Lion at the Venice Film Festival. Complex and intelligent, the movie temporarily made Jackson a respectable film-maker in the eyes of mainstream critics and Hollywood powers who had previously dismissed him as simply another cult film-maker.

FORGOTTEN SILVER (1995)

A co-write/direct with friend and fellow New Zealand film-maker Costa Botes, *Forgotten Silver* is a brilliant fake documentary which owes more than a little to Orson Welles's *F is for Fake* (1976) and Woody Allen's *Zelig* (1983). The subject of the documentary is (fictional) Kiwi film-maker Colin MacKenzie, who invented 'talkies' in 1908 and made a colour picture in 1912. It is a smart, witty film packed with 'interviews' with real film personalities (such as critic Leonard Maltin, producer Harvey Weinstein and actor Sam Neill) who talk about MacKenzie's 'forgotten career'. When it was first broadcast on New Zealand television it managed to fool much of the population into believing that their own claim to a film figure as influential as DW Griffiths or Cecil B de Mille had been found. Unfairly, the film itself is the least well known of Jackson's productions, despite being one of the best realised.

THE FRIGHTENERS (1996)

A horror comedy in which Michael J Fox can commune with the dead, *The Frighteners* works on pretty much every level except basic coherence. Opulent, funny, smart and well acted, the film descends into near gibberish in the second half, and an audience's ability to enjoy it depends on its ability to cope with that. Fox teams up with three ghosts, with whom he is friends, to run a ghostbusting service/protection racket involving dead people; he gets into trouble when he encounters the spirits of the murdered. Although it performed dismally at the box office (largely because of the lack of sense), many film-buffs hold a soft-spot for it due to the presence of R Lee Ermey as the ghost of a drill sergeant who bears an uncanny resemblance to that actor's memorable turn as Gunnery Sergeant Hartman in the first half of Stanley Kubrick's Vietnam war flick *Full Metal Jacket* (1987). Dismissed by critics and audience, its release saw Jackson's perception in Hollywood on the wane.

Jackson first started to ponder making a film based on Tolkien's writings in 1995, but Saul Zaentz still held the film rights. After the failure of Ralph Bakshi's animated version of the tale, Zaentz had assumed that no one would attempt to put the books on celluloid again, and had ended up sitting on them for nearly twenty years.

The idea came to Jackson and Fran Walsh one Sunday during the shooting of *The Frighteners*. The pair were idly considering projects that would keep the digital arm of their special effects studio WETA (added to WingNut to do the effects on *The Frighteners*) busy, and fantasy and science fiction films seemed to be the obvious options. Walsh was keen to do something 'like *Lord of the Rings*', but any such pastiche would run the risk of being little more than George Lucas's widely disliked *Willow* (1987) – a perfunctory, yet expensive, fantasy pastiche which appealed only to the very young. It slowly dawned on the pair that they should cut to the chase and simply attempt to 'do' *The Lord of the Rings* itself. As Jackson recalls, Walsh's argument was that Tolkien's tale 'was the prototype [for the genre] and if we can't think of something better, we shouldn't bother'. Eventually the pair came to the obvious questions: 'What's happening with . . . *Rings* itself? Why don't we try doing that?' To an audience now it seems so simple. Why not indeed?

The rights were the first solid reason why not. Another obvious problem was getting backing for what would almost certainly *have* to be a series of films in a genre which had generally been held to be expensive box office poison (with the sole exception of the dreadful Arnold Schwarzenegger vehicle *Conan the Barbarian* (John Milius, 1982), this type of film usually did not do as well as expected). After all, even Ralph Bakshi's quixotic attempt to make the book as a two-film series in the late seventies had collapsed halfway through, and in a manner that caused some parties to continue to display rancour decades later.

Why, despite Jackson's new-found respectability, enthusiasm and undoubted talent, would anyone take the risk of either (a) making an open-ended film which needed a sequel that would only be made if the first was a success or (b) making two or even three films back to back at potentially extraordinary cost? The Bakshi film had demonstrated the flaws with the first option. The second option could leave a studio facing the spectre of bankruptcy with one or two semi-completed sequels to a box office disaster in the can.

Jackson and Walsh contacted Zaentz's company and made an appointment with the man himself. They convinced him, with a combination of sheer passion and energy, to give them an option on the rights, although the literate and worldly Zaentz's appreciation for *Heavenly Creatures* certainly didn't do the bid any harm.

Jackson and Walsh's belief that the story could not be done in one picture sealed the deal. The couple were also adamant that the film could be made in their home country, a place of vastly contrasting weather and impressive landscapes, thus far underutilised by the film industry. For, while Jackson had always wanted to be a film-maker, Hollywood had never been part of his dream. He knew the movie could be made in New Zealand; all he had to do was convince someone with access to American money. New Zealand could provide scenery that many filmgoers had never seen, and a skilled workforce that had trained not only on films by Jackson and others of the Kiwi New Wave but on Universal's cult fantasy television series *Hercules: The Legendary Journeys* (1994 to 1999), and *Xena: Warrior Princess* (1995 to 2001).

These series were consistently the top-rated two hours of syndicated US television during their runs, drew large audiences, spawned merchandise and theme park attractions and created a mini TV fantasy boom in the mid 90s. (The series, particularly *Hercules*, are more self-aware and deliberately comic than many will credit. One late episode of *Hercules* is called 'Yes, Virginia, There is a Hercules' and is a comedy about the making of the TV show itself. Another is a remake of *Some Like It Hot* (Billy Wilder, 1959) entitled 'Men In Pink'. *Evil Dead* star Bruce Campbell writes, directs and guest stars in many episodes and both series were produced by *Evil Dead* and *Spider-Man* director Sam Raimi.) These shows' successful use of New Zealand scenery to represent not only an ancient land but also a whole ancient world, plus their often enormous battle scenes and the impressive array of ancient weapons, costumes and settings manufactured by the Kiwi costumiers and armourers over half a decade must have had an impact on Jackson's confidence in the Kiwi industry's ability to mount fantasy on a large scale. Before *The Lord of the Rings*, these two series were the first and last things of their kind to be made in New Zealand. As well as artisans and technicians, Jackson would also recruit much of the New Zealand-based cast of the series. Most notably Karl Urban, *Xena*'s Julius Caesar (and *Hercules*' Eros), would take the significant role of Éomer.

With the rights, slides, storyboards and script ideas in hand, Jackson and Walsh courted and got a two-picture deal with Harvey Weinstein at Miramax. Shortly afterwards the company baulked at the cost and suggested that *The Lord of the Rings* could be made as just one (long) movie. Jackson and Walsh in turn baulked, and they asked Weinstein's permission to offer the project to other studios. Weinstein, perhaps no longer keen on the project, agreed – but demanded two caveats. First, the other studio would have to reimburse Miramax's US$12 million investment in developing the project and, second, Miramax would, should the film(s) be made and released, receive 5% of the gross takings. (Weinstein and his brother Bob also receive Executive Producer credits on the finished movies in deference to their early work.)

Thanks to the intervention of producer Mark Ordesky, with whom they had become friends while in Hollywood, Jackson and Walsh were able to make a deal with New Line Cinema. What New Line Cinema understood was that making the films together, as a unit, minimised their costs. As well as obvious savings on costuming, sets, location hiring and the like, actors would not charge three movies' fees for doing The Lord of the Rings – they would work for two, or even one and a half, times their normal salaries. New Line Cinema's normal business model was also suited to the production. The studio habitually pre-sold international rights to their pictures in order to raise the money to get them made, and did so with The Lord of the Rings. Executive Producer Michael Lynne considered the property, with its millions of fans worldwide, to be pre-sold and, correctly, did not anticipate difficulties in securing advance international rights – despite the project's scale.

While the cost would be enormous, estimated at US$270 million, the combination of the international advance revenue and handy tax incentive, provided by an obliging New Zealand government eager for the films to be made on Kiwi soil, reduced the initial outlay to US$75 million. In terms of movie budgets these days, that is not really all that much – especially for what turned out to be in excess of nine hours of motion picture. (Sam Raimi's Spider-Man (2002) for Columbia Tri-Star cost at least $139 million, and that is only a few seconds over two hours long.)

While the total outlay would swell to closer to half a billion US dollars by the end of production, by then the gamble had already paid off. The films were a rampant commercial (not to mention critical) success.

Of course, when New Line Cinema announced their commitment in August 1998, Jackson, Walsh their co-writer Philippa Boyens and the rapidly swelling cast and crew did not know that. But Jackson and Walsh had made the deal. All they had to do now was make the films.

THE LORD OF THE RINGS: THE FELLOWSHIP OF THE RING (2001)

New Line Cinema Presents
A WingNut Films Production
The Lord of the Rings
The Fellowship of the Ring
Directed by Peter Jackson
Screenplay by Fran Walsh, Philippa Boyens, Peter Jackson
Based on the book by JRR Tolkien
Producers: Barrie M Osborne, Peter Jackson, Fran Walsh,
   Tim Sanders
Executive Producers: Mark Ordesky, Bob Weinstein, Harvey
   Weinstein, Robert Shaye, Mark Lynne
Director of Photography: Andrew Lesnie, A.C.S
Production Designer: Grant Major
Film Editor: John Gilbert
Co-producers: Rick Porras, Jamie Selkirk
UK Casting by John Hubbard and Amy MacLean
US Casting by Victoria Burrows
New Zealand Casting by Liz Mullane
Australian Casting by Ann Robinson
Costume Designers: Ngila Dickson, Richard Taylor
Music composed, orchestrated and conducted by Howard
   Shore
Associate Producer: Ellen M Somers
Special Make-up, creatures, armour and miniatures by
   Richard Taylor
Visual Effects Supervisor: Jim Rygiel

Released: 10 December 2000 (London premiere)

STARRING: Elijah Wood (Frodo Baggins), Ian McKellen (Gandalf), Liv Tyler (Arwen), Viggo Mortensen (Aragorn), Sean Astin (Sam), Cate Blanchett (Galadriel), John Rhys-Davies (Gimli), Billy Boyd (Pippin), Dominic Monaghan (Merry), Orlando Bloom (Legolas), Christopher Lee (Saruman), Hugo Weaving (Elrond), featuring Sean Bean (Boromir) and Ian Holm (Bilbo) with Andy Serkis as Gollum. Marton Csokas (Celeborn), Craig Parker (Haldur), Lawrence Makoare (Lurtz). Featuring Alan Howard (Voice of the Ring).

NOTE: These chapters follow thematic and structural elements and conceits across all three films with the information contained within the film chapter to which it is the most relevant. They are, however, cross-referenced as and when necessary.

THE SCRIPT: Structurally, the screenplay by Jackson, Boyens and Walsh is elegant in its simplicity and occasionally ruthless in its dispensing of details. (It is worth noting that another New Zealand-based screenwriter and mutual friend of Jackson and Walsh, Stephen Sinclair, is a credited co-screenwriter on *The Two Towers* only. He was, however, involved in the adaptation of *The Lord of the Rings* at an early stage and all parties happily agree that he contributed to all three films. This book tends to refer to the screenwriters of the film series as Jackson/Boyens/Walsh. This is not intended to denigrate Sinclair's involvement, even if the precise details of it remain unclear.)

Generally, the screenplay doesn't utilise Tolkien's own dialogue if it can help it, with a pithy, straightforward speaking style used for the most part rather than the writer's own lengthy declamations of a few hundred words or so in length. The way it manages to seem authentic is by using Tolkien's own vocabulary in shorter sentences than the author's own and by taking some small sentences and key phrases out of the book's long, long passages of dialogue and using them to its own purposes, often shifting dialogue to different characters and contexts. The result might be *faux*-Tolkien, but it works.

Throughout *The Lord of the Rings: The Fellowship of the Ring*, the overarching shape and sense of the story are entirely Tolkien's; the dialogue, the details, even the scene transitions, are from the Boyens/Walsh/Jackson troika. At points, these details are radically different. The dialogue, as noted, is rarely even similar. Scenes are frequently invented or dispensed with, but overall the screenplay is a small triumph. Anyone who has read the book once, whether it be a long time ago or recently, will recognise every set piece and every character, and come away feeling that this has been an almost impossibly faithful dramatisation. Anyone familiar with every dot and comma of the book, and of all its apocrypha, should understand that the demands of the medium have occasioned every departure from it.

PROLOGUE: The first film begins with a prologue which draws on elements of Book I, Chapter I, the appendices, some ideas from

The Silmarillion and details from *The Hobbit* in an attempt to bring the audience up to speed with Middle-earth and the soon to be unfolding story.

Before considering the success (or otherwise) of this sequence, it is worth pointing out that both the Bakshi film and the BBC Radio serial began in the same way. That this is a convenient, even necessary, way to introduce a mainstream audience to the background details of a story that is only a small part of a millennia-spanning fictional universe is not in any doubt, but it is also certain that Jackson and/or Sibley were aware of Bakshi's use of the same technique. While the fact the same information is conveyed can be, in part, explained by the simple fact that this is the information that *needs* to be conveyed, this is perhaps the clearest example of each successive adaptation building on the earlier ones.

Although heavy on exposition, Jackson's prologue sequence is easily comprehensible by anyone. The narration over this long montage is pieced together from various dialogues spoken by various characters – including Gandalf, Elrond, Frodo and Galadriel – at many points in the book. Here it is read out by Cate Blanchett in character as Galadriel. (Cate Blanchett, incidentally, only worked for three weeks on the film series, despite being billed sixth on the end credits of each picture.) This condensation of various disparate pieces of essential background information into a single, bite-sized chunk is actually a very impressive achievement, as any attempt to find all the various bits and pieces in the texts will attest to. Even a viewer with absolutely no familiarity with Middle-earth and *The Lord of the Rings* is entirely up to speed within minutes. Had Jackson not included a sequence such as this at the very start – as he did at one point contemplate – it would have been rather more difficult to convey all the necessary backstory to those unfamiliar with Middle-earth. It also acts as a handy trailer for the sort of scenes and themes the audience can expect in the rest of the movie series.

The narration introduces a couple of concepts to the audience that it might have been difficult to suggest otherwise: the Ring's ability to give 'unnatural long life' to its owner and the suggestion that the Ring is in some sense sentient (see **THE RING** in **The Return of the King**). An interesting aspect of this sequence is that it is never said who made the other Rings of Power. It is implied, heavily, that Sauron made them all and that he gave many of them away: giving three to elves, seven to the dwarf lords and nine to men ('who above all else, desire power' – see **BREE**) was a trick (they were 'deceived', says the narration), a part of his plan to take over all of Middle-earth, the same plan that led to the creation, in secret, of the 'Master Ring' as it is called here. This is a neat solution to the confusing implications in the book that only the One Ring was made by Sauron, but that it had the power to 'rule them all' despite the fact that the elves, and not he, made the other rings. (Bakshi's solution was different, and has been unfairly criticised – see **JRR Tolkien's The Lord of the Rings**.) The introduction then uses a few seconds from Gollum's discovery of the Ring (Book I, Chapter II, although this is examined in detail in the third film *The Return of the King*) and then makes use of elements from Chapter V of *The Hobbit* ('Riddles in the Dark') to show Bilbo's discovery of the Ring.

THE SHIRE: Rivendell and Lothlórien are magical places. Though beautiful and hospitable, they present no real warmth, and they are both characterised by the distance and aloofness of the elves. They are two of the only three places in the book and film that are seen to be unaffected (at least directly) by Sauron's growing might. The other is the Shire.

Warm, friendly and eccentric, the Shire epitomises all that will be lost if the coming darkness is triumphant. Each of the hobbits in turn comes to realise that, if they are weak or give up on their quest, it and everything that they hold dear will be lost. It is deliberately the least outlandish and most recognisable land encountered during the Fellowship's fragmented journeys through Middle-earth.

Gondor is falling, Rohan has been corrupted and nearly shattered, the lands of the elves are being abandoned, and Moria has already succumbed to the orcs, but the Shire endures as the last hope for the hobbits of an unspoiled safe haven. In the films, they return at the end of their journey to find it just as it ever was (including old Proudfoot eyeing them suspiciously, as he does Gandalf at the start of *The Fellowship of the Ring*) and they seem quickly to slip back into their old ways with a drink down the pub. The other hobbits of the Shire have noticed nothing, and continue as they ever have. This is the ultimate proof of the success of Frodo's mission. (In the book, it is a different story, but that is dealt with elsewhere.)

As the one place that remains unaffected and pure, the Shire is the most important of all the lands through which the journey passes. Although in Jackson's films a hobbit is seen being beheaded by one of the Black Riders, and though Sauron's spies make their way within its borders, the hobbits are so insular as to remain unaffected by these strange visitors. The simple assumption is that *all* foreigners and 'big people' are like that, and it is only to be expected that they are odd and have no manners. (If that seems unlikely, in 1805 the people of Hartlepool in England tried and executed a monkey washed up after a shipwreck under the assumption that it was a Frenchman – they had never seen either before, and the country was at war with France, so it seemed a safe bet that the solitary simian was part of an invasion force.)

It is also notable that the Shire is the most green and fertile of all the lands through which the journey runs (see **THÉODEN** in **The Two Towers**). It is a land of plenty, laughter and happiness, where young and old alike delight in good food and pleasant company, and all revel in the beauty of nature (see **TREEBEARD** in **The Two Towers**). Frodo is first seen sitting peacefully under a lush tree, enjoying the sunshine and the simplicity of it all. Hobbit children run in delight after Gandalf, hoping for fireworks and other treats, and their parents secretly enjoy it all too, despite their misgivings about the 'disturber of the peace'. Birds sing, flowers grow, crops are ready to be harvested, and everyone is ready for a big party, which all are determined to enjoy. The removal of the Sackville-Bagginses from the cinematic cut further heightens this idea of the Shire as a place of peace and tranquillity.

It is with the Shire that the soundscapes of Middle-earth, created for the films by Howard Shore, are first imprinted in the mind of the audience. It is the Shire theme that returns whenever hope and friendship resurface during the dark journeys ahead, often in a mournful minor key as the pull of duty reminds the hobbits of what they have to do. But the theme also highlights *why* they are doing what they are doing. It all comes back to the Shire.

The chief characteristics of each of the hobbits are honesty, decency and a love of the simple things in life – as elves are wise, dwarves are tough, orcs are cruel and men are in need of leadership (see **LET'S HUNT SOME ORC** in **The Two Towers**). It is clear that the resilience of Frodo and Bilbo (and Sam) to the

Ring's evil stems in a large part from the simplicity and purity of their Shire upbringing.

FRODO 1: The audience's initial sight of Frodo is of him seated on his own, reading under a tree. This is not present within the book, but is an easy visual symbol for the fact that Frodo is considered odd among hobbits because he has some learning. Anyone objecting to this visual conveying of character (as some self-proclaimed Tolkien fans have done online) has no grasp of film technique or the remotest sense of perspective.

The following scenes in which Frodo accompanies Gandalf in his cart on his way to Bag End have also been added. On the page, Gandalf approaches Bag End on his own but this on-screen addition clearly strengthens the audience's perception of the bond between Frodo and Gandalf. The physical affection and easy, comfortable dialogue between Frodo and Gandalf again clue the viewer into the fact that this is a pre-existing relationship of some depth and warmth. This naturally adds further pathos and emotion to Frodo's mourning of Gandalf's (apparent) death later in the film, as well as helping to set up Gandalf as a jovial and pleasant old man for those audience members unfamiliar with either *The Lord of the Rings* or *The Hobbit* (see **THE GREY PILGRIM**). While this backstory is conveyed through prose on the page, and through the assumption that the majority of the readers will already be familiar with Gandalf from *The Hobbit*, the only way to achieve the same effect on screen is through dialogue and performance (see **BILBO**).

While a superficial reading may cause the viewer/reader to see no real change between the on-the-page Frodo Baggins and the character as played by Elijah Wood, there are important differences to consider. These do not, however, fundamentally alter the function or form of the character as laid down by the author and are, instead, modifications made in order to ensure that the most important aspects of the character and his role are transmitted to the audience.

First, let us consider age. As Book I of Tolkien's story begins, Frodo is 33 years old – it is stated that he shares the date of his birthday with his Uncle Bilbo, who leaves the Shire at the age of 111 in the first chapter. A further seventeen years passes before Frodo leaves the Shire, intending to take the Ring to Rivendell (this is how long it takes Gandalf to correctly divine the Ring's identity and return with confirmation). This means that on the page, the Frodo who leaves for Rivendell, and accedes to going to Mount Doom, is a mature hobbit of 50 years of age. He has been master of Bag End and a respectable (if slightly odd) member of Hobbiton society for nearly twenty years. Elijah Wood, who plays Frodo in all three films, was 18 when cast (he was born 1981) and looked a little younger. Although Wood was already an experienced movie actor in bit parts and supporting roles (including the younger son in *The Ice Storm* (Ang Lee, 1997)), it was his role in *The Faculty* (Robert Rodrigeuz, 1998), via a campaign on his behalf by Internet geek Maestro Harry Knowles, that brought him to Jackson's attention. Jackson had wanted a British actor for the lead role but was won over by Elijah Wood's audition and the home-made tape Wood sent to him containing a self-shot screentest. Wood had previously played that other great icon of corruptible pastoral innocence, the lead in *The Adventures of Hucklebery Finn* in a Stephen Sommers-directed TV movie in 1993.

In the film, it has clearly not been a matter of years between Gandalf's departure and return. Sam, Merry and Pippin are all seen at Bilbo's party looking the same age as they are when they join Frodo in setting out for Rivendell. All the (short) scenes between Gandalf's leaving and returning take place one night, then during the day, then during an evening. Certainly the sequence of the Black Riders setting out from Minas Morgul takes place on screen *before* Gandalf arrives at Minas Tirith to research the Ring (which happens in daylight). The Ring Wraith(s) then arrive in the Shire *after* Gandalf reaches the library. A Wraith then questions a bystander about 'Baggins!' in a scene which takes place in the evening. (This scene with the Nazgûl and the bullied hobbit, which is implicit but not present in the book, seems to be derived from a scene in Episode Two of the BBC Radio serial. It explicitly has to take place at most a few hours before the Wraiths reach Hobbiton.) The clear implication here is that all three of these events take place on the same day. This implies this 'one-day' timescale very strongly indeed. In terms of essential filmic logic, no other interpretation is possible.

In the book, Frodo is not unlike the Bilbo of *The Hobbit*: a middle-aged person of some experience, who is somewhat set in his ways. On screen, Frodo is played by an actor who aged from 18 to 20 during principal shooting, and appears to leave the Shire for Rivendell within days – possibly even hours – of Bilbo's departure. One can, obviously, draw parallels between the hobbit age of majority (33) and the humans' (18 or 21 in the West), and conclude that the casting reflected the 'fact' that hobbits mature and age slower than humans (as expressed frequently in Tolkien's writings). However, it also needs to be reflected that the Frodo of Book I is not that different in age and appearance from the Bilbo of *The Hobbit*, but the Frodo of *The Lord of the Rings: The Fellowship of the Ring* is visibly and strikingly different from the Bilbo seen in on-screen flashbacks to *The Hobbit*. In these, Ian Holm plays Bilbo with darkened hair and without ageing make-up, but he does not look of a similar age to Elijah Wood (Holm was in his late 60s during filming). The difference is pronounced and must be deliberate.

The reason for the alteration is simple and clear. On the page, Frodo's simplicity is partially conveyed through his pastoral nature, as well as the fact that he is a hobbit, and hobbits are a simple folk. His innocence and idealism are invoked by associating him with, in the reader's perceptions, romantic notions of environmental harmony within a rustic, Arcadian paradise. He is simple and innocent because he lives in the country, the Shire.

Tolkien's association of the countryside with innocence is only a part of our present culture in a greatly reduced form. What the Jackson/Walsh /Boyens screenplay does is to evoke a different, more contemporary idea of innocence by associating Frodo not with pastoralism, but with youth. Elijah Wood is not just young; he is the youngest, shortest and most slender of the actors playing the hobbits. He has large, wide, blue eyes, which the camera often focuses on. Frodo is being intimated to the audience as a child, to be sympathised with because of the burden that the Ring places upon a child.

Frodo's childlike nature is very different to the book's portrayal of a hobbit well into his inheritance and approaching middle age. (It should also be noted that to convey the idea that seventeen years has passed, even if Frodo has hardly aged thanks to the Ring, to a cinema audience unfamiliar with the book would be very difficult to pull off without a clumsy and intrusive use of caption cards, something Jackson was keen to avoid.) What the change does manage to retain is the most important aspect of Frodo's character, albeit expressed in a different manner, while speeding up the pace of what is, in the book, a very slow passage.

Being more childlike is something that is not only true of Frodo but also, to a greater or lesser extent, of all of the hobbits as portrayed in the Jackson films. In the book, these characters are often addressed as 'Mister' followed by their surnames. On screen, their forenames, and the diminutives of their forenames (Sam not Samwise, Merry not Merriadoc, Pippin not Peregrin), are used almost exclusively. When their surnames are invoked (such as by Gandalf's repeated 'Fool of a Took!'), it just emphasises further the characters' lack of seniority, for there is something schoolmasterish about the use of a surname without any prefix.

When interviewed as a group after the release of *The Lord of the Rings: The Return of the King*, the other hobbit actors made it clear that Billy Boyd spoke for all of them when he said that their characterisations were based on 'innocence and *naiveté* . . . a lot of that came from watching children . . . if you watch a child who's just learning to talk, they'll sit and look at someone as if they hear every word that they're saying, and understand it, but they're not'. The innocence of the hobbits is their prime characteristic. This is what makes the fact that they are forced into such horrendous situations all the more powerful. Billy Boyd (born 1968) and Dominic Monaghan (born 1976) were largely unknown before being cast as Pippin and Merry respectively. Their unknown status combines with their deliberate childlike naiveté in performance to make the hobbit characters entirely 'real' in a way that more famous actors might have had trouble with. There are no earlier star roles to work against the performers here as there would have been if a more famous actor of a similar age (for example Macauley Culkin) had been cast in either role.

BILBO: Part of the problem with making a movie version of *The Lord of the Rings* without first having filmed *The Hobbit* is that the sense of it being a continuation of a story is in danger of being lost. Most people who read the book do so after first reading *The Hobbit*, and are thus already familiar with, and have affection for, Bilbo Baggins. The fact that the affable hero of the first book is shown, at the start of its sequel, to have started to act irrationally and to have become quick to anger – even with a powerful wizard, his old friend Gandalf – is the first indication that all is not right. While only being able to show a short glimpse of Bilbo's earlier adventure in the prologue, Jackson's film has to convey the fact that Bilbo is a decent chap, that he is thought of as a little strange, and that he has started to act oddly even by his standards, all in a very short space of time.

Jackson largely succeeds, and does so primarily thanks to the presence of Sir Ian Holm in the role. Since entering middle age, Ian Holm's unimposing stature and expressive face have meant that he excels as unlikely villains, or charming characters with dark secrets. His best-known film roles in the run-up to the release of *The Lord of the Rings: The Fellowship of the Ring* include Jack the Ripper suspect Sir William Gull in *From Hell* (Albert Hughes, 2001) and as (possibly) the devil himself in *A Life Less Ordinary* (Danny Boyle, 1997). He has also had a number of screen roles in which he plays bumbling but essentially good-willed types, as in *The Fifth Element* (Luc Besson, 1997) and the BBC's television version of the sickly sweet Mary Norton children's novel *The Borrowers* (1993). However, two of his best-received well-known roles in the decade running up to his turn as Bilbo combined aspects of the two extremes: his portrayal of King George III's well-intentioned but hard-hearted doctor in the film version of Alan Bennet's play *The Madness of George III* and his remark-able, award-winning turn as a particularly pathetic and sympath-etic *King Lear* in the National Theatre's 1997 production (which was an even more impressive performance on the intimate stage of the National's Cottesloe Theatre than when filmed for televi-sion by the BBC).

As Bilbo, Holm has the difficult task of demonstrating why the younger hobbits respect and love him so much, while also making clear the morally corrosive effect ownership of the Ring has had on him.

Casting Holm almost compensates, emotionally speaking, for their being no *Hobbit* film made before this. The audience's affection for actor and character are already there because of Holm's previous associations with Middle-earth. He is assisted in this in part by the metatextual frisson that he had previously played Frodo on the radio in 1981 and thus much of the audience is already fond of him in that capacity. It is certainly to be hoped that Ian Holm returns to the role of Bilbo Baggins if (or when?) Peter Jackson makes a film of *The Hobbit*.

Even with Ian Holm's wonderfully subtle performance, due to the sheer lack of screentime that the character can be afforded, the risk remains that those unfamiliar with the books may get the wrong impression about the character. The Extended Edition helps set Bilbo up as a kindly, absent-minded old man far more, largely thanks to the longer introduction to the Shire, revealed in a Bilbo voiceover. He is evidently very fond of his fellow hobbits, even while recognising that they might seem comical to outsiders, and this alone is enough to demonstrate that he is not simply the angry and confused figure who confronts Gandalf when it is suggested that he give up the Ring.

In the theatrical cut, Bilbo's love of the Shire is also evident from the scenes at his birthday party, but here is introduced another potential problem: in Jackson's version, Frodo does not know of Bilbo's plan to leave. It is clear that the suspicion is there, but it is Gandalf who confirms Frodo's feeling that Bilbo wants to set off on another of his adventures. This serves to make Bilbo seem rather more odd and secretive than he is portrayed as in the book.

Later, the amount of time Bilbo has spent at Rivendell seems odd in the context of the week or so that seems to have passed since he left Hobbiton and how long it should have taken him to get to Rivendell. It is possible that Gandalf is away for longer than it seems on screen after Bilbo's party (perhaps a matter of months) but what actually happens in those sequences and the logic of the way they are edited does not support such an idea at all. Perhaps this slip-up is an unintentional, and difficult to spot, side-effect of shortening Tolkien's timescale to such a large extent. Something was always going to not quite fit. Or maybe the answer lies in the books' explanation that time works differently in elven lands, and the implicit idea that without having the Ring in his possession its powers of longevity are wearing off, so he is rapidly approaching the physical state that more befits his advanced age.

Even with such minor potential problems, it is difficult to believe that another actor could make the shifts from fearful to fear-inspiring as effectively as Holm does at both Bag End and Rivendell in this movie. This is an actor completely in control of his performance, and aware of when and how to switch from endearing to disturbing and back again without ever losing the audience's sympathy. His grasping lunge for the Ring when Frodo shows it to him at Rivendell foreshadows both Frodo's descent and the sequence at the start of Jackson's *Return of the King* in which Gollum's gradual physical and mental collapse is shown, but within less than a second Holm manages to revert to the weak, sad, loveable old man that Frodo and the other hobbits know him to be.

Bilbo's ability to overcome the Ring's influence, though obviously a struggle, is one of the key things that give Frodo the strength to carry on. If Bilbo can continue to live a contented life after being in the Ring's power, perhaps Frodo can as well. It is also implicitly thanks to Bilbo's recovery that Frodo later comes to have sympathy for Gollum, and to try to bring out the good in him (see **SMÉAGOL** in **The Two Towers**).

SAM 1: Far from simply being Frodo's gardener, and so both socially inferior and necessarily deferential thanks to his status as an employee, in the Jackson films Sam is introduced as one of Frodo's friends. The first time we see them together, Frodo is helping him to get a dance with Rosie Cotton, his future wife, at Bilbo's party; next, Sam and Frodo are having a drink together at the pub. This is not a normal master–servant relationship, which is how the two are presented in the book. It is also worth noting that whereas in both book and film Gandalf tells Frodo that he need not go on his quest alone if he can think of someone he can trust, in the book Frodo can trust Sam because he is a loyal servant; in the Jackson film the trust is that of a friend (see **SAM 2** in **The Return of the King**).

Sam eavesdropping on Frodo and Gandalf's conversation about the Ring is not innocent or inadvertent in this version (in the book it is both) because it cannot be. The scene takes place at night as it does in the Bakshi film, not in the morning as it does in the book. This adds a further level of menace to the unfolding threat thanks to the encompassing darkness, but it also makes the likelihood of Sam actually doing some gardening at such an hour highly unlikely. He is not 'trimming the hedges' as he claims, and Gandalf picks him up on this fib ('it's a little late . . .').

In the book, as Gandalf's revelation about the Ring takes place during the day, it is entirely possible that Sam would be doing a bit of gardening, and Tolkien mentions that the sound of shears can be heard on a number of occasions during the passage. In Jackson's version, Sam 'heard raised voices', as he himself admits, and continued to listen because he was interested. This is made convincing on screen by the use of a short, wordless sequence of Sam walking Frodo back home from the pub moments before Frodo finds Gandalf in his house. Gandalf also explicitly sends Sam with Frodo both because he knows that he cares about him and because he knows too much to be safe on his own – this is also implicit, but not stated, in the book. Sam and Frodo then seem to leave Hobbiton the next morning.

TIME: Beyond the reduction of the timescale between Gandalf's departure and return with confirmation of the Ring's identity, there are a number of other changes made to the timing of the early part of the film. Most of these are through the desire to add dramatic urgency to the gradually unfolding plot. As Fran Walsh explains on the DVD commentary, in the book, after finding out the nature of the Ring, Frodo 'spends another six months just thinking about it . . . that tends to completely undermine any sense of dramatic urgency'. Most of the alterations in the early parts of the first film were made for this reason, to add urgency and increase the sense of danger.

All of the attendant flummery of Frodo selling Bag End to the Sackville-Bagginses and moving to Buckland with the secret intention of eventually heading towards Bree and/or Rivendell is entirely abandoned. (This thread runs through Book I, Chapters III–VIII.) It is very clear on screen that Frodo and Sam leave Hobbiton on the morning after the night on which Gandalf returned with his information rather than waiting months before they go as they do on the page.

After this, Gandalf visits Saruman (in a scene related by Gandalf in Book II, Chapter II) and explicitly arrives there a day after leaving Frodo and Sam (the audience sees the hobbits camp for one night). It is thus 24 hours since Gandalf and Frodo parted, around 12 hours after Gandalf came back from the library, and about 24 hours after Bilbo left. The two months that the literary Gandalf spends trapped at Isengard after his fight with Saruman seems to be reduced to him being unconscious for a few hours and then remaining atop the tower for a further whole day. (Gandalf sending a moth to find a larger creature to carry him from the tower is an invention of the screenwriters to save having to include the wizard Radaghast the Brown, who has the ability to communicate with beasts and who is using them to watch the world at Saruman's suggestion. Radaghast does not know that Saruman has thrown his lot in with Mordor and sends Gwaihir the Eagle to report to Saruman; when Gandalf explains the situation to Gwaihir, he rescues him. On screen, it is easier for Gandalf to simply summon help. That he can do it on his own also makes his own powers more impressive.)

The hobbits (who now number four, accompanied as Sam and Frodo are by Merry and Pippin) seem to reach Bree on the night of the same day that Gandalf fights Saruman. With seventeen years thus reduced to perhaps less than seventy hours, the script establishes a pace and structure for the film which is appropriate to the action-adventure (cum road movie) genre in which the picture belongs.

There are many further simplifications and condensations: for example, Bilbo has 'gone to stay with the elves' rather than set out to travel on a 'holiday' as in the book. Gandalf tells Frodo that this is the case. This cuts out much long exposition, but why Frodo is then surprised when he finds Bilbo at Rivendell is a mystery.

According to the chronology helpfully provided in 'Appendix B' of *The Lord of the Rings*, the hobbits reach Bree on 29 September, having left Bag End six days earlier; it takes a further six months before their quest is completed. The bulk of Chapters III to VIII are abandoned entirely – forming as they do the house-selling and moving subplot, the encounters with Old Man Willow, Tom Bombadil (see **TREEBEARD** and **FARAMIR**) and the Barrow-wight, as well as the appearance of Farmer Maggot, which is rendered impossible by the screenplay's method of Frodo and Sam being joined by the other two hobbits. Merry and Pippin (not here stated to be Frodo's cousins as they are in the book, although he later refers to them as his 'kin') are encountered while they are stealing from Farmer Maggot's field. In the book, this is something that Frodo did when young, but has not indulged in for many years. On the page, Merry and Pippin are great friends of Farmer Maggot and so are unlikely to be pillaging his fields for root vegetables.

Once the hobbits reach Bree and the inn of the Prancing Pony, there are fewer wholesale deletions and alterations because, from this point on, the narrative progresses far more quickly. All Jackson, Walsh and Boyens have really done is to try to present events as closely as possible in chronological sequence, with occasional pieces of intercutting between simultaneous events. There are a few lost aspects, but these are mostly minor and due primarily to the constraints of time placed on all films by the simple and vital consideration of the audience's patience.

BREE: In terms of filmic logic, the hobbits arrive at Bree on the same night that they flee the horsemen at the Bucklebury Ferry –

it is, after all, still nighttime. However, Peter Jackson has noted that just because the Tom Bombadil sequences are not shown does not mean that the hobbits did not have adventures in the woods and on the Barrow-Downs, and that the audience can, if they so wish, choose to believe that these events did still happen, but are simply not shown. The fact that it is raining when the hobbits arrive at Bree, but it is not at the Ferry, could suggest – again in terms of filmic logic – that it is a different night. As such, Jackson's contention is plausible.

However, the simple fact is that nothing that happens in the book between the hobbits leaving the Shire and arriving at Bree advances the basic narrative of the quest to destroy the Ring. In fact, rather than simply distracting from the principle plot, the encounter with Tom Bombadil actually detracts from the sense of the Ring's threat, and thus from one of the central premises of the entire story (see **FARAMIR** in **The Two Towers**).

The reason for the lack of advancement in the early stages of *The Lord of the Rings* is simple – Tolkien himself had no idea where his plot was leading him when he wrote the first half of Book I. On 31 August 1938 he wrote to his publishers explaining that the book was 'flowing along, and getting quite out of hand. It has reached about Chapter VII and progresses towards quite unforeseen goals.' He is on record as admitting that he had as little idea as the hobbits about who Strider was on their first meeting, and in the first draft Aragorn's place was filled by a 'queer-looking' hobbit called Trotter. It was only *after* Tolkien had written the journey as far as Bree that he came up with the idea that Bilbo's ring was in fact the One Ring.

This necessitated a certain amount of rewriting, but much of what had already been put down remained in place, bar the hero's name changing from the rather childish 'Bingo Bolger-Baggins' to the more serious-sounding 'Frodo'. The detailed descriptions of the Shire and its inhabitants in the first five chapters seemed important to underline what was at risk, as well as to provide a few hints about the danger of the Ring; the events of the next three chapters (taking the hobbits from the Shire to Bree) appear to have remained largely for sentimental reasons.

The essential elements of Chapters VI–VIII (Old Man Willow, Tom Bombadil, Goldberry, and the Barrow-wight) all appeared in Tolkien's poem 'The Adventures of Tom Bombadil', published in the *Oxford Magazine* in 1934. The character of Bombadil himself was based on one of Tolkien's children's toys, and had first become the centre of an unrecorded bedtime story during the 1920s. In other words, by the time the overall plot of the professor's sequel to his hit children's story had become clear to him, Tolkien had had Tom Bombadil waiting in the wings for well over a decade – the character deserved his turn in the limelight.

As part of a long work of written fiction, the clash with Old Man Willow and the Barrow-wight are diverting enough episodes, hinting at whole other aspects to Middle-earth beyond the basic narrative. In particular, the concept of the ancient, forgotten kings who lie beneath the Barrow-downs seems highly appropriate to a tale that purports to be from a long-forgotten past in our own world. Old Man Willow gives an early glimpse of the unknown world of intelligent trees that adds an air of menace to Merry and Pippin's first meeting with Treebeard (Book III, Chapter IV). Also, the sword Merry takes from the Barrow (it transpires in what seems a fairly half-hearted paragraph tagged on to the end of the sequence in which Éowyn confronts him before Minas Tirith – Book 5, Chapter VI) is enchanted to break the power of the Witch King of Angmar.

However, unlike later diversions, the whole section, from the moment the hobbits enter the Old Forest until Bombadil leaves them, seems to detract more from the central story of the Ring than it adds. Unlike the Watcher in the Water outside the entrance to the Mines of Moria or the Lady Galadriel in Lothlorien, neither Old Man Willow nor the Barrow-wight seem especially interested in Frodo or what he carries (they both attack the other hobbits first) and Bombadil remains entirely unaffected by, and largely uninterested in, the Ring when he tries it on. The fact that Bombadil's precise nature remains unclear, and that he insists on spending most of the time talking in near-nonsense verse, has ensured that these sequences have proved very hard to adapt, and have also been the parts where many first-time readers of the books decide that they have had enough.

Looking back from the end of Frodo's journey one has to wonder what the chances are of finding three creatures with no interest whatsoever in the Ring within a few miles of his home, when practically everyone else who is encountered along the way can think of little else. To have the first creatures encountered outside the Shire unconcerned by the Ring's evil – indeed, to have anyone unaffected by the Ring's evil (see **FARAMIR** in **The Two**

Towers) – severely undermines the sense of threat emanating from Mordor. Add to this the fact that the Black Riders remain unseen during this little diversion, and that both Old Man Willow and the Barrow-wight seem like much more direct threats than shuffling, whispering horsemen, diminishing even the menace of the Nazgûl, and even Tolkien expert and fan TA Shippey admits that these chapters 'could almost be omitted without disturbing the rest of the plot'. Dramatically, such a long period without any plot advancement makes little sense; this is why most of the dramatisations of *The Lord of the Rings* to date have not included this section.

In the Jackson films, the omission of the Tom Bombadil passages has actually helped highlight an aspect of Middle-earth that remains rather more implicit in the books – the nature of Man. The first non-hobbits Frodo and party encounter (aside from Gandalf) are the grotesque, weather-beaten, drunken faces at the bar of the Prancing Pony. The questioning gatekeeper, the darkness, rain and mud, and the apparent hostility and suspicion of everyone in Bree (including the innkeeper as he asks Frodo's name and later listens with interest to Pippin giving the game away), creates an immediate jolting change from the lush tranquillity and beauty of the Shire. As they walk up Bree's main street they are leered at by a belching drunk (played by Peter Jackson himself), nearly run down by a horse and cart, and angrily told to watch where they are going by a local.

Despite Merry and Pippin's delight in the beer at the Prancing Pony, the world of Man is hardly very welcoming. After the introduction of the 'dangerous' Strider, sitting menacingly in the corner, his eyes glowing red in the light of his pipe, various close-ups of the denizens of the bar flash up in a montage of Frodo fondling the Ring as the Black Rider's voice repeats 'Baggins'. As Jackson says in the Extended Edition commentary, 'we wanted to get the most unusual, odd, seedy-looking people that we could find . . . I wanted to make it feel quite ominous'. As men are first introduced in the prologue, Galadriel refers to them as 'the race of Men, who above all else desire power', and explains the whole problem faced by Middle-earth in one short statement: 'the hearts of men are easily corrupted'.

Bree, and by extension the world of men, is evidently full of potential danger. This fact is heightened, as Frodo trips in his haste to stop Pippin imperilling their quest, by the first extensive appearance of the Eye (see **THE ENEMY** in *The Return of the King*).

STRIDER: Aragorn is a hero straight out of Anglo-Saxon legend: true-hearted, practically fearless, and noble. He is the epitome of selfless heroism, and has his closest parallel in extant myth in Tolkien's conception of the character of Beowulf – although Aragorn, like Beowulf, exists in a world without Christianity, he embodies many virtues associated with Christian kingship.

By far the most obvious piece of Christian symbolism surrounding Aragorn that remains in the Jackson films is the fact that, though a king (indeed, *the* king), his appearance is not that of a monarch. Ensconced at the back of the bar in the Prancing Pony at Bree, he appears no more than 'a strange-looking, weather-beaten man' (Book I, Chapter IX) whose face is hidden under the hood of his travel-stained coat. Like Christ, Aragorn does not pronounce his status, but trusts to the ability of those he encounters to judge him for what he is, rather than how he appears. Frodo shows his decency of character in part because he can see through Aragorn's 'Strider' persona. The human denizens of Bree do not trust 'Strider' at all – yet another example of how Mankind is shown to be easily misled. (The fact that Sam does not trust Strider either can be put down to an oversight on Tolkien's part, the fact that Sam's primary concern is to protect Frodo, or to the fact that Tolkien may not, as with so many readings of his work, have intended this interpretation.)

The symbol of the kings of Gondor is the White Tree of Minas Tirith. The tree was adopted as a Christian symbol during the spread of the religion through Europe thanks to the extant symbolism of the cross (see **ENTS**). The flag of Gondor features the tree haloed by seven stars. These have been taken, by some, to represent the seven seals of the Book of Revelation, which the returning Christ shall break open at the end of the world. In the book, one of the things that proves Aragorn's identity as the true King of Gondor on his arrival at Minas Tirith is that, like Christ, he has the power to heal through the laying on of hands. (Although it may be noted that this was a frequent claim of Western European monarchs up until the seventeenth century, this claim itself stemmed from a desire to link the monarchy directly with Christ.) Much as it is possible to identify allegories of the Second World War into *The Lord of the Rings*, it is possible to identify any number of Christian allegories as well.

Does the decision by Jackson, Walsh and Boyens to make Aragorn reluctant and doubtful of his destiny (see **ISILDUR'S**

HEIR) detract from this? No – it is implicit at various points in the text, which are themselves based on that passage in the Bible where Jesus wonders whether his crucifixion is really necessary, just as the temptation of the Ring is based on the passage where Jesus is tempted by the devil in the wilderness. The whole thing is biblical – it cannot be coincidence that the Fellowship leaves Rivendell on 25 December, Christmas Day, and the Ring is destroyed on 25 March, the date of the Annunciation.

Jesus Christ, in the Christian tradition, is the 'King of Kings'; in Middle-earth, which existed in a time before Christ according to Tolkien's conceit, Aragorn fulfils this role. Despite the fact that Gondor has not been ruled by a king for centuries, this respect for the office – which in Western European tradition was often argued to have stemmed from the direct appointment by God of the first of the dynasty – is such that the country's current rulers refrain from adopting the title (much like Oliver Cromwell following the execution of Charles I), even though they are king in all but name. They are instead 'stewards' – a term evolved from the word 'shepherd', another appellation of Christ. (This idea, incidentally, stems from Scottish history, where the Stuart dynasty that also inherited the throne of England after the death of Elizabeth I were initially the 'Stewards' of the crown of Scotland, acting as such for two centuries before finally adopting the crown in AD 1371. Through the corruption of various Scottish dialects, the title gradually became 'Stewart' and then 'Stuart', before being adopted as a surname.) At the very end of the *Fellowship* movie, when Boromir lies dying in Aragorn's arms, the son of the Steward sees the error of his ways, and accepts Aragorn as his lord and king. It is a classic Catholic deathbed confession, and the final proof that Boromir is, despite all, a decent man. With his very last breath he accepts Aragorn – Christ – for what he is, and as such is saved.

Aragorn never knew his father; neither did Christ; neither did Frodo; neither did Tolkien. It would be possible to read any amount of pseudo-Freudian pop-psychological significance into the fact that the author of *The Lord of the Rings* was made fatherless (and then an orphan) at an early age, and that his two principle characters suffered a similar fate. One thing that is certain is that the concept of fatherhood is yet another central theme, and one that has been made far more of in the Jackson films than in the book (see **FATHERHOOD**).

Absolutely key to Aragorn's character is the moment where his paternal ancestor Isildur goes into Mount Doom and decides not to destroy the Ring. Although hinted at by comments made by Gandalf in Book I, Chapter II and Elrond in Book II, Chapter II, this scene is nowhere present in Tolkien's original text. In fact, other details in Book II, Chapter II, where Elrond recalls that he, Gil-galad and Cirdan were the only people (OK, elves) close to Isildur when he took the Ring for himself and that he ignored their advice to destroy it, explicitly excludes the idea that Isildur ever considered destroying the Ring, or saw the need to do so after Sauron's defeat, let alone got as far as holding it over the crack of Mount Doom.

This 'invented' sequence is vitally important to the Jackson films. It makes Isildur's taking of the Ring a moment of weakness, the end of a quick but still gradual seduction of this man by the Ring's power rather than an immediate desire. In terms of both camera angles and theme, it foreshadows Frodo's gradual seduction by the Ring, and his decision to keep it for his own is a direct echo of Isildur's earlier weakness. It is unclear from the book's recounting of Sauron's fall whether Isildur always intended to take the Ring or whether he did so as a result of its influence on him. The additional scene leaves no room for doubt. The Ring corrupts all who hold it.

The idea that it was Isildur's failure to destroy the Ring that has led to all the chaos and death that Sauron has been able to cause since also introduces the idea of the line of kings being fallible in a strong, compelling way. It sets up Elrond's line at the Council of Elrond (which is not in the book) – 'I was there . . . when the courage of men failed' – and helps create the idea of Aragorn's fears of assuming kingship and his doubts about his own suitability for leadership. 'Strider' becomes, in Jackson's films, not simply a name by which Aragorn is known in Bree, but a persona that he uses to hide from what he fears to be his true nature (see **ISILDUR'S HEIR**). Viggo Mortensen (born 1958) gives a complex performance that seeks to reconcile Aragorn's obvious heroism with his reluctance to assume his responsibilities and to make the reluctance more than a simple fear of responsibility. Mortensen replaced the originally cast Stuart Townsend at short notice and insisted on doing his own stunts, losing a tooth and breaking a foot during filming as a result. There is little in Mortensen's not-exactly-extensive previous movie CV to suggest that he would be capable of conveying the screenplay's complex character of Aragorn but he pulls off the difficult task with aplomb.

These alterations to Aragorn's character, especially considering how central he is to the overall plot, are yet another example of how Jackson's films managed to make sensitive alterations to the original while maintaining the basic intent of the author. In so doing, not only is Aragorn made a more complex, interesting, likeable and sympathetic figure, but also the casual fan of the book is left wondering how it will all play out. Frodo is, to all intents and purposes, pretty much identical to the Frodo of the book; as such, Elijah Wood was presented with the unfortunate prospect of having to live up to expectations. Viggo Mortensen as Aragorn had the chance to create an entirely new character – one based on Aragorn, but more human.

By altering certain aspects of the story, Jackson was able to bring something new to those people who had read the books, something beyond the simple pleasure of seeing what had previously only been imagined portrayed on a massive cinema screen in full Technicolor. Making changes to detract from the predictability of adapting a widely known extant work is always a temptation for film-makers; what Jackson managed to do was make changes that remained entirely faithful to the spirit of the original. That was no mean feat.

ARWEN: One of the major differences between film and book often comes down to casting. By choosing a certain actor, their physical characteristics can supersede their character's original description in the source material. However, Tolkien keeps the physical descriptions of most of his principle characters very vague – the hobbits have little to physically distinguish them from any other denizen of the Shire (at least until Merry and Pippin have drunk the Ent draught, but even then they remain physically indistinguishable from each other – see **MERRY AND PIPPIN** in **The Two Towers**). This is largely because Tolkien was not especially interested in the physical attributes of his characters, instead concentrating on their moral nature; all dwarves and all elves are pretty much like any other. The reason we know that Arwen is beautiful is not through detailed physical description (beyond the fact that her hair is dark and her eyes bright), but through the comparison to Lúthien, the most beautiful woman on earth (Book I, Chapter XI), and the fact that Frodo had never seen or even imagined anyone so lovely (Book II, Chapter I). This is a lot for any actress to live up to, for how can any real person be more beautiful than anything the audience has ever imagined? Whether or not then 22-year-old Liv Tyler comes close depends on each individual viewer's own predilections, but the fact that she had already established herself as an international sex-symbol through films such as *Armageddon* (Michael Bay, 1997) and modelling work before the films were cast certainly lends authority to the general idea that Arwen is impressively beautiful.

In the films, Arwen is the first elf the hobbits, and therefore the audience, encounter. Galadriel's voiceover does not really count, as it is (in terms of film logic) only with hindsight that the audience recognises her as explaining the history of the Ring during the prologue. In the Extended Edition, Frodo and Sam witness a group of elves passing west through the Shire, but do not speak with them (unlike in the book).

The beautiful Arwen is thus the audience's introduction to the chief characteristics of the elves – much as the grotesque customers at the Prancing Pony in Bree are its first introduction to those of men. Furthermore, Gimli's stout-hearted attempt to destroy the Ring at the Council of Elrond is the audience's first introduction to dwarves, and the screeching mass of writhing flesh which attacks the Fellowship in Moria is its first introduction to orcs.

Arwen epitomises everything the elves stand for: beauty, kindness, sorrow, and yet – through her facing up to the Nazgûl – hidden strength. She is the epitome of an archetype (see **LET'S HUNT SOME ORC**). She also first appears on screen surrounded by an aura of pure white light, like an angel. This is the first indication that, in a move again extrapolated from hints within the book, the elves are in some way holy creatures in the Jackson films. In the book, Elbereth Gilthoniel (the Star-Queen, one of the Valier or female Valar, in other words a kind of god) is invoked by various characters at moments of extreme hardship, much as God might be invoked by those who believe in Him. In the Jackson films, it is usually to Galadriel that the hobbits' thoughts turn – most obviously while Frodo is lost within Shelob's lair.

Does it matter, in the end, which particular elf it is that meets Frodo in the wild and sees him safely to Rivendell? No. But it *is* significant that it is *an* elf, as it is highly suggestive of a sudden divine intervention just as the quest seems to have failed. Both filmings of this sequence have changed the elf in question from a minor player to one of the major elves of the story. Bakshi's film makes the elf Legolas, seeking to increase the film's exposure of that heroic figure; the Jackson trilogy uses Arwen.

This is not the only way in which the character's role is expanded. The sizeable action sequence where Arwen carries Frodo away from a group of pursuing Ring Wraiths is entirely the production's invention. (In the book, Frodo rides off alone on the horse of the elf Glorfindel.) It is, however, a hugely effective sequence and Arwen's abilities immediately introduce the idea of the elves as being somehow magical, able to take on the worst of the Enemy's minions single-handedly, just as Aragorn does at Weathertop. It almost makes Arwen a supernatural action-heroine, able to both revive Frodo from illness with her tears and boil water with her words. DC Comics' original Wonder Woman is the most apt comparison.

The fact that it was 'not supposed to be' Arwen who rescues Frodo did, however, led to fears among some fans that Holly-wood had insisted on the creation of more and larger female characters in what is an almost exclusively male story (see **MERRY AND PIPPIN** in **The Two Towers**). The rumours that Arwen would be present at the Battle of Helm's Deep only added to these worries, although eventually this planned alteration was dropped.

The 'love interest' has been a clichéd requirement of Hollywood films since the earliest silent shorts. Arwen is, in the book, the closest Tolkien comes to providing one, and the Jackson films certainly expand the character into this kind of role far more than Tolkien did. But this is entirely understandable and excusable (see **ARAGORN AND ARWEN**), especially considering that Liv Tyler was one of the biggest names on the marquee when the first film appeared. (The other big female name, Cate Blanchett, also found her character given slightly more to do than she does in the book, and again for entirely understandable and thematically sympathetic reasons.)

In the last two decades of the twentieth century, thanks to the increasing acceptance of previously revolutionary ideas that (just perhaps) women were not the weak and pathetic creatures that they had always been portrayed as, another Hollywood cliché emerged – the 'action heroine'. Sparked largely by Sigourney Weaver's superb turn as Ripley in the *Alien* films (introduced in

Ridley Scott's 1979 masterpiece of sci-fi horror/suspense), and popularised further during the 1990s by characters such as Michelle Pfeiffer's Catwoman in *Batman Returns* (Tim Burton, 1992), the computer game character Lara Croft and innumerable others, the principle fear of Tolkien fans was that this would be Arwen's fate. Shortly after the release of the first film in the trilogy, tie-in merchandise became available, including life-sized replicas of her sword and action figures of Arwen in battle poses, which only heightened these fears.

However, the end result of the alterations was simply to give the character slightly more screentime than the book would warrant. Thanks to the dropping of the 'Action Arwen' sequences planned for Helm's Deep, the changes to the character are all entirely in sympathy with what Tolkien had originally written about her. It was instead another female character that would bare the brunt of the changes (see ÉOWYN).

THE FELLOWSHIP: On the page, Bilbo attends the council of Elrond and he offers to take the Ring to Mount Doom and destroy it. He sees this as his responsibility. Elrond and Gandalf both state that the Ring is no longer his and that he therefore no longer is responsible. This places Frodo in a position where he must, effectively, take the Ring to Mount Doom as it is a task that is his already, even if he does not know it.

On screen, this is quite different. Elrond says that 'one of you' – meaning one of the council, but not specifying which – will have to take the Ring to Mordor. Bilbo is not there and Frodo volunteers to take the Ring entirely of his own volition, without any pressure from Gandalf or Elrond (indeed in an earlier scene, one not present in the book, Gandalf says that Frodo has suffered too much already and should have to do no more). This scene is a development of Frodo's initial offer, at Bag End, to take the Ring to Bree for Gandalf (the offer which prompts the wizard to soliloquise about the fine qualities of hobbits). Frodo's 'I will take the Ring to Mordor, though I do not know the way' is a line of Tolkien's dialogue that is unaltered and uncut in the film. These are rather rare.

The screenplay's Council of Elrond is neater and shorter than Tolkien's, with much of the long backstory and plot exposition removed (although parts do crop up elsewhere in the films when necessary). The descent into bitter argument is the screenplay's invention, another example of the Jackson team's decision to play up the threat of the Ring (see THE RING in **The Return of the King**). It is clear from Frodo's expression, and the numerous close-ups of the Ring, with the Council reflected on its surface as the arguments begin, that it is through its power that the petty rivalries are blown out of all proportion. It is also at this moment that the Ring clearly first starts to gnaw away at Boromir's mind, his intent stare and suspiciousness of the other characters coming to the fore only once the Ring is revealed. Boromir thinks they should use it, and that is why he can be corrupted (see **BOROMIR**).

What the Council still does is introduce the principle members of the Fellowship of whom the audience is as yet unaware, and their relationships to one another. It is here that the republican Boromir is introduced to the rightful king of his country, setting up a tense rivalry between the two men, and – thanks to Legolas's revelation of Aragorn's royal status – forcing Aragorn to confront directly his birthright for the first time. His reaction is one of embarrassment, which makes clearer another alteration to the character (see **ISILDUR'S HEIR**).

In the films, Merry and Pippin, like Sam, have snuck in on the Council of Elrond to find out what is going on. This is not the case in the book, where the Fellowship is not even decided at that meeting – they wait for a further two months before finalising the party and setting out. However, it does make more sense as, by having the hobbits barge in unexpectedly and demanding to go, Elrond's acquiescence can be put down to the fact that he is a little bit flustered by the presence of so many little creatures running about the place. In the book, they are allowed to go thanks to the frankly defeatist notion that considering that the quest has so little chance of success they might as well send a lot of small and weak hobbits as a select group of strong and powerful elves. This is dropped in the film because it is, quite frankly, a bit silly. In the films, the idea of the quest having little chance of success is only revived later, by Gandalf, just before the Battle of the Pelennor Fields. This is a far more sensible place to include this notion, as it adds further tension and uncertainty to the final sections of the story.

During the chaos brought on by the Ring's influence at the Council, Gimli shouts out 'I will be dead before I see the Ring in the hands of an elf!' – giving interest to two characters who otherwise risk doing very little. Despite the fondness many fans of the book have for the two characters, Legolas and Gimli hardly feature, and remain unmentioned for large chunks of the story, even though logic dictates that they are present at certain events where Tolkien neglects to tell the readers what they are up to. The vaguely drawn character of Prince Imrahil (who does not even appear in the films) has more to do at the Battle of the Pelennor Fields and before the Black Gate of Mordor than either the elf or the dwarf, who during the course of Book VI may as well not exist for the impact they have on the story.

Does this mean that Peter Jackson, by expanding the two characters from the bit-part background players they effectively are in the books into more major players, is betraying the core of Tolkien's story? Or is he (sensibly and sensitively) emphasising the inclusive nature of the 'good', which was Tolkien's apparent intention in having representatives of all the 'good' races make up the Fellowship? (Jackson's decision to present Legolas as single-handedly capable of taking out an Oliphaunt in *The Return of the King* is perhaps less justifiable, but that is another matter entirely.)

By setting up the initial violent rivalry between dwarf and elf, Legolas and Gimli become, in Hollywood terms, 'buddy cops'. They are effectively Riggs and Murtaugh, as played by Mel Gibson and Danny Glover in the original *Lethal Weapon* (Richard Donner, 1987). One – Murtaugh/Legolas – is straight-laced and serious; the other – Riggs/Gimli – is impulsive and incapable of taking anything seriously. Gradually, during the course of the films they come to see the merit of the other's way, and both experience subtle shifts in their characters as they take on aspects of their companion's personality, ending up best friends along the way. The then unknown Orlando Bloom – who had previously only been seen falling out of a helicopter in the halfway decent *Blackhawk Down* (Ridley Scott, 2000), but became a star after this trilogy – and experienced supporting player John Rhys-Davies – *Indiana Jones and the Last Crusade* (Steven Spielberg, 1989) and *The Living Daylights* (John Glen, 1987) – certainly choose to play their scenes together in a manner which invites the viewer to see them as 'buddy cops'.

The only other real changes to the characters are minimal. Legolas gets a few more fancy action sequences than the book would warrant, but these were largely because Orlando Bloom seemed to appeal to the female members of the audience. Gimli gets a few more jokes, and becomes the comic relief for much of the Battle of Helm's Deep. Gimli also introduces the idea of going through Moria rather than over the mountain. This is obviously because it seems neater dramatically for Gandalf to reject Gimli's plan in favour of his own and then later acquiesce to Gimli's when all else fails. In the book, it is Aragorn who fears to enter Moria, not Gandalf. By shifting this reluctance to the Fellowship's leader, a taste of dread is added. What is down there that even Gandalf should fear? It also prepares the audience for Gandalf's 'death' – he seems to know that something will happen to him, as his advice to Frodo would suggest that he is preparing the hobbit in case he is not around for much longer.

THE GREY PILGRIM: Chapters IV and V of Book II (the passage through the Mines of Moria) are adapted more clearly and faithfully than virtually any others in the novel. It is a good example of the subtle differences in tone which occasionally surface between the on-screen and on-page tellings of the same story that the on-screen Gandalf's 'last' words are spoken quietly and with resignation in the Jackson version, unlike the literary Gandalf's loud cry which might have been bathetic if presented literally on screen. All the dialogue that follows Gandalf's apparent death is also cut, leaving the Fellowship's escape wordless and instead scored with high-pitched choral music. It further underlines the sense of loss, and the significance of the loss, that Gandalf's 'death' has on the rest of the Fellowship, and particularly on Frodo. (The battle with the Balrog is, incidentally, paced almost exactly as it is in the book, and takes a similar amount of time to play out on screen as it takes to read from the page.)

In the work of JRR Tolkien, Gandalf is a Maia – a kind of deity, perhaps most closely resembling the angels of Christian tradition. (The Maiar are described in *The Silmarillion* as being beneath the Valar – the Valar are 'The Powers' who guard and govern the world, and the Maiar/Ainur are 'The Holy Ones', the first beings created by Ilúvatar, the creator, or God.) Gandalf has lived for centuries, perhaps even longer, and had many names – of which 'Mithrandir', as he is known to the elves and the people of Gondor, and 'Gandalf (Stormcrow) the Grey Pilgrim', which is his favourite persona, are only the most recent. When Gandalf dies at the Bridge of Khazad-dûm in Moria, this angelic presence/

host eventually re-coalesces and finds new life. Gandalf the White also speaks of being 'sent' back and the implication is that he has been returned to Middle-earth by a higher power in order to assist in the hoped for destruction of Sauron. On screen, this is perhaps not the case as Gandalf says he has 'come back' rather than been 'sent back' and while Gandalf the White is a more straight-backed, less mischievous and more militarily inclined figure than Gandalf the Grey, they are the same person. Perhaps because the first people whom it encounters knew its previous iteration, it takes on a personality and persona not unlike its most recent one.

Ian McKellen certainly chooses to play the two incarnations of Gandalf as if they are the same person. They share the same physical quirks and repeated gestures, the same nods and shrugs; the merest glance at any of McKellen's other screen performances, let alone his acclaimed stage work, will demonstrate to any viewer that any such consistency has to be deliberate. McKellen (born 1939) was a leading figure in the Royal Shakespeare Company for decades but his film work was infrequent and rarely showcased his abilities. This changed in late middle age with a string of great screen roles for the actor, including the title role in *Richard III* (Richard Loncraine, 1992), film director James Whale in *Gods and Monsters* (Bill Condon, 1998) and, most famously, villain Magneto in *X-Men* (Bryan Singer, 2000) and its sequel. McKellen's performance as Gandalf is passionate, subtle, avuncular and full of power. Gandalf the White does not move like Magneto or James Whale or Richard III, but he does move like Gandalf the Grey, albeit quicker.

On screen, it is not clear whether Gandalf dies at all. It seems more like a near death experience, one resulting in some loss of memory and faculty (temporarily at least). At the very beginning of *The Two Towers* what may, or may not, be a dream of Frodo's shows far more of his battle with the Balrog. It shows that fight going on in such a way that it is far from inconceivable that Gandalf could have survived it due to his magical abilities (he survives a physical beating in *The Fellowship of the Ring* that would have killed a human being, after all).

This is one of the film trilogy's few real failings: that the audience does not really seem to grasp how, why, or even if, Gandalf has come back from the dead (even if he did die). The film seems content to let them be unsure; safe in the knowledge that either an understanding of the book or an acquiescence to the fact that the film is in a genre where characters are frequently resurrected/turn out not to have been dead all along will pull the viewer through. It is also yet another partial Christian allegory – Gandalf returns from the dead just as Christ did to come and save the world. (In the films, Aragorn also 'returns from the dead', following the invented sequence in which he falls off the cliff after the Warg attack in *The Two Towers*. This sequence has little narrative function, and seems to exist purely to underscore the Aragorn/Christ parallels set up in the first movie – see **STRIDER**.)

As well as being one of the films' few narrative failings, Gandalf's appearance in front of Aragorn, Gimli and Legolas is also one of its few visual ones. The entire audience knows that Gandalf will return. If they have not read the book, they will have seen the trailer or at the very least the poster. Treebeard's references to a 'white wizard' in previous scenes seem clumsy, so clearly designed to possibly mean Gandalf or Saruman; that the ambiguity is the point becomes blindingly obvious. (Éomer's earlier revelation that there are rumours that Saruman walks 'here and there' disguised as an old man seem an equally half-hearted attempt to introduce an element of uncertainty.) There is no reason at all, even within this fiction, for Gandalf to speak with Saruman's voice for a few seconds when the remainder of the Fellowship first encounter him. It is there to fool the audience, but it has no function, and makes no sense, within the plot. At best, it is dramatic sleight of hand; the two characters are not ever really linked on screen except by rank, and are obviously very different characters in terms of both vocal and physical appearance.

Fortunately for the film and its audience, Ian McKellen is magnificent in this scene and this ameliorates any problems. Again, the emotional sense of the story, in terms of Gandalf's confusion and Aragorn, Legolas and Gimli's joy at seeing him, moves the audience empathetically onwards when sense and logic briefly falter. They even draw attention from, though do not excuse, the quite appalling shot continuity that is present in the sequence – and even more so in the Extended Edition DVD.

BOROMIR: On screen, the film of *The Fellowship of the Ring* drifts nearly a full chapter into the literary *The Two Towers* to present much of 'The Departure of Boromir'. While Aragorn's shift to more kingly behaviour here (see **ISILDUR'S HEIR**) is

Tolkien's, his shout 'Let's hunt some orc!' – both rousing and comical – is the screenwriters' own.

Boromir is not Isildur's genetic heir, but he is still the heir of the man now fulfilling his role in society. When Boromir holds the Ring on its chain and says to himself 'that we should suffer over such a little thing', the actor's physical positioning and the camera angle recall Isildur's failure to destroy the Ring in the prologue.

This reiterates once more the fallibility of men and reminds the audience of the ease with which the Ring can corrupt even someone who is genuinely noble. The particular wording, shifted forward from its place in the book, implies that Boromir is referring to both the Ring and to Frodo – its bearer, the creature that stands in the way of him possessing it and using it, as he thinks he can, to save his city. This scene is an invention of the screenwriters that places Boromir's gradual corruption far sooner in the narrative. In the book, he only sees it once, at the Council of Elrond. Later, just before entering the Mines of Moria, Gandalf warns Frodo to be on his guard, even against members of the Fellowship, giving a knowing pause just as Boromir passes them by.

Boromir is clearly being set up as another threat to the mission in the Jackson films. Frodo suspects on the mountainside that Boromir wants the Ring, and Gandalf's warning heightens this. Boromir later confirms that these suspicions were justified.

The choice of Sean Bean to play Boromir, especially as he is presented in the Jackson films, was a superb one. Bean has proved himself capable of playing a truly heroic character in the excellent *Sharpe* series of Napoleonic War-era TV movies that were made during the mid 1990s, and could easily have portrayed Boromir as another Sharpe. But he was, before the Jackson films, probably best known to international audiences for his roles in *GoldenEye* (Martin Campbell, 1995) and *Ronin* (John Frankenheimer, 1998). In both of these big-budget blockbusters, Bean played men who initially appear to be heroic and decent, but turn out to be either dishonest or corrupt. This is more the kind of performance he gives throughout his time as Boromir (although a more Sharpe-like version of the character can be seen in a superb additional scene in the Extended Edition DVD of *The Two Towers*). As with Bernard Hill (see **THÉODEN**), it is highly likely that Bean's best-known roles played a large part in his casting in this role, as audiences who know his work would instantly relate him to one or all of those three roles.

The fact that Frodo suspected that Boromir might try to take the Ring (and this proved to be the case) should, one would think, have prepared him for Gollum's eventual betrayal. However, the parallels between the two characters are certainly ones that Frodo was aware of, albeit subtly. Frodo only really starts to get close to Gollum, and to begin to truly trust him, *after* he has learned of Boromir's death from Faramir. Frodo seems to associate Boromir's death with his redemption (which, in Catholic terms, it may be – see **STRIDER**). He recognises that Boromir was a decent man, temporarily led astray, and that he paid dearly for his moment of weakness. Partially because of this, he seems to decide to give Gollum more of a chance to become the good creature he once was.

Boromir's death is deeply moving on screen, thanks partially to Sean Bean's performance, but it is also a good scene to illustrate the difference between Tolkien's dialogue and that of the script.

On the page, after telling Aragorn that he tried to take the Ring from Frodo, Boromir apologises for his failure saying that the Orcs have taken the Hobbits and begging Aragorn to save his people at Minas Tirith. Aragorn denies that Boromir has failed and tells him that he has won a victory. Boromir then smiles and dies without speaking.

On screen, Boromir and Aragorn's talk of fighting and honour explicitly has a double meaning. Here it is both about not yielding to the temptation of the Ring and about protecting the other members of the Fellowship from marauding orcs. This is implicit in Tolkien's words, but it is brought out more clearly for a different medium.

In both versions, Boromir recognises his failure, but the film recognises Aragorn's moral superiority over him as well as his own failure. On screen, Aragorn is prompted to promise to defend Gondor against all foes by Boromir's despair. On the page, Boromir demands it of him. On screen, Aragorn offers the promise freely ('I do not know what strength is within my blood, but I swear to you I will not let the White City fall'). The on-screen Boromir also does not know that Frodo is not dead; Aragorn gives him this information and the impression is that Boromir has been trying not to succumb to death until he is satisfied that at least some of his task has been accomplished. The on-screen Boromir's talk of 'darkness' ('It is over. The world of men will fall. And all will come to darkness . . . and my city to ruin') conjures up thoughts of universal Armageddon in the audience, making Boromir less selfishly obsessed with his own people and more concerned for the fate of the whole world. It also provides a link with the on-screen Saruman's reason for allying with Mordor (see **SARUMAN** in **The Return of the King**) and again implies that the race of men is predisposed towards despair. It is Aragorn's recognition of the men of Gondor as 'our people' (i.e. his and Boromir's, not Boromir's alone), and his equally important recognition of their common humanity and common potential weakness ('The Ring is beyond *our* reach now') that enable Boromir to express what he has been feeling all along, and what Aragorn's ability to do 'what I could not' has just proved to him. Aragorn is the King and with his last breath Boromir tells him this – 'I would have followed you my brother, my captain, my King.'

Production Notes and Number Crunching

New Line Cinema announced its commitment to a trio of films based on *The Lord of the Rings* in August 1998. They were all to be directed by Peter Jackson and released in three successive years, despite being made as one production. This follows a model used on the second and third *Back to the Future* films (Robert Zemeckis, 1989/90) and by Richard Lester on the first two Musketeers films (*The Three Musketeers – The Queen's Diamonds*, 1973, and *The Four Musketeers – The Revenge of Milady*, 1974) and the first two Superman pictures (*Superman – The Movie*, 1978, and *Superman II*, 1980, in collaboration with Richard Donner).

Principal photography took place between October 1999 and December 2000. Within this period, there were 274 days on which film was actually shot (around 3 million feet of film). Most of the footage was shot on industry standard Super 35 Kodak Film, approximately 78 per cent of which was then scanned into a computer in order to be altered digitally. This was not simply a matter of adding special effects but also of altering lighting and colour contrasts in many shots. Jackson also shot some of the film on Hi-Grade lightweight digital video cameras rented to the production by the camera's inventors at Lucasfilm.

All the production's locations were, as Jackson had always planned, in New Zealand and often locals unused to the film industry were used as extras. Principal locations were Recreational Reserves such as Arrowtown and Regional Parks such as Kaitoke (which stood in for Rivendell). The Battle of the Pelennor Fields was fought near the amusingly named Twizel. All in all, 100 different parts of New Zealand were used.

The production had not only an unusually long shoot plus two (previously planned) additional periods of re-shooting (July 2002 and August 2003), but it also required some thinking ahead on the part of the production team. The exterior set for Helm's Deep took three months to build and the plants, shrubs and trees around the Hobbiton sets were all planted over a year before the first shots there were filmed so that they could take root and look as though they had been part of the landscape for some considerable time.

All told, the production required 48,000 pieces of weaponry, more than 20,000 extras, 15,000 costumes, a crew of 2,400 (including a wardrobe department of 24), and 1,600 or so pairs of latex hairy hobbit feet.

Design

The look of Jackson's Middle-earth has struck a chord with many Tolkien fans, largely thanks to the fact that the production managed to hire two of the most widely respected of the many artists who had provided visions of the world of *The Lord of the Rings* in the decades before the New Line Cinema films went into production: Alan Lee and John Howe. By basing the look of his Middle-earth on designs that had already graced the covers and interiors of numerous versions of Tolkien's works, and various other collections of paintings and drawings inspired by them, Jackson was able to feed into the imagined worlds of a vast number of readers who had, perhaps subconsciously, taken their vision of the places and characters of the book from the works of Lee and Howe.

Alan Lee, a graduate from the Ealing School of Art, is a noted illustrator of fantasy books, winning the Carnegie medal for his illustrated edition of a translation of Homer's *The Iliad*. Although hired for his experience with fantasy artwork rather than any particular film expertise, Lee had previously worked in movies, serving as a conceptual designer on both *Legend* (Ridley Scott, 1985) and *Erik the Viking* (Terry Jones, 1989), the latter of which is entertainingly stupid and the former of which is dire.

The New Line Cinema trilogy's other conceptual designer, John Howe, had no movie experience before coming on board Jackson's production. A Canadian who graduated from Ecole des Arts Decoratifs de Strasbourg, he went on to work on *The Lion, The Witch and The Wardrobe*, the first of a series of five projected adaptations of Tolkien's friend CS Lewis's Narnia books.

The other crew in the design department also had strong backgrounds in 'fantasy' design. Production designer Grant Major, a veteran of Jackson's *Heavenly Creatures* and *The Frighteners*, spent some time as art director on the New Zealand-filmed *Hercules* TV series and, like Howe, moved on to work on the first Narnia movie. Art directors Philip Ivey and Christian Rivers and costume designer Ngila Dickson had also done stints on both *Hercules* and *Xena*; Ivey had also worked on *The Frighteners*, as had another of the art directors, Simon Bright, with Rivers adding *Heavenly Creatures* and *Braindead* to his Jackson CV. None of the design team had ever worked on any film with as large a scale or as big a budget before, and all did a stand-up job, all overseen by WETA head Richard Taylor, alongside Jackson himself.

The masterstroke in the look of the films was certainly the collaboration with Lee and Howe. This decision ensured that Jackson's *The Lord of the Rings* had over thirty years' worth of pre-production sketches and paintings available for the design and effects teams to work with as soon as the films were greenlit.

Both Lee and Howe are fans of Tolkien first, artists second; their designs have all been sympathetic and as accurate as they can make them to what Tolkien described. As such they, and the three-dimensional versions of them rendered by the WETA Workshop, manage to explore and expand aspects of Middle-earth that it is impossible to glimpse on the page. As Tolkien used language to hint at deeper roots for his various races, Lee and Howe use their own designs, bringing in Celtic, Saxon and Norse traces to costumes and architecture, ensuring that each race, each place, has a unique and thoroughly worn-in look. They have helped Jackson's films to create visually what Tolkien was only able to hint at on the page – a fully functioning world full of danger and beauty and wonder, but one that is, first and foremost, a real place. Middle-earth was brought to life.

One of Lee's sketches formed the basis for the initial confrontation with Gollum at the start of *The Two Towers*; the shot of the hobbits hiding under a tree root in *The Fellowship of the Ring* was taken by Jackson, and Bakshi before him, from one of Howe's paintings. The tower of Orthanc at Isengard and Gandalf's underground battle with the Balrog were from Lee's designs, the shot of the Nazgûl peering out over Osgiliath and the basic look of Gandalf from Howe's. Combinations of both their pre-existing art noticeably fed into the look of Bag End and Minas Tirith, and, in places, extant sketches by Lee and Howe were imitated right down to the angle from which a particular scene from the book was filmed.

THE LORD OF THE RINGS: THE TWO TOWERS (2002)

New Line Cinema Presents
A WingNut Films Production
The Lord of the Rings
The Two Towers
Directed by Peter Jackson
Screenplay by Fran Walsh, Philippa Boyens, Stephen Sinclair,
  Peter Jackson
Based on the book by JRR Tolkien
Producers: Barrie M Osborne, Fran Walsh, Peter Jackson
Executive Producers: Mark Ordesky, Bob Weinstein, Harvey
  Weinstein, Robert Shaye, Michael Lynne
Director of Photography: Andrew Lesnie, A.C.S
Production Designer: Grant Major
Film Editor: Michael Horton with Jabez Olssen
Co-producers: Rick Porras, Jamie Selkirk
UK Casting by John Hubbard and Amy MacLean
US Casting by Victoria Burrows
New Zealand Casting by Liz Mullane
Australian Casting by Ann Robinson
Costume Designers: Ngila Dickson, Richard Taylor
Music composed, orchestrated and conducted by Howard
  Shore
Associate Producer: Ellen M Somers
Special Make-up, creatures, armour and miniatures by
  Richard Taylor
Visual Effects Supervisor: Jim Rygiel

Released: 5 December 2002 (New York premiere)

STARRING: Elijah Wood (Frodo Baggins), Ian McKellen (Gandalf), Liv Tyler (Arwen), Viggo Mortensen (Aragorn), Sean Astin (Sam), Cate Blanchett (Galadriel), John Rhys-Davies (Gimli), Bernard Hill (Théoden), Christopher Lee (Saruman), Billy Boyd (Pippin), Dominic Monaghan (Merry), Orlando Bloom (Legolas), Hugo Weaving (Elrond), Miranda Otto (Éowyn), David Wenham (Faramir), Brad Dourif (Wormtongue) and featuring Andy Serkis as Gollum, Karl Urban (Éomer), Craig Parker (Haldur), John Rhys-Davies (Voice of Treebeard).

NOTE: These chapters follow thematic and structural elements and conceits across all three films with the information contained within the film chapter to which it is the most relevant. They are, however, cross-referenced as and when necessary.

TWO TOWERS? There are considerably more than two towers in Tolkien's *The Lord of the Rings*. There is the Tower of Cirith Ungol; the Tower of Barad-Dûr – aka the Dark Tower; the Tower of Orthanc – aka Isengard; the Tower of the (Setting) Sun – aka the Tower of Ecthelion, aka the Tower of Guard, aka the White Tower, aka Minas Anor, aka Minas Tirith; the Tower of the (Rising) Moon – aka the Tower of Sorcery, aka Minas Ithil, aka Minas Morgul; the Towers of the Teeth – aka Narchost and Carchost; and the elven structures on the Tower Hills to the west of the Shire, to name but a few.

It is never clear which of these many structures are the two towers of the title of the second volume. This is partially because Tolkien wrote *The Lord of the Rings* as a single large book. It was only published in three instalments due to paper shortages – plus his publisher Stanley Unwin's desire to both hide the sheer size of the tome and garner three sets of reviews rather than one for something he was certain would be a great success. (Incidentally, he was right about the advantages of the multiple reviews: WH Auden reviewed the first and third volumes for *The New York Times* using glowing, but very similar, words on both occasions.)

The titles of the individual volumes were arrived at after some negotiation. Tolkien was determined to keep *The Lord of the Rings* as the overall title, and *The Fellowship of the Ring* as the title for the volume containing Books I and II was easily agreed upon. Tolkien wanted *The War of the Ring* for the third volume, feeling that *The Return of the King* was what we would now call a 'spoiler'. He was persuaded otherwise by his publisher. Several of Tolkien's own letters make clear that he himself was not certain which two towers should be *The Two Towers* and the question has been the topic of much discussion among Tolkien fans – largely pointless discussion if the professor's own papers provide no answer.

Different adaptations have taken different approaches. The 1981 BBC version seems to opt for Minas Tirith and Minas Morgul – the towers of the two cities that face each other across the valley of Ithilien (with the city of Osgiliath lying in between). This is as sensible a choice as any, considering that Minas Morgul is the home of the Witch King, responsible for breaking the line of Gondor's Kings, and who leads the attack on Minas Tirith in the third volume, as well as that these are the two towers of the Moon and the Sun, and so set up as opposites. However, Minas Tirith does not feature in the second volume of Tolkien's book as originally published, except for a few brief mentions. The BBC version, however, dispenses with the three-part structure, opting instead for thirteen hour-long episodes, so the whole idea of there being any significance behind the 'two towers' is effectively lost.

Especially in the light of genuine public and Internet pressure to change the title of the second film due to the unfortunate coincidence of it being reminiscent of the term used to describe the 'Twin Towers' of the World Trade Center, the Jackson film has to come up with a very convincing explanation. Thus, early in the film, Saruman is given a line of dialogue whereby he explicitly refers to an alliance between 'The Two Towers' – the tower of Barad Dûr in Mordor and his own tower of Orthanc at Isengard. This makes at least as much sense as any other explanation for a title that was seemingly chosen by Tolkien's publishers simply because it was alliterative, and so likely to be remembered easily by the book-buying public.

In the grand scheme of things, *The Two Towers* is an arbitrary third of *The Lord of the Rings*. In and of itself it is two books, Book III and Book IV, of the overall work. Book III follows Aragorn, Legolas and Gimli as they search for Merry and Pippin (climaxing at Helm's Deep) and also contains Merry and Pippin's adventures with the Ents, leading up to the fall of Isengard. Book IV is Frodo and Sam's continued journey towards Mordor, including their discovery of Gollum, his betrayal of them, and Sam and Frodo's separate fights with Shelob the spider. Book IV ends with Frodo comatose and Sam vowing to rescue his 'Master' from the orcs, who have carried him off. The events of these two books run roughly contemporaneously but they are told in two individual continuous streams.

The film *The Lord of the Rings: The Two Towers* does not actually adapt all of the book. Book III, Chapter I has already been covered at the end of the on-screen *Fellowship* and Book III, Chapters X ('The Voice of Saruman') and XI ('The Palantir') are left to the film of *The Return of the King*, as are Book IV, Chapters VIII–X. The two strands of Books III and IV are intercut with one another in a manner essential to film storytelling but alien to Tolkien's structure. In doing this interlacing, the screenplay re-orders the events roughly in line with the chronology in 'Appendix B' of the book, provided by Tolkien himself.

There are some additional changes, however. The film begins with Frodo and Sam (parts of Book IV) rather than Aragorn and company. The screenwriters also invent a long sequence of Frodo and Sam being taken, as captives, by Faramir (Boromir's brother) to Osgiliath. In the book, Faramir is not tempted by the Ring and he simply sends them on their way with some food. This alteration is partially so that the audience is spared the confusion of the notion of a character that can resist the Ring (see **FARAMIR**). It is also so that Frodo and Sam have something to do. The deferring of the Shelob plotline to the next movie means that without this expansion Frodo and Sam would feature in even less of the film than they do, and their screen-time is very limited as it is.

As in the film of *The Fellowship of the Ring*, time is telescoped so that events seem to take place over a few days at most and it is never truly clear on screen how many days pass and how the chronology of one set of events truly dovetails with one another. (In the book, it is explicit that thirteen days pass between Boromir's death and Gandalf and Pippin's arrival at Minas Tirith, even though it seems much longer both to the reader and the characters.) Again though, the journeys of all three sets of characters make emotional sense to the audience. The Ents' destruction of the dams on the river Isen, leading to the drowning of Isengard (in part also an invention of the film, as this is only related after the fact in the book) is now the story's climax. The final scene, where Sam and Frodo talk about the nature of stories and myths, is Tolkien's, but it has been re-positioned here (from Book IV, Chapter VIII – 'The Stairs of Cirith Ungol').

LET'S HUNT SOME ORC: The orcs and uruks who attack the Fellowship at the end of the first film, killing Boromir and splitting up the company, are vicious, howling and single-minded creatures who exist for one purpose alone – killing. Those who attack in the Mines of Moria are even more animalistic, like cockroaches crawling over the walls, jabbering incoherently, scuttling through the darkness, and utterly bestial. The fact that they are also dark-skinned has led to some people raising a worrying question: was Tolkien racist?

In the book, goblins and orcs are the same thing and the uruk-hai seem to be a sort of orc/goblin SAS – better-trained and tougher monsters with more military nous. There are also several different cadres of orcs/goblins, such as Sauron's orcs of the Red Eye and Saruman's orcs of the White Hand. These distinctions are partially lost because, on screen, orcs and goblins seem less obviously interchangeable. The beasts in Moria look very different from the orcs that fight at Helm's Deep, and appear to be smaller cousins of the orcs, or goblins. The uruk-hai, which Saruman breeds out of the ground, are said to be a mix of orc, goblin and men. They are more horrific partially because they are the product of a Nazi-style eugenics programme, but also because that makes them mixed-race – the 'ultimate horror'.

Much has been written about the racist interpretation of *The Lord of the Rings*. An article in the *Guardian*, published just before the release of the second film in Jackson's trilogy, stated this categorically: 'The Lord of the Rings is racist. It is soaked in the logic that race determines behaviour.' The arguments can seem compelling. The side of the good is populated by white-skinned, beautiful races; the bad side is also the 'dark', and populated by dark-skinned, ugly races. Gandalf becomes 'the White' to symbolise his purity; in the book, Saruman's corruption is symbolised by his adoption of the new title 'Saruman of many colours'. The 'white city' of Minas Tirith is pitched against the 'black land' of Mordor. The men who fight for Saruman are the Arabic/Islamic-sounding Haradrim, and are described in the typical terms of 'savages' – brown-skinned and covered in war paint.

Tolkien's creation was based upon a mythical Anglo-Saxon past; so was much of the theory invented to support Nazism. The Nazis aspired to turn Europe into a single 'pure-blooded', fair-skinned, blond-haired, blue-eyed 'Aryan' nation, and chose to do this by exterminating those who did not fit this ideal, be they Jews, Slavs, the Romany, or any number of other 'impure' races. Tolkien's heroes aim to defeat Sauron, and return the West to the rule of men, driving out races they claim are 'evil' – most obviously the dark-skinned orcs. The fact that the most obviously superior race, the elves, have traditionally been represented in adaptations of Tolkien's work as classically Aryan (and in Peter Jackson's films are primarily played by good-looking actors often in blond wigs) has added to this interpretation. The books and the films have also been consciously adopted by certain reprehensible far-Right groups to promote their ideas – notably the fascistic, racist and one-time Holocaust-denying British National Party's claims in early 2004 that Tolkien's book is an allegory of the 'great real-life battle to save the West', by which they meant the supposedly superior white European 'races'.

To take the orcs to be a mere racial stereotype and to present the battle against the Dark Lord as one of Aryan supremacy is to miss Tolkien's intention entirely. Thanks to his studies, Tolkien was more than aware that Hitler's invented Aryan mythology was based on lies, distortions and a single fundamental untruth: the Aryans were not white-skinned Europeans, but brown-skinned Indians. Tolkien utterly disagreed with the Nazis' ideology but he also repeatedly made clear that he was uninterested in creating a simplistic allegory. If anything, what Tolkien had witnessed being inaccurately appropriated by eugenicists over the previous half century set the record straight about the true nature of the 'Anglo-Saxon inheritance' and 'great Northern spirit'.

It is also necessary to point out that in the 1930s and 1940s, when the books were being written, the modern-day conception of 'racism' simply did not exist in the way in which it is now understood. It is utterly anachronistic to apply modern definitions to a period in which, in America, black people were still forced – by law – to use different modes of public transport. Another obvious point was that Tolkien was creating a myth for England, set in an approximation of Europe; there are no indigenous dark-skinned people in Europe, hence making the central characters white.

The presentation of the orcs is not an indication of any Nazi tendencies on the part of the author, which did not exist, but represent another obsession entirely: his hatred of industrialisation and mechanisation. Nazism was an industrial ideology, whereas Tolkien was an early environmentalist. The orcs are proletarian; they have been twisted and corrupted by the mechanised, smoke-spewing factory land of Mordor, just as the Industrial Revolution in Britain brought the peasants of the fields into towns and put them to work in factories, spewing out pollution, and expanding to destroy the countryside. This view might be naive, pastoral and invoke class stereotypes, but it is not racist.

Jackson's films make the industrial, artificial nature of the orcs very clear. We see them being spawned deep in the machine-filled fiery pits beneath Isengard, spewed out on an organic production-line amid the foundries and armouries that prepare their weapons of war. They labour hard but in terrible conditions, mostly underground – like miners. They refer to their leaders as 'boss', rather than 'master'. The squabble at the Tower of Cirith Ungol makes plain that they are after profit, not subsistence, like the good old peasants of the Shire. The way they speak is a further indication of this. They are all working-class – not working-class in the sense of Sam Gamgee or his father, who are effectively industrious, hard-working peasant farmers with wholesome, rural, West-country accents, but industrial working-class with approximations of Cockney accents.

Furthermore, Tolkien's different races are not stereotypes; they are mythic archetypes. They represent different aspects of Tolkien's conception of European humanity – hobbits represent the love of the good things in life; elves, the love of culture; dwarves, the love of hard work; orcs, the possibility of corruption; and men represent a combination of all of these things. Tolkien's 'races' are not races in the sense the Nazis used the term; they are simply a convenient way of presenting aspects of human nature in a condensed, unadulterated form. Tolkien's races are fragments of his perception of the twentieth-century's white, post-Enlightenment European. If their positive traits are exclusively drawn from that perception then so too are all of their negative ones.

The orcs are presented as dark skinned not to associate their corrupt nature with any actual ethnic group in the modern world, but because it has been a feature of myths from all parts of the world that darkness is associated with evil, and light with good. The idea of light versus dark is also a central theme of the Bible. If *The Lord of the Rings* is racist because of this conceit of light and dark, so too is Christianity.

MERRY AND PIPPIN: As an illustration of how film studios did not understand *The Lord of the Rings*, Peter Jackson has often mentioned that it was suggested to him more than once that he should cut one or more of the hobbit characters – or perhaps make one of them female.

While loudly chuckled at by Tolkien fans, these suggestions have, in screenwriting terms, much merit. They would be an easier solution than the one that Jackson found for two very simple problems with the on-the-page nature of the hobbits: first, Merry and Pippin do very little in the story's first two-thirds and, second, they are really very difficult to tell apart. (The lack of female characters in Tolkien has been discussed already (see **ARWEN** in **The Fellowship of the Ring**), and again Jackson's solutions are elegant.)

Before they become separated, following the incident with the Palantir, the only distinctions between the two characters are that Pippin is a little more shifty and foolish and Merry is a little more straightforward and brave. In the book, half the time even these distinctions are not clear. By casting actors that are physically similar in Billy Boyd and Dominic Monaghan and ensuring that their hair, clothes and costumes resemble each other more than they do those of Sam, Frodo or Bilbo, the films turn what would normally, cinematically speaking, be a weakness into a strength. Despite the fact that Billy Boyd's Pippin has a Scottish accent (which is down to the actor being Glaswegian and has no basis in the original text, despite some attempts to claim the contrary), even in the film the two characters remain largely indistinguishable. The characters' very alikeness becomes part of the point – they are typical hobbits.

It is only when the ways in which they are not alike are later made clearer by the screenplay that their characters become more tangible. On screen in *The Two Towers* Merry, and particularly Pippin, play a key role in getting the Ents to agree to go to war with Saruman's forces. On the page, Treebeard has already made the decision to fight, and the hobbits are only observers to his efforts to persuade his fellows (and even then they are not present for much of the discussion). However, in both book and film it is only after they are separated, following their reunion with Aragorn, Legolas and Gimli at Isengard, that they become obviously separate characters, and that is largely thanks to geography. But they both have an opportunity to make a difference – Pippin by helping to save Faramir and Merry by helping Éowyn kill the Witch King (although he is less involved on screen than he is on the page). Like Sam, they are not natural heroes (see **SAM 2** in **The Return of the King**); like him, they do what is right.

Characters are often, especially in adventure fiction, reader substitutes, and the reader is accustomed to being interiorised within a character's perceptions, even when the narrative is not in the first person. In Jackson's films, Merry and Pippin become the audience identity figures far more than they are in the book. Their reactions are those of any regular person when presented with incredible, frightening, near-incomprehensible situations – initially they do not seem to realise how much trouble they have got themselves into; this is followed by nervous humour, horror and fear. But they both come through and do what is right in the end – a fact that is entirely in keeping with Tolkien's central message that even the smallest, most insignificant person can, if they do what is right, make a major difference.

ENTS: Ents, at least in name, can be found among the old Anglo-Saxon poetry that served as much of Tolkien's inspiration, although they do not originally appear to have had any particular association with woodland. However, much of Anglo-Saxon poetry, even after the introduction of Christianity to the British Isles, is concerned with the power of trees. Probably the most powerful extant Anglo-Saxon poem, 'The Dream of the Rood', is a deliberate conflation of this kind of pagan nature worship with the then emergent Christian tradition, an attempt to couch the appeal of Christianity in terms that could be understood within the cultural norms of the time. It presents the crucifixion as a battle between Christ and the cross (Rood means Tree, and is used as a synonym for cross in this instance) with the cross initially victorious, before Christ's triumphant resurrection. Symbolically, Christ is defeating the old pagan woodland spirits, the worship of which was prevalent in much of pre-Christian northern Europe. It is an attempt to use the imagery of a warrior culture to introduce the conceptually alien idea of a peaceful victory.

The Ents of Tolkien's books are described as being almost like trolls, very tall – about 14ft – with long heads but very short necks. The tree-like aspects to their appearance are their toes and beards, which look similar to roots, twigs and moss (Book III, Chapter IV), but they are not quite so arboreal as their representation in Jackson's films. Nonetheless, the decision to make the Ents look more like their charges is a logical one, as this is hinted at in the book and the majority of fans have accepted the WETA design team's Ents as a faithful rendition. In any case, if the Ents were rendered more closely to how they are described in the book, not only would they be shorter (and so far less visually impressive), but they would most likely look rather silly, much as Treebeard does during his brief appearance in the Bakshi film.

TREEBEARD: In the Jackson films, Treebeard is (according to Gandalf) the oldest creature in Middle-earth, a wise and solid, unchanging being. Under Peter Jackson's direction, he has taken on much that was Tom Bombadil's in the novel – a fact that is made clearer in the Extended Edition of *The Two Towers* when he is even given some of Bombadil's dialogue as Merry and Pippin are attacked by a version of Old Man Willow deep in Fangorn Forest.

Tom Bombadil's place in the novel is a confusing one. He is the Eldest, the Master, and was around even before the Elves went to the West and before the Dark Lord appeared (Book I, Chapter VII). Unusually, Tolkien never fully explained who or what Bombadil was – he is immortal, but is he a god, one of the Maiar (like Gandalf and Sauron), the physical manifestation of the spirit of Middle-earth, or something else entirely? Tolkien scholars and fans alike seem unable to agree. This confusion seems to have been intentional on Tolkien's part: 'I think it is good that there should be a lot of things unexplained . . . even in a mythical Age there must be some enigmas, as there always are. Tom Bombadil is one (intentionally).'

Bombadil predates much of Middle-earth in the chronology of Tolkien's writing as well as in his fictional world's internal history. First appearing in 1933 in the poem 'The Adventures of Tom Bombadil', the character was based on a toy belonging to Tolkien's son Michael, which might explain his simple, childlike joy and singing. Bombadil was there before Tolkien had realised how dark the tale of Frodo's quest would become (see **BREE** in **The Fellowship of the Ring**). He seems slightly out of place and is referred to only infrequently during the rest of the narrative (at the Council of Elrond, as Merry and Pippin recount their adventures to Treebeard, as Frodo and Sam approach Shelob's lair, and then near the very end, as the hobbits pass his lands again on their way home).

The decision not to include Bombadil in the film is certainly understandable. Ignoring the fact that the Bombadil passages fail to advance the narrative (see **BREE** in **The Fellowship of the Ring**), how many modern moviegoers, unfamiliar with the books, would be able to put up with a character that spends half the time talking in riddles and singing nonsensical strings of syllables? Although he may work on the page, on film Bombadil could have alienated a sizable section of the audience.

However, although Tom's precise nature remains unclear, his role in the book is more certain. Although the way in which Tolkien presents the concepts he encapsulates would be difficult to pull off on film, they remain important to give the events of the War of the Ring a wider context. Considering the whole of Tolkien's life-long construction of the world of Middle-earth, the loss of such context would be to lose much of what has enabled *The Lord of the Rings* to appeal to successive generations of readers and, now, moviegoers. As Tolkien was later to write, 'I would not have left him in if he did not have some kind of function.'

By endowing Treebeard with some of Bombadil's qualities, Jackson was able to reinstate the ideas of permanence and immutability that the Master brings to the novel, and so restore his 'function' that would otherwise have been lost. When Treebeard bemoans the fact that 'nobody cares for the trees anymore' he is expressing a desire for a system like that in which Bombadil lives, where man/Ent/whatever Bombadil actually is and nature can live side by side in perfect harmony. Whereas Tom apparently has the power to stop evil from causing too much damage within his lands, Treebeard discovers that his Arcadian realm is being destroyed by the encroaching forces of industrial production of Isangard. (Here it is perhaps worth noting the similarity between the name 'Isengard' and that of Victorian England's pre-eminent engineer, the man who, more than any other, was responsible for the spread of the railway, and thus of industrial production throughout the world: Isambard Kingdom Brunel. Considering Tolkien's appreciation for and interest in names, and dislike for the encroaching of town and industry into the countryside, this surely cannot have been an accident.)

In the book, the destructiveness of industrialisation is most clearly presented in Book VI, Chapter VIII, 'The Scouring of the Shire'. This sequence was omitted from the Jackson films for the simple reason that it would be likely to prove a somewhat anticlimactic ending after the impressive, grand-scale manoeuvrings of the Battle of the Pelennor Fields and the destruction of Mordor. As Dominic Monaghan (Merry) has said, 'four hobbits riding into the Shire on horses and kicking a lot of people's asses would have been brilliant. We would have loved that. [But] It wasn't necessary. The emotional endpoint is the destruction of the Ring. You can't have a whole forty-minute subplot after that.' But the significance of the 'Scouring' was an important concern for Tolkien, as is noted elsewhere.

Much as Jackson's films have imbued Treebeard with the environmentalist qualities epitomised by Tom Bombadil, they have also (through his horrified reaction to the destruction on the edges of Fangorn Forest) imbued 'the last march of the Ents' with much of the significance that 'the Scouring of the Shire' had in the book. The significance of the 'Scouring' is that the Shire has been perverted by the forces of industrialisation and modernisation; trees have been cut down and anything natural defiled; the hobbits' traditional way of life has been destroyed. It takes the return of the four hobbit members of the Fellowship – and primarily the battle-hardened Merry and Pippin – to rouse the other inhabitants of the Shire from their complacency and inspire them to overthrow Saruman's regime (for it is Saruman who is responsible for the Shire's defilement).

In the book, the majority of the Ents do not see the need to tackle Sauron; in the film, Treebeard becomes the mouthpiece of this feeling. As with the hobbits in the 'Scouring of the Shire' sequence in the book, once his eyes are opened to what is being done to his lands, and once Merry and Pippin have roused his anger and outrage, he shakes off his complacency and isolationism and decides to act. Again, Jackson's films have managed to retain an important aspect of Tolkien's book, albeit in a different place and slightly different context.

What the Ents and the hobbits of the Shire have in common is that they feel that events outside the borders of their realm are none of their concern. If one is looking for an allegory, the 'Scouring of the Shire' sequence can be seen as a rejection of 1930s American isolationism and British appeasement. It is a reminder that no matter what we may choose to believe, we are all, as Merry tells Treebeard in the film, 'a part of this world'. Far-off events may well be our concern, whether we like it or not. If we ignore them, this may come back to haunt us when the perpetrators of far-off cruelties finally begin to encroach upon our own existences. As previously mentioned, this message was taken by some as an endorsement of the US-led invasion of Iraq in 2003.

THÉODEN: As with so many characters, the Théoden of Peter Jackson's films is somewhat different from that of the book, but again the changes have been made with a distinct thematic purpose. Originally a heroic kingly archetype, temporarily led astray by the evil council of Grima Wormtongue, the King of Rohan on celluloid becomes a flawed, distraught, and apparently scared figure – at least in *The Two Towers*. Although beloved to his people, he is no true leader, and even after his recovery from Saruman's spell, he remains weak and confused, forcing Aragorn to take charge at Helm's Deep and retreating into defence when it is strongly suggested that he should be moving to attack.

In the book, we first hear of Théoden as Aragorn, Legolas and Gimli encounter Éomer and his men during the pursuit of the orcs who have taken Merry and Pippin (Book 3, Chapter II). There are some hints that all is not well with Théoden, but nothing too explicit. Éomer mentions that the king is angry with Gandalf for taking Shadowfax from him, that some of Théoden's counsellors do not advise him to be aggressive; much like the hobbits of the Shire and the Ents of Fangorn, Rohan only wants to be left alone to live their lives. Éomer's ride to the north did not have Théoden's agreement. None of this should give any real cause for concern – the loss of Shadowfax would be great indeed, especially as he is described in the books (where he is the lord of all horses, almost a horse god). In times of peril, a king would usually be wise to bide his time; if your homeland is threatened, it makes sense to keep your best troops close at hand in case of attack. Equally, as Gandalf arrives at Edoras to confront Théoden and Wormtongue, the king's mistrust could be written off as the superstition of a people who have had few dealings with wizards, and know Gandalf only as a powerful being who appears in times of trouble (as Théoden himself tells Gandalf). It is the classic scenario of the messenger being confused with the message. At the Council of Elrond in the book, Gandalf reports that Gwaihir the Windlord – the eagle who had rescued him from Isengard – thought that Rohan was paying tribute to Sauron, but this Boromir disputes, and the allegation remains unproven.

Further evidence that the Théoden of the book is a nobler creature than that of the second of Jackson's films comes as Aragorn asks the horsemen whether they support or fight against Sauron and Éomer responds that he serves only Théoden. Such an introduction, replete with the ceremonial address and full title-giving that he includes, suggests a noble and lordly figure reigns over the troubled land. Aragorn responds in kind, just one of innumerable examples where he shows he has accepted his birthright sooner in the books than the films (see **STRIDER** in **The Fellowship of the Ring** and **ISILDUR'S HEIR**), using all his genealogical names and titles. Aragorn's titles are more impressive, but that is only to be expected of the true King of the West. It is clear that Aragorn considers himself and Théoden, whom he knew during his time in Rohan as a younger man, as equally regal (see *The Two Towers* Extended Edition, Scene 32, as taken from 'Appendix A' and 'Appendix B' of the book).

Through Éomer's description of his countrymen's feelings, their desire to live their lives as they always have, the spirit of the Shire is invoked again. Like the hobbits (and the Ents in the films), the Rohirrim do not wish to risk their way of life and the land they love by becoming involved in affairs outside their borders. Yet, in another example of the weakness of men, even when their borders are threatened they do not, apart from Éomer and his troop, make any effort to resist. Despite the fact that Rohan, unlike the Shire, has its fair share of warriors and is directly under threat, still Théoden does not act. Contrast this with the response of the four principal hobbits, on learning of the peril of the Ring. Frodo decides he must do what must be done, and his friends leap to his aid without hesitation or consideration for their own safety, simply because it is the right thing to do (see **SAM 2** in **The Return of the King**). Under the council of Wormtongue, Rohan would wait until all others have fallen, and no one is left to come to their aid.

Nonetheless, the failure of Théoden and Rohan to act could be seen, in the books, as little more than a typical flaw of men. History is littered with examples of the failings of rulers being blamed on bad advice from their counsellors, be it the Duke of Buckingham during the reigns of James I and Charles I of Great Britain, or Rasputin during the time of the last Tsar of Russia. Théoden is simply another misled monarch. Although Gandalf puts on an impressive light show – the flash seems as if lightning has broken open the roof (Book III, Chapter VI) – there is nothing in the book to suggest that the king has been possessed by Saruman, or even that he was under a spell. He was simply taken in by the depressing and ill advice of the aptly named Wormtongue; once he receives better advice from Gandalf, his strength and wits rapidly return. Within moments of grasping his sword, he is calling his men together to ride out to war, to hunt down those who have threatened his borders. In short, he is a true king, temporarily led astray.

Contrast this to the introductions of Rohan and Théoden in the film. Saruman is the first to mention the kingdom as he sends the wild men off to burn the Westfold: 'The horsemen took your lands. They drove you into the hills to scratch a living off rocks. Take back the land they stole from you!' Saruman may be a highly untrustworthy source for this information, but the poor picture of Théoden's realm continues to build. Next, a village is evacuated under Saruman's onslaught. Compared to the previous lands the film has shown us, most notably the happiness and plenty of the Shire, the people are poorly dressed and undernourished, little more than the peasants Saruman accuses them of being. It hardly seems like a very pleasant land in which to live – it is characterised by bleak, windswept moors and marshes, and seems positively inhospitable, with little or no sign of agriculture or nourishment. It is more like Mordor than the Shire.

Théoden appears for the first time. He looks by far the oldest of any of the humanoid characters in the films (except perhaps the wizened Bilbo at the end of *The Return of the King*), and sits mute and apparently unaware as he is informed of his son Théodred's injuries and Saruman's attack. Éomer tells him that 'Orcs are roaming freely across our land, unchecked, unchallenged, killing at will' – a far more serious situation than that faced by Rohan in the book – yet Théoden sits by, seemingly half asleep, and too old and frail to be of any use at all.

In Peter Jackson's version, Théoden has become the embodiment of everything that can go wrong with having a hereditary system of government – if the sovereign becomes incapable of ruling, the country can fall into ruin, as no one else has the authority to order the people to do something about the situation. (The United States managed to rectify this potential problem with the nature of the presidency in 1967 with section 4 of the 25th Amendment, which provides for the cabinet and Congress together to remove a medically incapacitated President.) Seemingly, the only order Théoden has given is the banishment of Éomer, who has already been introduced as a noble and heroic character wanting the best for his people (see **ÉOMER**). When Aragorn and his friends confront the riders, Éomer warns them: 'Théoden no longer recognises friend from foe, not even his own kin.'

Later, as Gandalf and his party approach Edoras, the banner of Rohan falls to the ground as they enter – a symbolic reference to the fact that the kingdom is failing, further underlined by the previous scene in which the heir to the throne is seen lying dead, his father seemingly unaware. (To add to the symbolism, the banner hits the ground just as Aragorn, a truly kingly monarch, enters the gates.) It is soon revealed that Théoden is under a spell of Saruman's, the wizard of Isengard being in such control that he can even speak through the king – a much more potent indication that the king is not himself than is given in the book.

However, unlike in the book, the breaking of Wormtongue's hold over his master is not the end of Théoden's weakness. After a truly excellent transformation scene, in which Bernard Hill's consistently superb performance is perfectly complemented by subtle shifts in make-up and computer effects, in the film version Théoden's first thought on recovering his senses is not to ride to war for the sake of his people and the rest of Middle-earth, but revenge. Grasping his sword, his eyes turn to Wormtongue cowering on the floor; the king has his former adviser physically hurled from his hall, before raising his sword to kill him. It is only Aragorn's intervention that spares the snivelling Grima – a kingly act of mercy that, in the books, belongs to Théoden, who tells his men, 'do not hurt or hinder him. Give him a horse if he wishes it.'

In Jackson's version, Théoden looks bewildered at Wormtongue's departure, staring into the middle distance and having to lean on Aragorn for support, before turning his back on his people and staggering indoors. He is still weak, even after the spell has been broken. This is only the first example in which Aragorn appears nobler than the king of Rohan. Others include the decision to withdraw (to Helm's Deep) rather than ride out and fight (as Aragorn does after the Battle of the Pelennor Fields), and the fact that it is Aragorn who is in effective command at Helm's Deep, something Théoden himself acknowledges in *The Return of the King*. Yet immediately after the departure of Wormtongue comes an explanation of the changes in the king's character: 'That I should live to see the last days of my house . . . no parent should have to bury their own child.'

This last line remains the most moving of any in the three films, thanks again to Bernard Hill's utterly convincing portrayal of a grieving father. Born in Manchester in 1944, Bernard Hill's most notable role is as the psychotically violent, unemployed scouser Yosser Hughes in Alan Bleasdale's *The Black Stuff* (1980) and *The Boys From The Black Stuff* (1982). In terms of film exposure, he was limited to small roles (sergeants, desk clerks) in pictures such as *Ghandi* (Richard Attenborough, 1981) until late middle age when he was cast as Captain Smith of the *Titanic* in James Cameron's Oscar-feted, but bloated, boat picture. A strong performance as a decent, ageing man crippled by responsibility, afraid of failure and ultimately not up to the task at hand, it is inconceivable that the invitation to play King Théoden was not related to his role in one of the highest grossing, most-watched films of all time. Hill is brilliant as Théoden, and it is to be hoped that the success of *The Lord of the Rings* gains him further big-screen, big-budget roles.

In *The Two Towers*, Théoden is a distraught father witnessing the loss of everything he holds dear, in much the same way that Denethor is in *The Return of the King* (see **FATHERHOOD** in **The Return of the King**). Théoden is mentally shattered by the loss of his son, almost as much as he was by Saruman's enchantments, and has lost almost all hope for himself and his people. The end is near and, as far as he can see, there is no escaping it. Rather than ride out to fight off his foes, he decides to retreat to a safe haven, his only remaining hope being that at Helm's Deep his people may be able to survive. Once there, the solidity of its walls gives him momentary cheer, but once the outer defences are breached, he soon calls the retreat. His part in the battle seems primarily to be to distract Aragorn, nearly causing his death, and to get stabbed in the shoulder by a spear while recklessly heading to the frontlines (something a good general in theory should really never do, although Aragorn is also guilty of this on a number of occasions).

Heroism in Tolkien's Middle-earth is pre-medieval, unthinking brute masculinity. In Jackson's films, this style of heroism is epitomised by Gimli's aside before the march to Mordor: 'Imposs-ible odds . . . certain chance of death . . . what are we waiting for?' In the books, Théoden's response to finding himself and his country in such a dire situation is to ride out seeking enemies to kill as soon as he can. Not heeding any tactical considerations, he tries to cause as much damage as he can before death takes him, but he leaves no warriors to guard the fleeing women and children he sends into the hills. His actions are not those of a man who expects to live, yet they are presented by Tolkien as being evidence of a truly kingly, truly heroic spirit. In many ways, the moral of *The Return of the King* can be summed up as uninhibited appreciation for, and acceptance of, monarchical (even apostolic) succession. This is even more problematic in an early twenty-first-century context than a mid twentieth-century one.

What the changes to Théoden's character in the films do is very simple – they make him a weaker leader and a more complex, tortured figure. This is a transition helped greatly by Bernard Hill's remarkable performance in the role. What is more complex is the effect these alterations have on other characters. It makes Aragorn stronger, even more 'film-heroic' in comparison. Aragorn himself can see this, even though he unconvincingly denies it in *The Return of the King*, when Éowyn effectively tells him that he is now the leader of the Rohirrim and cannot leave them in their time of need. Aragorn, by rights a king himself, encounters a man who is also a king, and finds him to be weaker than Aragorn fears himself to be. By witnessing Théoden's weaknesses at Helm's Deep, Aragorn comes closer to accepting that it is his destiny to ascend the throne of Gondor, and that he has the qualities that would make a good ruler.

ISILDUR'S HEIR: In the book, Aragorn is in no doubt as to his duty and ultimate destiny – he is the heir to the crown of Gondor, and one day he will claim the throne. What Tolkien fails to cover in the main text is the single most obvious question: why hasn't Aragorn, or one of his ancestors, decided to return to Gondor sooner?

The reason for the breaking of the line of kings can be found in 'Appendix A' of the book. In short, following a civil war similar to that of England's Wars of the Roses, King Eärnur (a descendant of Isildur in direct line) was captured by the Witch King of Angmar, by then set up in the former Gondorian city of Minas Ithil, now renamed Minas Morgul. Eärnur did not leave a son to automatically succeed him, and even if he had done, there was no proof of his death: there could not be two kings, after all. As time dragged on and it became clear that he would not return, an heir was sought, but thanks to the earlier civil war no one could be found who was willing to claim the throne and risk further bloodshed, and so the rule of the stewards took the place of the kings.

In some versions of the Arthurian myth, the king is prophesied to return again at a time of dire need for his kingdom; the prophesy that the King of Gondor will one day return is an obvious reworking of this idea. But the prophecy, as presented in the text – that the King will return when the broken blade is mended – gives no indication of precisely when, or under what circumstances, the line of kings will be restored.

Isildur's broken sword, Narsil, is the blatantly Arthurian proof that Aragorn is both who he says he is, and that he is heir to the throne – it is Middle-earth's Excalibur. In the book, Aragorn carries it with him at all times, despite the fact that a broken sword is hardly the most suitable implement for someone who spends much of their time fighting dark forces in the wilderness. (It is also unclear how he came to possess the sword, but that will just cause further confusion.)

Tolkien introduces the idea of the significance of the sword but then fails to capitalise on the idea. Aragorn's decision to claim the throne is not given any added significance by the time he and the hobbits reached Rivendell – it is here that the 'prophecy' is revealed to be no more than a rhyme made up by Bilbo. But aspects of the prophecy storyline are maintained throughout, despite this dismissal.

In the book, when Aragorn gets to Rivendell with the hobbits the sword is unceremoniously reforged and then hardly mentioned again. Considering the lack of fuss made over this hugely symbolic act, it might as well have been remade at any point in the preceding 2000 years – it does, after all, seem to have magical qualities and would no doubt have come in handy for any number of Aragorn's ancestors.

What Jackson, Walsh and Boyens did was to capitalise on this concept that the restoration of the line of kings has some kind of symbolic significance. In this version, the suggestion seems to be that it was on Isildur's death that the line of kings was broken, and the reason for this was Isildur's weakness in taking the Ring.

Boromir's frequent description of Aragorn as 'Isildur's heir', in Jackson's version, carries with it the implication that Aragorn is heir of Isildur's worst qualities, his weakness and his corruptibility as well as his right to the throne. As much as Arwen tells Aragorn 'You are Isildur's heir, not Isildur', it is the fear of weakness that holds sway over both Aragorn and the audience. When Aragorn himself speaks of 'Isildur's blood' he also speaks of the 'weakness' that goes with it. Aragorn is reluctant to accept his birthright due to his fear that he has inherited the bad qualities of his ancestor as well as the good, and the shards of Narsil remain preserved in a shrine in Rivendell until the third film – they are only reforged when the time is right, when Aragorn is ready to assume the crown.

In both the Arthurian and Christian prophecies, the 'King' will return at a time of great need, at the end of the world – just as he does here, at the end of the Third Age of Middle-earth. This is so evidently what Tolkien was originally intending: Sauron is loosely the Antichrist, and the whole of Middle-earth is threatened. In the Jackson films, the Ring itself is placed in the Antichrist's role (see **THE RING** in **The Return of the King**), and Aragorn loosely in Christ's (see **STRIDER** in **The Fellowship of the Ring**) – there is even a statue of his mother in Rivendell that looks suspiciously like the Virgin Mary.

At the end of *The Lord of the Rings: The Fellowship of the Ring* (in a scene actually taken from Book III, Chapter I), moments after Boromir has died, Aragorn rallies his remaining comrades around him. On screen, as he does so he begins to speak in the plural personal pronoun ('we'). It seems possible, initially, that he is referring to the remaining three of the Fellowship: himself, Gimli and Legolas. As his words go on though, it becomes clear that this is not the case. This is the moment where, ultimately, he begins to acknowledge his kingship – it is the royal 'we'. Coming as this does moments after the heir to the Steward of Gondor has recognised Aragorn's primacy over him, it is impossible not to make the connection. But it is not until after the Battle of Helm's Deep that Aragorn truly accepts his destiny, and who he is.

The weakening of Théoden may not be in the interests of the character, but it does have a palpable thematic point. It does build up Aragorn, yes, but not solely so that he becomes the film's undisputed heroic lead. What it also does is transform Aragorn from the book's presentation of a man who is great because he is a king into a man who will be a great king because he is a great man. The film then, while endorsing continuity and heredity, stops short of endorsing absolutist monarchy, by presenting characters (especially Théoden and Denethor) whose hereditary rights are similar, if not actually equal, to Aragon's own, as unworthy of their rights and incapable of living up to their responsibilities.

ARAGORN AND ARWEN: Purists might argue that the love story of Aragorn and Arwen has no place within the main body of the story, as it featured solely as a part of an appendix. This is, arguably, simply another example of the structural unorthodoxy of the original.

If Tolkien were not interested in the relationship, he would not have included it within the pages of the book in the first place. All the information in the appendices to *The Lord of the Rings* expands the reader's understanding of the world of Middle-earth, but only 'the tale of Aragorn and Arwen' from 'Appendix A' contributes greatly to the reader's understanding of one of the central plots of the story of the War of the Ring. It is arguably by far the most important part of any of the appendices.

Tolkien's omission of this insight into one of his two principle characters from the main body of the text was, in terms of character development, a grave one indeed. Perhaps, had he been writing with the benefit of modern computer technology – enabling swift restructuring and rewriting – he might have worked it into the main story. As it was, he would have had to type his entire 1,000-page book, two-fingered, on his own. Such major alterations, after fourteen years of writing and typing, would have been a daunting task indeed, as he hinted in the Foreword to the second edition.

Far from being simply a crude Hollywood device to introduce a female lead (although such considerations no doubt played their part – see **ARWEN** in **The Fellowship of the Ring**), Jackson's restoration of this central aspect of Aragorn's life to the main narrative both broadens Aragorn's character and provides a further route into the heart of his story which, in the original, is a rather sterile, emotionless place. Rather than simply having to battle with his own doubts and fears about his ability to do what is expected of him and take up the throne, Aragorn is also worried about his personal life. He risks losing everything that he holds dear.

It has been suggested by certain fans that Elrond's claim (i.e. if the Ring is not destroyed, Arwen will die) perverts Aragorn's noble motives by introducing a hint of selfishness into them. This demonstrates a misunderstanding of the information as presented on screen. Elrond is immortal, as is his daughter. If she decides to be with Aragorn, she must renounce her immortality. Before Elrond comes to Aragorn at Dunharrow, bearing the reforged sword (now renamed Andúril), Arwen has made her choice – she will become mortal and, if he survives the coming battle, be with Aragorn.

For a member of a race that rarely experiences death, the very fact that one of their number, previously immortal, will now definitely die at some point in the future would be unbearable. Death is inconceivable to the elves, except in war; they simply do not die natural deaths. Thanks to their immortality, time for elves also seems to pass much faster – what would be a lifetime for a human would, for an elf, seem but a moment thanks to the relative lengths of their existences. So, for Elrond, the fact that he knows that Arwen will now die would be the same as a human father discovering that his daughter has some terminal illness. When he looks into her future, he can see only death – this is because, for him, that is all that matters; his daughter is now going to die, where before she was not. This is why he ignores the fact that he also can see that Aragorn and Arwen will have a child – this is not as important to him as the knowledge that she will die. (In *The Silmarillion* it is revealed that Elrond has already experienced a similar loss when his brother, Elros, opted to become mortal, becoming the first King of Númenor at the end of the First Age, and thus founding the dynasty that spawned Isildur and then Aragorn. This, incidentally, makes Aragorn his future father-in-law's great-nephew several times over, and Arwen is therefore Aragorn's second cousin umpteen times removed.)

Thanks to her decision, Arwen's fate *is* tied up with that of the Ring – but not directly, as some have inferred from Elrond's speech. Her fate is, to an extent, already sealed – she has already chosen mortality. Where the Ring comes in is that, if the mission to destroy it fails, Sauron will overcome Middle-earth. If the Ring is taken by Sauron, Aragorn will doubtless be in the frontline of the then futile attempts to stem his advance. If he is constantly involved in battle, he can never be with Arwen, and her sacrifice will have been in vain. Furthermore, now that she has become mortal, Arwen cannot pass into the West with the rest of her people, but must remain in Middle-earth come what may, so she will have to face his onslaught as well, and will doubtless be killed in the process. Elrond is talking in riddles, but this is what he means.

Many people have experienced the loss of someone they love, and it is a terrible experience indeed (see **FATHERHOOD** in **The Return of the King**); few have been placed in the position Aragorn is in through his relationship with Arwen. To be in a situation in which you love someone but fear that your relationship can never work through no fault of either of you, and that it may in fact hurt or even (in Aragorn's case) kill the one you love, can be even worse than the loss of a loved one through death, or even through their own decision to leave. At least if someone dies, or decides they no longer love you, there is no possibility of it ever working out. If the person you love leaves through no choice of theirs or yours, and continues to live somewhere out of reach, there is the constant gnawing idea that somehow you might find a way to be together again, even though it is impossible. The best-known version of this story, *Romeo and Juliet*, suitably enough ends in tragedy.

Aragorn somehow finds the strength at Rivendell to tell Arwen that she should leave with the rest of her people. For a relationship to end when both parties are still in love, when it is not their choice and both still live, leaves no possibility of recovery. To try to focus on anything else when at the back of your mind you know that you should be strong, do what seems to be right, and give up your love for their sake, is well-nigh impossible. It is yet another example of his strength of will, and of his selflessness. It also foreshadows his decision in *The Return of the King* to march on Mordor, even though he knows it will most likely be suicide, in an attempt to help Frodo in his quest.

Aragorn is strong enough to do what is right even when it will cause him harm. That is truly noble, truly kingly. When he is united with Arwen towards the end of the film, this then becomes a far more satisfying conclusion thanks to the knowledge of the difficulties their relationship has had imposed upon it by events and circumstances beyond their control. Whereas taking up the throne of Gondor is something Aragorn does not really want, but sees as his duty, his marriage to Arwen is his reward.

FARAMIR: The Faramir of the films is another character that is far more complex than that of the book. As David Wenham, the actor who played him, has said, 'The problem with Faramir as a character is that, in *The Two Towers* at least, he's a pretty dead character, dramatically.' The principle reason for this is that, in the book, Faramir is never even slightly tempted by the Ring. Some fans have expressed outrage that the pure, heroic yet sensitive character that is Faramir has been 'corrupted' during the process of adapting the book for the screen but, dramatically, keeping him as written makes little sense.

Earlier in the book, the hobbits encounter another character that has no interest in the Ring: Tom Bombadil. He even tries it on, yet he remains visible and unphased by its malignancy. At the Council of Elrond, Gandalf explains that, although this immunity from its powers might mean that Bombadil may be able to protect the Ring, his mind is beyond it – he might either forget he had it or, even worse, discard it (Book II, Chapter II). This reasoning sounds rather more like an attempt to excuse a major plotting problem than a real explanation – let it not be forgotten that Tolkien wrote the Bombadil passages long before he had decided that the Ring was to be as evil as it ended up (see **BREE** in **The Fellowship of the Ring**).

By having any character that is not tempted by the Ring's evil, its power and malignancy is diminished. But in the book, there are several. In the original, on learning of the Ring, Faramir states that he wouldn't take the Ring even if he found it lying on the road; if he were to be tempted by it he would stick to his vow of not taking it (Book IV, Chapter V). Likewise, in the books, Sam, despite having tried on the Ring (which he does not in the films), only shows the briefest hint of reluctance in giving it back to Frodo after describing it as a huge burden (Book VI, Chapter I). This reluctance is expressed as much as from a desire to spare Frodo the pain of carrying it as from any Gollum-like avarice.

The Ring is the source of all the violence and hatred of the story, and is in many ways the chief protagonist (see **THE RING** in **The Return of the King**). To introduce the idea that some characters may be immune to its power to corrupt hugely lessens the threat it poses. In the books, neither Faramir nor Sam show more than the smallest of signs of the temptation that drove Boromir to his ruin, and Tom Bombadil shows none at all. He will, it is suggested, carry on quite happily as before even if Sauron succeeds in overrunning the whole of Middle-earth.

Part of the message of *The Lord of the Rings* is that people should do what is right, no matter what may happen to them in the process. It is about overcoming temptation. In the Bible, Jesus is tempted by the devil and overcomes it. But the vital point is that even Jesus, God in human form, is tempted. Were Jesus to remain unphased by Satan's promises, not only would he become less human (and therefore harder to relate to), but also Satan's power would be diminished. If the devil can even tempt God, no one is immune, and his power must be terrible indeed.

SMÉAGOL: Gollum (Sméagol) is a far more sympathetic character in the film series than he is in the book, or in any previous adaptation. This is achieved through two separate but complementary threads: one, making him more of a victim; two, making him more understandable. The fact that no one who comes into contact with it is immune from the Ring's influence only heightens this.

The brief appearances of Gollum in *The Fellowship of the Ring* set the tone for much of how the cinematic audience are invited to see him. As viewers first lay eyes on him, he is being tortured for information by Saruman's forces so that they may ascertain the whereabouts of the One Ring. The piteous screams that echo around this scene would move the most hard-hearted of moviegoers, and the audience is thus set up for feeling pity first, revulsion second, for Gollum. The fact that in *The Fellowship of the Ring* the whole character is never seen, just his grasping, pawing hands in the torture scene and his wide, glinting eyes in Moria, further diffuses the notion of the character being a completely malevolent one.

By shifting Gandalf's comment to Frodo from their discussion at Bag End about how Bilbo pitied Gollum to the moment when he first starts following the Fellowship, the point is underlined further. In the book, there is a hint that Gollum is following the party through Moria, but it is only once they reach the borders of Lothlorien that the suspicion is confirmed. His first appearance is as the hobbits sleep on the wood's borders, climbing the tree in which Frodo is lying to try to claim back the Ring before being scared off by the elves. In the film, by shifting his first appearance forward not only can Gandalf point both Frodo and the audience in the right direction – pity – but also the significance is not lost among the shock and horror of Gandalf's apparent death (see **THE GREY PILGRIM** in **The Fellowship of the Ring**).

Andy Serkis's performance as Gollum, both in terms of his physicality and vocal work, is outstanding and cannot be praised highly enough. Serkis keeps Gollum psychologically real, even when WETA's digital trickery (occasionally) fails to make him physically so. (Lighting is an incidental problem of Gollum's CGI status, particularly around the back of the character's head, and on occasions he seems to float more than walk, particularly when on all fours – although this is hardly noticeable to the casual observer.)

From all the vast amount of information about the production of the Jackson films that is available, it appears that the decision to hire Andy Serkis to play Gollum was one of the single most influential casting decisions of all time. Practically unknown when the films went into production, despite a number of film credits to his name, he was cast purely on his vocal versatility. Serkis's interpretation is a far more childlike, high-pitched take on the character than Peter Woodthorpe's version in both the Bakshi and 1981 BBC adaptations, which had shaped many people's idea of how Gollum should sound. The voice alone would have been enough to make Gollum seem less threatening and more sympathetic. But the sheer energy Serkis put into his voiceover work, contorting his face and body and fully entering the character, to achieve the right vocal expression, was soon picked up on by Jackson and his team.

Gollum was originally intended to be a combination of stop-motion and CG, animated in the studio and inserted digitally into the film. However, when watching Serkis perform, it was evident that the facial expressions he was making in delivering his lines were exactly what the team required to make Gollum seem more real. Before *The Two Towers*, there had been several attempts to create realistic and believable CG characters, but most had been unsatisfactory for the simple fact that it is so difficult for animators to effectively convey emotion in three dimensions. By deciding to use Serkis's face as the basis for Gollum's own expressions, layers of subtlety that otherwise would have been lost were added to the character. The decision also necessitated a complete redesign of the character's head to more closely resemble Serkis's own muscle structure, and shift it away from the more Bakshi-like original models. This is why the glimpse we get of Gollum's face in Moria seems to look different to the one that turns up in *The Two Towers*. From this it was a natural step to get Serkis to don a skin-tight suit and place him actually within the frame with the other actors, digitally removing him after filming and replacing him with a motion-captured Gollum based upon his own movements.

The scene around the forbidden pool in *The Two Towers* in which the character is allowed to be almost cute is hugely impressive, because that sweetness is achieved without damaging the character as a threat. It is as effective as the comic interplay Gollum demonstrates with Sam over the issue of food, pulling faces, spitting and wailing because Sam has insisted on cooking a meal rather than consuming the dead animal's flesh raw. A moment that could have been a commentary of Gollum's pseudo-vampiric nature is instead a funny, but sad, indication of how near and far he is from being the hobbit-like creature he once was.

Gollum's split personality, which is merely a small reference in the novel (a total of a little over a page in Book IV, Chapter II – 'The Passage of the Marshes'), and the sympathy that is elicited by his introduction, becomes the focus for much of the action related to him in the second film. The long monologue where Gollum argues with himself has been much praised, as has, rightly, Andy Serkis's delivery of it. This scene is absolutely key to the cinematic audience's understanding of, and sympathy for, the Gollum/Sméagol character.

FRODO 2: For a large part of the book, Tolkien neglects to mention Frodo's internal conflict. In the 1981 BBC version, Frodo (as played by Ian Holm) rarely seems conflicted about the Ring – even as he is climbing the stairs of Cirith Ungol, he seems as determined and strong-willed as he was on setting out from Bag End. This is psychologically highly improbable considering the hardships he has been through, and considering the occasional moments in the preceding chapters where he has told of how the Ring is becoming heavier, and he can feel the Eye searching for him; but it *is* how Frodo is written at this point in the story.

By further exploring what is, in the book, only a briefly mentioned idea that Gollum still has some good inside him, Jackson's films also make Frodo's character more complex. When asked by Sam why he puts up with Gollum, Frodo makes clear that he does so because he needs to believe that it is possible to shake off the Ring's influence. If Gollum can become Sméagol once more, then there is hope for Frodo as well.

The crushing of Frodo's spirit, his physical and psychological incapacitation as the burden of the Ring begins to take its toll on him across the films, was of prime interest to Elijah Wood when it came to creating and portraying his Frodo Baggins. On-screen make-up and performance have to carry that. The slow bleaching out of Wood's pallor to make him slowly resemble Gollum more and more also plays a big part. In a very brief scene that was filmed but then cut from both the cinematic and Extended versions of *The Two Towers*, Wood was placed under heavy make-up designed to make him even more closely resemble Gollum. That Wood has unusually large eyes also enables the audience to (unconsciously perhaps) draw parallels between he who carries the Ring and he who once owned it. Again Wood's thinness parallels Gollum's starved, almost literally famished, look to draw physical parallels. It is a marked contrast with the rather plumper Sam. When Frodo believes Gollum's word over Sam's in the third film it is a moment of horror and disappointment for the audience but not one of surprise. Film, as a visual medium, has prepared us for this. Elijah Wood described it as a 'trippy thing ... To watch yourself so deteriorated and so completely different from who you are'.

Frodo's journey is one of emotional collapse; that of the young man going to war and seeing and doing things that no one, in any sane world, should have to see or do. It is very different from, say, the portrayals of damaged soldiers that litter the works of veterans such as James Whale (*Journey's End*, 1930, *The Road Back*, 1936) or Oliver Stone (*Platoon*, 1986). This, although implicit in Tolkien, is brought out far more by the film-makers.

Tolkien was not aiming at realism – he was creating a myth, and his characters were largely ciphers, symbolic of a greater truth about the nature of mankind and the world at large. This lack of realism simply would not work on screen. While reading the book, it is possible to keep the idea of Frodo's gradual mental and physical decline always at the back of one's mind; on film, it has to be shown, or his eventual submission to the will of the Ring in the cracks of Mount Doom becomes utterly unbelievable. Through the constant comparisons between Frodo and Gollum/ Sméagol during the last two films, this internal struggle is rendered more clearly still.

HELM'S DEEP: While its originality has been somewhat overstated, the film's climactic battle at the siege of Helm's Deep has been rightly praised for its scale, ambition and superb special effects. The orcs performing a 'war dance' and making a threatening noise by banging their pikes into the ground and screaming in unison has been taken by some as an appropriation of Maori ritual, occasioned by the serendipity of the New Zealand shoot (it does not feature in the book). A movie precedent does exist, however, with the struggle from the end of the classic against-all-odds war film *Zulu* (Cy Endfield, 1962). This similarity is further heightened by the sight of the massed ranks of archers firing then kneeling to reload, so that a second rank of bowmen can fire from behind them, with the process then repeating. This manoeuvre is also familiar from *Zulu* – albeit with single-shot rifles rather than bows being reloaded.

Despite taking aspects of (or paying homage to) previous film battles, Helm's Deep was, when it first appeared, a truly inspiring display of cinematic action. The sheer technological medievalism and hand-to-hand brutality set the sequence apart from, for example, the equally impressive larger scale, but more impersonal, battle in George Lucas's *Star Wars: Episode II – Attack of the Clones*, which used much the same computer technology and was released six months previously. Lucas's war, with its vast tanks and starships, robots and Jedi, as well as massed armies of men, is a stunning riot of visual invention that is difficult for the eyes to keep track of. Helm's Deep, however, is an on-screen conflict in which the objectives and counter-objectives of the two opposing forces are entirely clear at all times – something that is not the case in the book (see **THE BATTLE OF THE PELENNOR FIELDS in The Return of the King**).

The darkness of the setting and the emotional reaction prompted in the audience by both the presence of children at the front and the rain-soaked visuals aid the sequence's impact. The battle is, in essence, a pathetic fallacy, with the misery and dread of the characters being evidenced in the weather and light conditions around them.

However, some Tolkien fans were somewhat disturbed by two significant changes between the battle as presented on film and on the page. However, there were few complaints about the decision to have the women and children of Rohan holed up in the caves behind the keep (in the book, they are some miles away at Dunharrow). Furthermore, the initially planned, much-derided scenes of Arwen arriving to kick ass with her sword-wielding Xena-style prowess (see **ARWEN in The Fellowship of the Ring**) were, perhaps thankfully, abandoned during shooting. What remained alterations was the decision to have a company of elves arrive to aid the Rohirrim, and the decision, taken straight out of the Bakshi version, to have Gandalf and Éomer ride to the rescue with reinforcements at the last minute.

The reason for the elves' presence is primarily that, having seen elves briefly in battle in the prologue to the first film, quite simply, they look cool when fighting. Although some fans have bemoaned the 'fact' that their fighting alongside men means that the 'last Alliance of Men end Elves' of the prologue is no longer the 'last Alliance', this is patently nonsense. It is only the 'last' in the sense that, up until Sauron's next rising, men and elves had not had any need to fight alongside one another (although actually, in *The Hobbit*, they have done – at the Battle of the Five Armies at the foot of the Lonely Mountain; technically this was not a formal alliance, but one of expediency). Nonetheless, justification for their presence can be found within the book. Although not mentioned in the film, in the book it is clear that Sauron's offensive is far more widespread than just an attack on Gondor. He also attacks the dwarves at the Lonely Mountain, the men at Laketown, the lands of southern Gondor, the lands of the Dúnadan in the north and, most importantly, the realm of the elves at Lothlorien. The elves are, in *The Lord of the Rings*, part of the war against Sauron. All Jackson has done is show this on screen, rather than casually drop it into the conversation after the war has been won, as Tolkien does.

The reason for having Éomer return with Gandalf to save the day is, based on a strict reading of the text, less easily excused. In the book, Éomer is not banished from Rohan, but briefly imprisoned, and released as soon as Wormtongue's hold on Théoden is broken. He then accompanies the king to Helm's Deep, fighting with the other Rohirrim from the inside of the defences. The people of Rohan then, on their own and despite being vastly outnumbered, manage to rout the vast army of orcs. (Although Helm's Deep, in both book and film, is based on the Battle of Rourke's Drift, as featured in *Zulu*, at Rourke's Drift there was not a rout – the Zulus decided to leave of their own accord.) The orcs then flee, to be consumed by the trees that have advanced from Fangorn Forest in a literal rending of the end of *Macbeth* (a scene that is restored to the Extended Edition of the film). The trees do not attack the orcs, but wait for them; the Rohirrim win on their own. In terms of numbers, as well as in how the action is described, this is impossible. That is why Éomer is kept away from the battle to return with reinforcements (and why the elves are present) – sheer believability (see **THE BATTLE OF THE PELENNOR FIELDS** in The Return of the King).

SAM 2: Again, the on-screen Sam is a subtle re-envisioning of the one in the book, the changes undertaken in order to make the character stronger, more psychologically complex and more appealing for an audience. In other words, to make him a character more appropriate for drama than prose.

This is achieved in a number of ways on a scripting level, although perhaps the most important contribution is Sean Astin's stellar performance. Astin plays against the obvious sense of his lines as often as he goes along with them, transforming lines that seem to emphasise Sam's stupidity into ones that reflect his bravery. When Frodo tells Sam that he is going to Mount Doom alone, Sam replies, 'Of course you are, and I'm going with you!' On the page, this seems like Sam does not understand the implications of what Frodo is saying. On screen, Astin turns the line into a declaration of faith, a refusal to acknowledge that Frodo's task is not Frodo's alone. Later, when Sam is trying to preserve their food supplies 'for the journey home', Astin's delivery and facial expressions make clear that, although he maintains a certain amount of hope that they may make it out alive, he knows deep down that such a possibility is highly unlikely. He is maintaining the charade that there is a chance of success as much out of an attempt to keep Frodo's spirits up as from any real belief. As the actor himself has put it, 'There's an element of Sam's personality that's staunch and stoic and re-served, and I preferred living in that space rather than the Ralph Bakshi interpretation' (Bakshi's film portrays Sam as a simple fool). Astin is assisted in this by a script that removes much of Sam's most foolish dialogue. Astin also delivers various lines that emphasise Sam's stupidity in a way that instead emphasises his protectiveness towards Frodo and his sense of duty. Astin again: '[His] job is to be in the service of the officer that's he working for.'

There is more to it than that, though. The screenplay takes out most of the references to Sam's father, Gaffer Gamgee, and (except in the Extended Edition) all of his appearances. There is no mention of the fact that Sam is the Gaffer's apprentice, and this means that on screen he is presented as a professional gardener and tradesman in his own right. His greater physical size (see below, a matter of much contention on set) also gives him seniority – in the Bakshi version, Sam is significantly smaller than Frodo. Of all the actors playing hobbits, Sean Astin is the only one who was, at the time of filming, a husband and father, a confirmed family man, and the actor has reiterated time and again that he was the paternally responsible one of the foursome both on and off set (see **FATHERHOOD** in **The Return of the King**). Sam is also consistently called 'Sam' in the films rather than 'Samwise', giving him a common forename rather than a comically archaic one.

Another important alteration between the on-page and on-screen Sams is the removal of his habit of calling Frodo 'Master Frodo'. The reasoning for this is simple. In the context of 1940s and 50s Britain, there are many connotations of 'Master' that could be seen as positive, or at least not overtly negative. A tradesman with an apprentice would be considered a 'Master'. Schoolteachers in English public schools would be referred to, and addressed as, 'Master'. These practices have now almost vanished. For a global audience, particularly one centred on America, the only possible connotations of someone being addressed as 'Master' are overwhelmingly negative.

The strongest and most obvious connection an audience is likely to make when a subservient character addresses a socially superior one as 'Master' is that of slavery – a particularly uncomfortable topic for many Americans. There are also connotations of S&M domination, which would fuel the already homoerotically tinged elements of the hobbits' relationships in an uncomfortable way. (The four hobbit actors have admitted to deliberately exploring 'queer' readings of their characterisations, and trying to imply on screen that Frodo/Sam and Merry/Pippin are couples, but claim to have done so largely because it was funny.) The on-screen Sam's use of 'Mister Frodo' or (mostly) just 'Frodo' is far more appropriate in an early twenty-first century, international context, and it makes Sam respectful and socially inferior without implying *actual* inferiority.

This raising of Sam's intellectual and social status becomes most clear towards the end of *The Two Towers*, when he stops Frodo from giving himself up to the Nazgûl in Osgiliath. Immediately after this moment, just one of many in which Sam proves himself invaluable to the mission (see below), he embarks upon a speech which demonstrates his ability to see and understand the big picture that Frodo has momentarily forgotten. His monologue, an invention of screenwriters Fran Walsh and Philippa Boyens, runs over a montage of scenes from the duel climaxes of Helm's Deep and the Ent attack on Isengard, lauding the values that are being fought for and pleading for 'the good in this world'. Thus, he brings Frodo back from the brink of madness and reminds the audience of how all the disparate storylines of the middle film of the trilogy are linked. His words are so effective that they even seem momentarily to touch Gollum who, by this stage, already appears to have decided to betray his 'master'.

According to Astin, Jackson initially resisted the idea of having an American play Sam, seeing that as anti-ethical to the character. This is why Astin affects a rural English accent throughout the film series (it is a surprisingly good rendition of a generic West-country one for an American actor). Jackson also wanted Sam to be fatter than Astin. Astin was 160 pounds in weight when cast, and was told to put on more bulk for the part. He peaked at 197 pounds, which the actor found both physically uncomfortable and inappropriate for the character: 'I couldn't see the character anymore, all I could see was that fat f***.' His weight was a cause of some creative contention between Jackson and Walsh. Jackson (a man of not inconsiderable size himself) saw no contradiction between Sam as fat comic relief and Sam as hero. Walsh and Astin did – 'When people say "Sam is the true hero of this story" . . . I want to be able . . . maybe if it is true . . . to own that. And at 197, I don't.'

So, is Sam actually 'the true hero' of the story? It is Aragorn's destiny to become king; it is (in the book at least – see **THE FELLOWSHIP** in **The Fellowship of the Ring**) Frodo's destiny to be the Ringbearer.

Neither Aragorn nor Frodo really have any choice in the matter – they have to be heroes thanks to these obligations having been placed upon them by fate; others are now relying on them to fulfil their duty. Aragorn and Frodo are also more at home with their responsibilities. Aragorn is prepared to selflessly give up his one chance of happiness despite the pain he knows it will cause him (see **ARAGORN AND ARWEN**), and is unafraid of death, as is made clear by his decision to enter the Paths of the Dead. Frodo also comes to be unafraid of death, accepting far sooner than Sam that the journey to Mordor is likely to be one-way, and smiling at Sam both affectionately and in amazement at his companion's apparent naivety when he says that he is trying to ration their supplies for the journey home. Near the very start of the film series, just after they have set out from Bag End, there is a scene where Frodo and Sam are trying to get to sleep out in the open – while Frodo is comfortable and gets to sleep easily, Sam tosses and turns, complaining about the lack of a bed. He is not cut out for adventure; he, unlike Frodo, is not a natural hero.

Furthermore, other than for the first part of the trip, when Gandalf sends him along with Frodo, Sam is never under any obligation to take part in the quest. By the time he breaks in on the Council of Elrond (eavesdropping again – see **SAM 1** in **The Fellowship of the Ring**) he is aware of the hardships that will be involved, but goes anyway. When offered the choice to return to the Shire by Galadriel, he again opts to stay with Frodo and see the quest through, even though (as revealed in his vision in the Mirror of Galadriel) this may mean that his beloved Shire comes under threat in his absence. Later, as noted above, when Frodo tries to slip off on his own after Boromir's attempt to take the Ring, Sam goes after him despite being fully aware of what this will mean. In the third film, when Frodo, corrupted by the Ring and Gollum's deviousness, abandons Sam again, he still does not give up, returning just in time to save the day.

Without Sam, Frodo would never have made it to Mount Doom. Not only does Sam save him from Shelob, but he also then rescues him from the orcs, and later literally carries him up the slopes of the volcano. Besides these obvious moments, throughout the second two films Sam constantly denies himself food and sleep to allow Frodo to maintain his strength, even though Sam is going through the same hardships as his friend. It is only at the very end, after the Ring is destroyed and the two hobbits are lying on the mountainside awaiting an apparently inevitable death, does the enormity of what he has done hit him, and Sam finally allows a thought for himself, pining at his lost chance to marry Rosie Cotton.

By the end of the film, Sam is as much a hero as either Frodo or Aragorn. Like Frodo, he has been a Ringbearer, and passed through innumerable dangers on the journey to and through Mordor. Like Frodo and Aragorn, he has accepted the possibility of death, and carried on regardless. Like Aragorn, he has met in battle with foes that seem to far advance him in both size and strength. Also like Aragorn, he has given up his chance for love and happiness to fulfil what he sees as his duty.

Galadriel's announcement that 'even the smallest person' can make a difference to the future of the world is not a phrase of

Tolkien's at all, although it does succinctly summarise one of his key messages. Although ostensibly directed at Frodo, by the end of the film it is clear that this piece of reassurance-cum-prophecy means Sam. Frodo, at the vital moment, gives in to his desire for the Ring. Sam never allows himself to give up until the job is done. The fact that this was not his job in the first place and that he, unlike Frodo, was never obliged to take it on, only makes this strength of character and will even more impressive. The heroism of someone who is weak is far more impressive and worthy of praise than the heroism of someone who is strong. For this reason, Sam is indeed arguably the 'true hero' of *The Lord of the Rings*.

THE LORD OF THE RINGS: THE RETURN OF THE KING (2003)

New Line Cinema Presents
A WingNut Films Production
The Lord of the Rings
The Return of the King
Directed by Peter Jackson
Screenplay by Philippa Boyens, Fran Walsh, Peter Jackson
Based on the book by JRR Tolkien
Producers: Fran Walsh, Peter Jackson, Barrie M Osbourne
Executive Producers: Mark Ordesky, Bob Weinstein, Harvey
    Weinstein, Robert Shaye, Michael Lynne
Director of Photography: Neil Cervis, A.C.S, Andrew Lesnie,
    A.C.S
Production Designer: Grant Major
Film Editors: Annie Collier, Jamie Selkirk
Co-producers: Rick Porras, Jamie Selkirk
UK Casting by John Hubbard and Amy MacLean
US Casting by Victoria Burrows
New Zealand Casting by Liz Mullane
Australian Casting by Ann Robinson
Costume Designers: Ngila Dickson, Richard Taylor
Music composed, orchestrated and conducted by Howard
    Shore
Associate Producer: Ellen M Somers
Special Make-up, creatures, armour and miniatures by
    Richard Taylor
Visual Effects Supervisor: Jim Rygiel

Released: 1 December 2003 (Wellington, New Zealand,
    premiere)

STARRING: Elijah Wood (Frodo Baggins), Ian McKellen (Gandalf), Liv Tyler (Arwen), Viggo Mortensen (Aragorn), Sean Astin (Sam), Cate Blanchett (Galadriel), John Rhys-Davies (Gimli), Bernard Hill (Théoden), Billy Boyd (Pippin), Dominic Monaghan (Merry), Orlando Bloom (Legolas), Hugo Weaving (Elrond), Miranda Otto (Éowyn), David Wenham (Faramir), featuring Sean Bean (Boromir), Ian Holm (Bilbo) and Andy Serkis as Gollum, Karl Urban (Éomer), Craig Parker (Haldur).

NOTE: These chapters follow thematic and structural elements and conceits across all three films with the information contained within the film chapter to which it is the most relevant. They are, however, cross-referenced as and when necessary.

GOLLUM: The third film begins with a long sequence that tells the story of how the hobbit-like Sméagol gained possession of the Ring and his murder of his friend Déagol in order to acquire it. This is taken from Gandalf's explanation of these events to Frodo in Book I, Chapter II. (This scene was, incidentally, shot for inclusion in the first film, moved into the second and then finally cut and used as an opening to the third – see below, **THE ROAD GOES EVER ON AND ON**). It is a very suitable beginning in many ways.

This opening is unexpected, surprising the audience that the film should begin in flashback. This surprise is heightened by the deliberate parallels of Sméagol here using a worm to catch a fish when the audience has seen Gollum himself eating a worm in the previous film – the difference between the two characters is immediately apparent. Positioned where it is, it seems like an 'origin story' for Gollum, not unlike the 'Secret Origin' of a comic book villain. These tales, a long tradition in the comic book medium, have become familiar to film audiences through their use in films such as *Batman* (Tim Burton, 1989), *Unbreakable* (M Night Shamalyan, 2001) and *Spider-Man* (Sam Raimi, 2002), among others. The use of this tradition is effective here; beginning with Gollum's genesis is appropriate for a film in which the pathetic creature is arguably the lead villain.

In this scene, the audience witnesses the body-horror of Sméagol's transformation into Gollum, which is viscerally disturbing and faintly sickening, and also sees him commit murder with his own hands. These two things together remind the audience of the danger that Gollum presents to Sam and Frodo and remove some of the sympathy the audience has felt for the creature up to this point. It is difficult for most viewers to empathise with a character that they have seen commit a coldly unpleasant murder, no matter how much they may intellectually understand the corrupting power of the Ring. It is also not hard to associate the hobbit-like Déagol and Sméagol with Sam and Frodo – Sméagol is even dressed similarly to how Frodo appears at the start of the first film and, like Frodo, has genuine affection for his companion before the Ring drives him insane.

Gollum is far more sinister here than in the previous film. His comic asides come less often and less screentime is given to his battling split personalities. This is all building up to his 'betrayal' of his 'Master' Frodo and his usurpation of Sam's rightful place at Frodo's side. This was hinted to the audience at the end of the second movie with his sinister closing line about allowing the unspecified 'she' to dispose of the hobbits. After the apparent downfall of Saruman a few scenes earlier, it is clear that Gollum is being set up as his replacement, as the figure for the audience to identify as the villain.

Gollum remains tragic, but the events of his corruption and his extreme actions make him less sympathetic while retaining the element of tragedy that lies in his character. It is worth noting that here, unlike in the book, it is clear that the Ring has taken possession of Déagol as well as Sméagol. The murder that begins Sméagol's journey to becoming Gollum begins in self-defence, as it is Déagol who first tries to strangle him. Nevertheless, Sméagol crosses a line in the audience's perceptions, maintaining his grip on his friend long after he has ceased to struggle.

Although in the previous film, during the debate between the Gollum and Sméagol sides of his personality, the evil side seems at one point to win the argument by calling him 'murderer' it is not until the opening sequence of the final film that the audience sees this with their own eyes. The superb combination of Andy Serkis's performance and the WETA effects have somehow managed to transform a creature that was, in the books, malevolent and repulsive into an ugly thing that is nonetheless somehow cute (see **SMÉAGOL** in **The Two Towers**). The audience has been set up to sympathise with Gollum, and to hope, like Frodo does, that he can be saved. But after seeing the murder, Sméagol is no longer a tragic anti-hero; he is now more simply the villain, one driven by his selfishness and his lust for the Ring. It is in this capacity that he causes Frodo to reject Sam, throws away their food, leads the Ringbearer to Shelob and, unwittingly, saves the whole of Middle-earth.

In the end, it seems, Gollum's obsession with the Ring is different to anyone else's. While everyone else tempted by it on screen (whether Frodo, Gandalf, Saruman, Boromir, Faramir or Sam) is tempted to *use* it, Gollum simply wants to be *with* it. There is no thought, in his last struggle with Frodo, as to what he can do with the Ring; he simply wants to possess it. In the book, he tells himself that once he has his 'precious' back he will reap revenge on those who he believes to have hurt him (although how likely it is he will try to go through with this plan is unclear); in the film, he simply wants to hold it again. His greed is so naked that it knows no expression except itself. This is pure selfishness, but it is also the reason that Gollum dies smiling – not knowing that he is saving the world, not knowing that he could do anything he likes, and not caring about either.

There is an irony there: for all the story's protestations about doing the right thing whatever the costs, the world is saved by an uncomprehending and selfish act. Is the world saved by accident? Well, actually, yes – although the point is more that the accident was only possible because, back in *The Hobbit*, Bilbo pitied Gollum rather than destroying him. It was mercy and kindness, not heroism, that made the difference in the end.

Special Effects

All the effects for *The Lord of the Rings* films were done 'in house' by New Zealand-based effects company WETA Ltd of which Peter Jackson owns part. Essentially, this followed the example set by George Lucas who started his Industrial Light & Magic company (now the pre-eminent effects house in the world) in order to do the effects for the first *Star Wars* movie (1977) in a manner whereby he could both control every aspect of the final look of the effects and personally keep an eye on the financial end of the (potentially exorbitantly expensive) effects production he required. (WETA is derived from the name of a native New Zealand insect, of the cricket family, which is about the size of the palm of your hand, the heaviest insect in the world, able to survive extreme conditions, and practically unchanged since the days of the dinosaurs.)

As well as Lucas, WETA's techniques also owe a debt to those pioneered by Jim Henson's Creature Shop, responsible for the Muppets as well as innumerable animatronic creatures in cult films such as *The Dark Crystal* (Jim Henson and Frank Oz, 1982) and *Labyrinth* (Jim Henson, 1986).

The company was founded in 1987 by Richard Taylor and his partner Tania Rodger in the back room of their flat in

Wellington, New Zealand, as RT Effects Ltd. It started out as little more than a low-budget, home-made attempt to fill a gap in the market. Its philosophy was much the same as Peter Jackson's when he was creating effects for *Bad Taste* in his parents' kitchen. Taylor and Rodger worked together for two years before meeting Jackson, with whom they immediately hit it off and collaborated with on *Meet the Feebles* (see **A Long Expected Party**). This was the start of a long and fruitful relationship, as they have contributed effects to every one of Jackson's subsequent films.

The name-change to WETA came in 1994, following Taylor and Rodger's first foray into computer animation on Jackson's *Heavenly Creatures*. They had leased a computer from the US to achieve the results, but realised towards the end of production that they could not afford to lose the machine. Pooling their resources, Taylor, Rodger, Jackson and producer/editor Jamie Selkirk formed the new company out of RT Effects, and continued to lease the computer. With the new technology, the company built up work via stints providing effects for the *Hercules* and *Xena* TV shows and a number of movies.

When Jackson started the *Lord Of The Rings* project it was in part thanks to some pre-production design work and animations WETA had been working on for Jackson's projected *King Kong* remake. The company then split in two to better handle the vastly increased workload, WETA Digital handling the visual effects work for the films and the WETA Workshop overseeing the construction of physical sets, props and practical, in-camera effects. However, the two companies remained (literally and metaphorically) under the same roof, overseen by Taylor and Roger within one large warehouse to aid the creation of a single visual style in the digital and physical effects and design work across all three films. Farming out effects work to other companies was quickly discarded because of its potential to introduce visual inconsistency in the standard of effects (*Harry Potter and the Philosopher's Stone* is a prime example of this problem. Work began two and a half years before shooting started to give enough time to get everything ready.

The statistics are impressive. For the first film of the trilogy alone, around 570 special effects shots were produced, with some of the more complex shots having over 300 input layers of various types, and thousands of separate pieces of computer code to make them all work together. The WETA Workshop made in the region of 48,000 separate pieces for the film – including 2,000 weapons, 68 miniature sets, 10,000 facial appliances, 10,000 arrows, 1,800 body and prosthetic suits, 1,000 suits of armour, and innumerable other interactive creature effects, models for the digital team to scan, and so on. The company built its own blacksmith's shop in order to beat the armour out of plates of steel and hand-grind the weapons. Every prosthetic piece was individually crafted, shaped and sized to fit the needs of the actors. By the end of filming, WETA had augmented its initial sole computer by well over a thousand others, all top of the range, initially licensing software and hardware from ILM and later pooling resources and data with the more established company. Lucasfilm producer Rick McCallum visited WETA in New Zealand and WETA's technicians spent time at Lucas' Skywalker Ranch in Marin County, California, to allow the two effects teams to more easily trade technology and ideas.

Especially for such a new operation, WETA's work on the films was consistently excellent, garnering the company numerous awards and many more nominations (see **Tolkien and Oscar**). The 'Massive' computer program, developed jointly by WETA and Industrial Light & Magic, enabled the creation of vast numbers of artificially intelligent characters for the battle scenes. The program allows the CGI figures to make their own (limited) decisions about how, and who, to fight. Even within the constantly evolving field of special effects 'Massive' is an enormous achievement.

It is the success of the CG creation that is Gollum which has stuck in most people's minds as WETA's supreme effects achievement. Although by no means the first wholly computer-generated character to appear in a major motion picture, Gollum was certainly the first to display a wide range of emotions. This was thanks to a technique which expertly spliced motion-captured facial expressions from an actor with CGI builds and texture mapping (see **SMÉAGOL** in **The Two Towers**). What Gollum has that the previous CGI-built characters lack is the ability to engage the audience on an emotional level. While Gollum's complexities are down to Andy Serkis's performance and the Jackson/Boyens/Walsh scripts, you would not *see* his performance without WETA's technology.

For the most part, the effects in New Line Cinema's *The Lord of the Rings* films are effectively blended into the environment with few visible joins. As in any film, there are some glitches, but they are few and far between. The simplicity and skill with which the live-action and effects work was blended is just one more example of the success of the Jackson world-building exercise. Combined with the work of Alan Lee and John Howe (see boxout, **Design**, page 131), WETA really brought Middle-earth to life.

THE ENEMY: In the commentary to the Extended Edition DVD of *The Fellowship of the Ring*, Peter Jackson makes the understated, fairly obvious, but often missed point that 'Having your central villain as little more than a flaming eyeball is a little bit of a problem.'

In the book, Sauron is a constant menacing presence, and is certainly the principle enemy of the Fellowship and their allies. However, he never actually appears or speaks, except (telepathically) to Pippin (through the Palantir recovered at Isengard) and (through his messenger) as Aragorn and company advance on the Black Gates (in a scene cut from the cinematic release of *The Return of the King*). The Eye is the closest he gets to a physical presence until the moment of his destruction, where he briefly manifests as a massive threatening shadow topped with lightning (Book VI, Chapter IV). The Eye itself is described as being yellow within a ring of fire, but the black pupil looks into nothingness behind it (Book 2, Chapter VII).

This lack of detailed description of Sauron as a physical entity greatly helps enhance the feel of a dark, brooding threat – after all, how can you fight something that remains so vague, yet is so powerful? But thanks to this very vagueness, which makes him such a good villain for a book, to render him visually from the descriptions given is practically impossible. Sauron is incorporeal for the entire course of *The Lord of the Rings*, represented solely by the Eye, which appears not to be a part of him so much as a tool of his. Although as a reader one can imagine a pupil that looks into nothing, how can this actually be represented on film without the pupil just being black, much like any other? In short, the concept of Sauron is fundamentally uncinematic: he is a psychological villain, not a physical or a visual one.

As film is a fundamentally visual medium, finding a physical enemy to act as the focus of the audience's attention – especially for the portion of it that had not read the books – must have been immensely desirable for Jackson and his team. Luckily for them, Tolkien populated Middle-earth with enough other evil creatures, mostly minions of Sauron, so that there are sufficient incidents of dramatic confrontation between good and evil for those responsible for adapting his work to provide innumerable physical confrontations. Each clash with a new evil (be it Old Man Willow, the Barrow-wight, the Nazgûl, the Balrog, the Witch King, Shelob, or a vast army of orcs) also helps enhance Sauron's threat. If the Nazgûl cannot be killed, and they are only his servants, and if he is more evil than either Old Man Willow or Shelob, who are only acting after their nature, then he must be powerful and terrible indeed.

The various adaptations of *The Lord of the Rings* have taken different approaches to get round this central problem of Sauron's vagueness as a villain. The Rankin/Bass version of *The Return of the King* chose to emphasise the orcs as Frodo and Sam make their way across Mordor, with the Nazgûl occasionally zipping about overhead on their flying horses to add an extra layer of threat. The BBC version gives the Nazgûl distinct voices and far more dialogue to their leader, helping them become a more constant menace than they are in the book during the first two-thirds of the tale, and additionally Peter Woodthorpe's Gollum remains far more threatening and devious than Andy Serkis's more sympathetic version of the character (see **SMÉAGOL** in **The Two Towers**). For the parts of the story where their two versions overlap (up until the battle of Helm's Deep), both Bakshi and Jackson opt to raise the prominence of the wizard Saruman.

SARUMAN: The decision to raise Saruman to the position of chief (physical) villain is a fairly obvious and, to an extent, sensible one. Although he hardly features in the book, where he is just another example of what can happen to those who give in to their temptation, Saruman nonetheless causes a great deal of trouble. Although he is not physically present, it is Saruman who is directing the attacks against Rohan in Book III and, as a wizard (and Gandalf's former boss), he is evidently a powerful foe. In the book, Saruman achieves little beyond his spiteful revenge of the Scouring of the Shire and the capture of Merry and Pippin (which, through their resultant meeting with Treebeard, leads to his downfall). In Jackson's films, the failure of the Fellowship to traverse the mountain of Caradhras is also attributed to him, and his machinations against Rohan, only reported in the book, are presented on screen for the audience to see.

The fact that in Jackson's films Christopher Lee was cast as Saruman may well have influenced the decision to give the character more screentime. Lee remains one of cinema's true icons. A great Bond villain, a fine Sherlock Holmes and the definitive screen Dracula, he has made over a hundred films in a career spanning more than half a century. A tall, gaunt, dignified figure with enormous screen presence, hypnotic eyes and sonorous voice, Lee excels as the film's version of Saruman. Thanks to his star status, practically everyone in the audience would immediately make the connection between him and his previous villainous roles. This makes the decision to increase the character's screentime as the physical embodiment of the evil that is threatening Middle-earth an entirely understandable one. You do not waste the talents of an actor like Christopher Lee on a walk-on part unless there is absolutely no way they can spare the time for a bigger role. And, given that Lee was such a fan of Tolkien's work, as soon as he heard that the films were being made, he determined to *make* time.

Yet even without the benefit of Christopher Lee, when making a trilogy of films it is necessary to have a sufficient hook to bring the audience back after the first instalment. The book of *The Lord of the Rings* was not supposed to be put out in three parts. It was written as a single entity (albeit one structured into six 'books' which are really just sections), and only put out as three separate volumes due to paper shortages left over from World War Two. Because of this, the first 'part', *The Fellowship of the Ring*, does not really have a central villain at all. Saruman is one of the major sources of potential tension in the second 'part', *The Two Towers*, and so it makes sense, as it is an attack by his orcs that breaks the Fellowship, to make him more prominent in the first, thus foreshadowing this cataclysmic event. The fact that Saruman has been highlighted as an active enemy of the quest makes the previous revelations of his 'treachery' seem to have more of a point much sooner. In the book, this is not fully revealed until the first chapter of the second volume (Book III, Chapter I – 'The Departure of Boromir'). Had the films followed the structure of the book more exactly, there would have been no real excitement at the end of the first movie, no cliff-hanger, and so no real incentive for the (non-Tolkien-fan) audience to come back for more in a year's time.

On-screen, it seems that Saruman's plan is very simple. He will, in his own words, 'serve Mordor'. He is creating in his eugenics pits 'an army worthy of Mordor' and he explicitly tells Gandalf that 'against Sauron the world of men cannot stand'. Saruman is initially presented, in the screenplays, as a wise and decent man who has decided to throw in his lot with evil because he has decided that it is impossible for good to triumph. If evil will reign then it is better to be on the side of evil. He is a quisling.

On the page, this is not the case. Saruman does not intend to serve Sauron; he intends to take the Ring for himself. He intends to use the powers of the Ring to defeat Sauron and rule in his place. This change in Saruman's character may be part of the reason behind the cutting of Book VI, Chapter VIII ('The Scouring of the Shire'), which was described by Tolkien as an outgrowth of Saruman's character. A Saruman who is merely a servant of Sauron, who has no hope once the Dark Lord is defeated, would have no reason to occupy the Shire and take what power he can for himself. He is a servant without a master. The game he was playing is over and there are no more moves to make. A Saruman who intends to rule by himself is a different matter entirely. He would risk all on a final seizure of whatever power and land is available to him because it is a scaled down version of his plan to rule the world.

The on-screen Saruman is more dynamic than the literary one, a war leader played by a great screen star, but he is also much less complex. In the book, the alternative term for Saruman the White, which the wizard adopts himself, is 'Saruman of Many Colours'.

It is fitting that the 'Many Colours' become one colour on screen and that that one colour is the simplest one, an absence of colour. White.

THE RING: Gollum finds himself struggling between his good and evil sides – the evil ending up triumphant in the final film. Gollum's 'evil' side is really the personification of his desire for the Ring. Gollum's split personality thus brings into sharper focus one of the key ideas of both book and film.

The real struggle for the heroes of the books is not a physical one against an external, physical enemy (the orcs, Sauron, Saruman or Gollum), but an internal one against their own desires and weaknesses. This is not obvious on the page but, especially through the alterations to the character of Aragorn, becomes far more so on screen. Aragorn, like all the 'good' characters (including the 'Sméagol' part of Gollum), is struggling against the temptation to give in. Frodo, in both book and films, spends day after day, week after week, desperately trying to resist his desire to take the Ring for his own. In the end, his willpower (like Sméagol's) is simply not strong enough. But Frodo's psychological collapse is not due to any direct effort of Sauron, the supposed enemy – at that time, his attention is fixed elsewhere. Frodo gives in purely though his own mortal weakness.

This is partly why Jackson's decision to show Sauron as a physical being at the start of *The Fellowship of the Ring* initially seems such an odd one. At first, some fans feared that this indicated a surrender to Hollywood, that this was simply the teaser, and that Sauron's appearance in the prologue indicated that he would return as a physical presence in the final film in betrayal of Tolkien's original work (see **THE BATTLE OF THE PELENNOR FIELDS**).

In fact, Sauron's initial appearance is nothing more than a MacGuffin (to use Hitchcock's term), a cinematic sleight of hand. Tolkien sets up Sauron as the major villain, but never delivers on the expected final showdown; Jackson does exactly the same. But whereas for Tolkien having a single physical villain was never the point, as the psychological and moral battle was for him the more important one, Jackson had another villain in mind for the central role: the Ring itself.

One of the most important changes between Tolkien's book and Jackson's films was the decision to turn the Ring from a symbol and conduit of evil into the personification of evil; in Jackson's films, the Ring is a character in its own right. He explains in *The Fellowship of the Ring* DVD commentary that 'we concentrated on making the Ring, and the threat of the Ring, foremost'. As Galadriel explains in Jackson's prologue, 'the Ring of Power has a will of its own'.

This is not immediately apparent. It is first hinted at in Bag End, as Gandalf returns from seeing Bilbo off on his 'holiday' and leans down to pick it up from the floor. The Eye flashes on screen with a menacing rumble and, as Gandalf sits smoking in front of the fire, the Ring remains in the background of the shot (effectively invisible when viewed on the small screen), preying on the wizard's mind. The Eye's appearance could simply be put down to the fact that it is calling to Sauron, and Gandalf's confusion to the Ring's powers of temptation. But at this point, Gandalf is unaware that the Ring is the One Ring. (He may suspect, but until he returns from his research trip to Minas Tirith and throws the Ring in the fire to reveal its hidden writing he does not know for certain.)

How can Gandalf be tempted if he does not know what the Ring actually is? All the other characters that are affected by the Ring's power, both in the book and in the film, are tempted by the Ring in the full knowledge of its powers. The fact that, beyond turning its wearer invisible (except, inexplicably, when Sauron wears it), these powers are never really explained is beside the point – they know that it is strong. Boromir is only driven to try to take the Ring thanks to his belief that it can aid Gondor; Galadriel and Gandalf both resist it because they know it would give them too much power and corrupt them; Sam is tempted (in the book) through the desire to turn Mordor into a wonderful garden.

The fact that Gandalf does not know what the Ring is, yet it still starts to corrupt him, suggests that it is a more powerful thing than it is in the books. In the DVD commentary, Jackson makes this clear: 'Gandalf had, up until this moment, no suspicions about this ring.' Gandalf is in the same room as it for just a few minutes, yet is so consumed by the Ring's presence that he doesn't notice Frodo enter; he even mutters 'my precious' to himself – and anyone who's read the book or seen the films knows what *that* means. In Jackson's version, the Ring is deliberately trying to come into contact with Gandalf. It is reaching out to him, trying to corrupt him before he knows to resist. As he later explains, if he took possession of it, he would become another Sauron. It would, though him, wield too much power. The Ring, in Jackson's version, seems aware of this. (This is an extrapolation from the very brief mention of how Gollum came to possess the Ring as mentioned in Book I, Chapter II – he is unaware of its nature, but is so consumed by his desire to possess it that he kills his friend. The Ring has influenced his actions without him being aware of how it can benefit him, unlike *all* of the other characters who consider taking it.)

The idea of the Ring determining its own course is much more prominent in Jackson's films. In the prologue, Galadriel's voice-over explains that when Bilbo picked it up, this was 'something the Ring did not intend'. It is more than just a powerful weapon – it is a conscious being.

This concept is taken from Book I, Chapter II ('The Shadow of the Past'). Gandalf explains to Frodo that 'A Ring of Power looks after itself . . . It was not Gollum . . . but the Ring itself that decided things. The Ring left *him*.' In the book, the Ring abandons Gollum because it is being called by its Master, who has woken and is telepathically calling to it – an idea that is retained in Jackson's films as the Ring '*wants* to be found'. In the same chapter, Tolkien describes how Isildur came to lose the Ring: it 'slipped from his finger'. In Jackson's films, this becomes far stronger, Galadriel's voiceover stating that 'it betrayed Isildur – to his death'. This again is extrapolated from a brief mention in the book where, at the Council in Rivendell, Elrond uses the word 'betrayed' to describe how Isildur lost the Ring. As written, this is not meant to signify an actual betrayal as much as a metaphorical one – it is clear that it was Isildur's own desire that betrayed him, not the Ring itself. In the Jackson films, the Ring is capable of treachery; it is capable of murder. This is far stronger than simply slipping from Isildur's finger. As Tolkien writes it, this might be an accident; in Jackson's version it becomes a deliberate decision on the part of the Ring.

Later in Jackson's *The Fellowship of the Ring*, when Gandalf and Frodo are discussing the Ring's origins and history, it seems to speak. The voice (that of actor Alan Howard) is hissing, malevolent and indistinct, but it is calling a name: 'Isildur'. It speaks again on various occasions throughout the three films, normally in the black speech of Mordor, which few cinemagoers are likely to understand, although its evil nature is clear from its pronunciation (something of which Tolkien would undoubtedly have approved). When the Ring's voice next becomes understandable to the layman, it is in *The Return of the King*, and it is again calling a name: 'Frodo'. In the DVD commentary, Jackson explains that the decision to give the Ring a voice was to enable it to interact more with the other characters. He also claims that 'ultimately, obviously, it is Sauron's voice', but in the way the voice is portrayed, this is not necessarily as apparent as Jackson may think. By making the Ring interact more with the characters, by emphasising its threat, and especially by giving it more screentime than Sauron himself and having *it* speak rather than its supposed master, the impression is more that the Ring itself is the one behind the menace, and that the voice is that of the Ring, not its maker.

Jackson's films play down the idea that Sauron is the Ring's master. Though Sauron made the Ring, he is more in *its* power than it in his – why else would the loss of it result in his destruction? Why else would he need the Ring so badly? He is addicted to its allure as much as Gollum is; he created something he could not control. As Gandalf explains to Frodo in Bag End, 'his life-force is bound to the Ring'. In the book, it is Sauron who has begun to regain his strength and call to the Ring; in Jackson's films, 'the Ring has awoken'. It is not simply that Sauron has regained some of his former strength and is able to call his creation to him, it is that the Ring itself has become more conscious and has started calling to others – to Isildur and, once it has realised that Isildur no longer holds it, to Frodo.

In the book, it seems far more apparent who 'the Lord of the Rings' actually is: Sauron. In Jackson's films, this becomes far more ambiguous. The Lord of the Rings is, if anything, more the One Ring itself than Sauron. (It, after all, is the thing that can control the other Rings of Power, and as a 'lord of men' is generally a man and the 'lord of horses' is Shadowfax – a horse – it logically makes sense that a 'lord of rings' would be a ring.) The Ring abandons Gollum and forces Frodo's final capitulation – it is always the Ring that is in charge, not the Ringbearer. Does this, in Jackson's films, apply to Sauron as well? Is he also just a tool of the Ring? The fact that the Ring seems to be trying to tempt Gandalf in that early scene, and that it calls to Isildur and to Frodo, would suggest that it has no loyalty to its erstwhile master;

it simply wants to be worn by someone through whom it can wield power.

In the book, the real enemy is internal and moral, and the characters' ability to resist depends upon their faith and strength of will to do good. In the films, they are tempted not just by the knowledge that with the Ring they might become great lords, stronger than all others, but also by the Ring's constant, conscious teasing. The Ring has become like Satan, promising the world to Jesus in the desert. With both Satan and the Ring, the promise is something that they cannot deliver. Were anyone to try to use the Ring to their own ends, it would consume them, as Galadriel and Gandalf know, and as both Gollum and Isildur's fates are testimony to.

Does the Jackson films' alteration of the nature of the Enemy alter the nature of what is being fought against in Tolkien's original work? No. The struggle is still the same: it is still a matter of the characters' moral fibre. With the sole exception of Faramir, the same characters still react in the same way to the Ring's temptation, and the change to Faramir's reaction has already been explained as one of dramatic necessity. The fight between the orcs at the Tower of Cirith Ungol over Frodo's mithril coat remains indicative of what would happen to creatures with stronger wills when confronted by the possibility of possessing the Ring. Boromir is a man of noble spirit – something that is made clearer in the Extended Edition of Peter Jackson's *The Two Towers* – but the temptation is too much, and he tries to take the Ring from Frodo by force, just as Shagrat and Gorbag come to blows over Frodo's mithril-coat. Yet Boromir is not a bad man any more than the fact that, in the end, Frodo is unable to resist the Ring's temptation makes Frodo a bad hobbit. It is simply that the Ring is, as Gandalf explains at the Council of Elrond, 'altogether evil'. As anyone who has read Milton's *Paradise Lost* will be aware, absolute evil, whether it is in the form of a circle of metal or Satan himself, is an attractive and compelling thing indeed.

The reason why it must have seemed necessary to make the Ring's allure more explicit was Christianity. Tolkien's story is not, as he repeatedly tried to make clear, an allegory. It is a parable. Its message is, though not exclusively, primarily a Christian one, taken from the Gospels of Matthew and Luke as Jesus spends forty days and forty nights fasting in the wilderness while being tempted by the devil. According to 'Appendix B' of *The Lord of the Rings*, Frodo and Sam spend only twenty-nine days in the wilderness (the Fellowship breaks on 26 February, a month that had thirty days in Middle-earth, and the Ring is destroyed on 25 March), but the symbolism of the temptation in barren lands is clear. The fact that the Fellowship leaves Rivendell on 25 December and that the Ring is destroyed on 25 March (the day of the Annunciation, when Mary was informed that she would be the mother of God) further underlines the Christian significance of their journey. Tolkien was, after all, a committed Catholic. His faith did creep into his work, even if not so explicitly as it does in the *Narnia* books of his close friend CS Lewis (whose lapsed and indistinct Christianity was awakened and reinvigorated through discussions with Tolkien himself).

Far fewer people are committed Christians in the early part of the twenty-first century than were in the 1950s, so the significance of the parable needs underscoring. By avoiding the obvious course of making Sauron more explicitly Satan (which would not, in any case, be faithful to that character's status as conceived by Tolkien), Jackson, Walsh and Boyens opted for the more subtle approach of using the Ring as a Satan substitute. In so doing, they heighten what was seemingly part of Tolkien's original intention by making the attempts of Frodo to resist the Ring's temptation more closely analogous to Christ's attempts to resist the devil's. But, most importantly, they do not do this obviously. After all, if Tolkien chose not to use his book to evangelise, why should Jackson, Walsh and Boyens? A far more subtle approach gets the point across more effectively than an obvious and explicit Christian allegory could ever do.

THE BATTLE OF THE PELENNOR FIELDS: There are three principal pitched battle sequences in Jackson's *The Lord of the Rings* that are taken directly from the book – The Battle of Helm's Deep, The Battle of the Pelennor Fields, and the battle before the Black Gates of Mordor. Only the last of these ends in the same way as Tolkien wrote it.

Tolkien's battles are, perhaps due to his experiences during the utterly chaotic and senseless Battle of the Somme in 1916, practically impossible to follow. The action is frenzied and confusing, and, as such, is probably a fairly accurate approximation of what it feels like to be in the frontlines. A by-product of this is that, when the vastly outnumbered forces of men at both

Helm's Deep and the Pelennor Fields emerge victorious, the reader is left wondering how this could possibly happen.

At Helm's Deep (Book III, Chapter VII), the men of Rohan are, as in the films, largely either too old or too young to be much use. The orcs are a vast mass of vicious destruction, intent only on their goal of killing everyone within the walls of the fortification. In the book, Théoden and Aragorn charge out from the Hornburg in a serious attempt to rout the orcs, despite being massively outnumbered, and succeed. They are not expecting any reinforcements – Gandalf has gone off on an errand, but where he is going is unclear, and he does not specify how long it will take him to return.

In the Jackson films, Gandalf is expressly setting off to get help, and even specifies a precise hour at which he will return – 'at dawn on the morning of the fifth day'. Just before he suggests riding out in the Jackson films, Aragorn glances up at a window high overhead. The sun is rising. The hour has come when Gandalf has promised to return. Aragorn is not suggesting riding out in a last, desperate effort to win, with little chance of success; he has faith that Gandalf will keep his promise to come to their aid. Whereas in the book Gandalf does arrive with a thousand foot soldiers, they do little, as the orcs are already routed by the time they appear. In the book, Gandalf has also informed Treebeard of the plight of the Rohirrim, and the trees from Fangorn have also come down to dispose of the orcs (a scene restored to the Extended Edition DVD). But the trees have not yet attacked either. The Battle of Helm's Deep is won solely by the men who were besieged. This is somewhat unlikely. Jackson, by setting up the idea that reinforcements are on the way, introducing the elves as a decent fighting force who significantly delay the advance of the orc army (see **HELM'S DEEP** in **The Two Towers**), and having the battle won by the charge of Gandalf and Éomer and their men, rather than by that of Théoden and Aragorn and theirs alone, makes the victory significantly more plausible, as well as visually satisfying.

A similar problem exists with the Battle of the Pelennor Fields (Book V, Chapters IV and VI). The defenders of Minas Tirith are vastly outnumbered, and have no hope of victory. Denethor's reaction on seeing the army before the city, though cowardly, seems entirely reasonable given the circumstances. The arrival of the Rohirrim momentarily seems to alter the course of the battle, but the Nazgûl and the Witch King soon shift the advantage back to the forces of Mordor. In the book, Aragorn does, as in the film, arrive by captured Corsair ship to save the day at the last minute, but the strength of his forces is unclear and they are, in any case, just men. Even though the Witch King has been destroyed, they would not be much use against the rest of the Nazgûl or, for that matter, any more effective against the trolls and *mûmakil* (or Oliphaunts in the Jackson version) than those men who had already nearly been defeated at the gates of the city.

In the book, after setting off through the Paths of the Dead and picking up the undead army (as he does in the films), Aragorn liberates the southern parts of Gondor (unseen and unmentioned in the films – see **HELM'S DEEP** in **The Two Towers**) from Sauron's forces, and gathers a new army from there to save Minas Tirith. He tells the Army of the Dead that they have fulfilled their oath and can be at peace long before he gets to the Pelennor Fields. Furthermore, all of this is only told later on – it is not recounted by Tolkien as if these events have any particular significance.

Gimli's suggestion that Aragorn is foolish to let the Army of the Dead go before the war is won is an acknowledgement of this change in the Jackson version of the battle. The scene of the undead soldiers sweeping across the water in a misty mass, and swarming like ants over the forces besieging Minas Tirith, is a very cool one. It would have been an utter waste to have their part in the war take place entirely off-screen, even though this would have been more faithful to the book. In terms of sheer believability (ignoring the fact that an undead army is hardly believable – it is, after all, a film with elves and wizards), Aragorn's arrival with a literally unstoppable army, a force that only he can fight back against, makes the comprehensive victory of the men of Gondor entirely feasible. Who would you rather have on your side in a fight – a man of flesh and blood who can easily be killed, or an ethereal, invulnerable soldier? Anything else would have rendered the whole 'Paths of the Dead' sequence irrelevant, and meant that another excuse would have to be found for Aragorn to abandon the Rohirrim. Hence the change.

Of course, there is a major problem with the claim that Jackson's versions of the battles are more plausible. In *The Fellowship of the Ring*, orcs swarm like cockroaches over the walls and ceilings in the Mines of Moria. If they can scale walls so easily in the Mines, why do the walls of Helm's Deep and

Minas Tirith prove so much of a problem for them? But, to be honest, both battle sequences are visual feasts – pure cinema – and that is all that really matters.

FATHERHOOD: The concept of fatherhood is a subtle theme in *The Lord of the Rings*, and it is easy to miss. It has already been noted that the two principle characters, Aragorn and Frodo, never knew their fathers, and that Tolkien himself lost his father at a very early age (see STRIDER in The Fellowship of the Ring). But in the Jackson films the idea of paternal relationships and duty becomes far more important – not least through Aragorn's fears that it is thanks to his paternal inheritance that he might not be up to the task that fate has allotted him (see ISILDUR'S HEIR in The Two Towers). There are two principal father figures in the story – Bilbo and Gandalf – and both have a great deal of influence on Frodo's personality and decisions; there are also four *actual* fathers – Elrond, Théoden, Denethor and Sam.

Thanks to the alterations to the character, Sam's relationship to Frodo becomes, in the films, a protective, almost paternal one. Frodo is not Sam's 'master', but his friend (see SAM 2 in The Two Towers). But as Frodo gets weaker and weaker, Sam becomes increasingly protective of him. He repeatedly makes clear his intent to look after his friend; he deprives himself of food and sleep so that Frodo can have more; he protects him from danger when Shelob and Gollum attack, and rescues him from the orcs at Cirith Ungol; he worries about him and fears for him to the extent that Sam is willing to put his own life at risk to save Frodo's; he even picks Frodo up and carries him when he has no strength left. His selflessness is not so much that of a friend as that of a worried parent who would do anything in their power to protect their vulnerable child. Sean Astin is the only one of the films' four principal hobbits who was an actual father at the time of filming and has said that he brought this experience to bear in his performance. The fact that Astin – is physically more prepossessing than the other hobbits adds to the feeling of paternal authority created by his performance.

At the very end of the film, Sam has his own children – and he is evidently a very loving father. It is partly because Sam now has his own children to look after that Frodo feels that it is time for him to leave. If Frodo stays, he knows that Sam's paternal instincts would be split between him and Sam's real family.

Frodo's decision to depart for the West is not just a 'selfish' desire to be at peace, but also a final selfless desire to help his most loyal friend move on from the hardships they have both endured, and settle into a normal life that Frodo knows can never be his ('the Shire has been saved, Sam, but not for me').

The other three fathers in the films do not have so happy a family life; nor are they so clear about what their responsibilities to their children are. All three experience, during the course of the films, the loss of a child. Théoden loses his only son, Théodred, during the course of his possession by Saruman (see **THÉODEN** in **The Two Towers**); Denethor loses Boromir and, he believes, Faramir (see **THE STEWARD**) and Elrond loses Arwen through her decision to become mortal (see **ARAGORN AND ARWEN** in **The Two Towers**). All three react very differently.

Théoden's line, 'no parent should live to bury their own child' is perhaps the most moving in the entire film trilogy; it is also at the heart of the movies' exploration of the nature of family and duty. Théoden and Denethor both discover that they have lost a son while their attentions were diverted elsewhere – Théoden's by Saruman's possession, Denethor by the preparations for war. Both of them react with abject, consuming grief and despair. Both also see the death of their heir as the harbinger of the end of days as well as the end of their line (Denethor hardly acknowledges Faramir as his offspring until he too seems near death). Théoden's grief leads him to retreat to Helm's Deep in a desperate attempt to survive a war he now sees no hope of, or point in, surviving; Denethor's grief sends him mad, and leads him to abandon another, essentially paternal responsibility – the defence of the city which is in his charge.

Théoden is presented as a better man than Denethor largely because, even in the midst of his despair, he does not forget his duty to his people. Denethor not only neglects his duties, but he also causes panic by advising the people of Minas Tirith to flee the city; in his grief he also neglects his remaining son, resenting the fact that he lives in the place of the favoured child, and sending him to his near-certain death.

Denethor neglects to think of what is best for his remaining son; Elrond reacts in a similar way on contemplating the possibility that Arwen might give up her immortality. For Arwen to choose a mortal life is, for Elrond, much the same as Théoden or Denethor's discovery that one of their children has *actually* died.

The thought of his daughter's death consumes Elrond – when he tells her that 'when I look into your future I can see only death' he is not lying. He can foresee her death because death is inevitable for any mortal, and for him that is by far the most important consideration. When Arwen has her own vision, and sees that she and Aragorn would have a son were she to stay, she confronts her father to ask why he did not tell her. The reason is simple – for him, the thought of losing her was more painful than any happiness he might feel at the thought of her having a child, so much so that it metaphorically – and perhaps literally – clouds his vision.

The reactions of Denethor, Théoden and Elrond on contemplating their children's deaths are all initially selfish. Denethor and Théoden worry about the end of their houses; Elrond worries about the grief he will experience on losing Arwen.

The message further underscores one of Tolkien's key concepts – the happiness of others should be put before your own. Just as Frodo puts the concerns of the whole of Middle-earth before his own interests, just as Aragorn puts his duty before his desires, and just as Sam goes without so that Frodo can fulfil his mission, Théoden and Elrond come to see that their own interests are not in the best interests of others. The message is one of Christian utilitarianism – a combination of the Bible's 'love thy neighbour' and social theorist Jeremy Bentham's 'it is the greatest happiness of the greatest number that is the measure of right and wrong'.

ÉOWYN: The expansion of Éowyn's character in the second film serves to make her far more memorable than she is in the book. She not only has a far greater physical presence, but she is also shown practising swordplay (preparing the audience for her confrontation with the Witch King of Angmar), she is given expository dialogue that belongs to Éomer or Théoden in the book, and she has a far more apparent romantic interest in Aragorn.

It seems highly probable that the principle reason for expanding the role of Éowyn was to provide the last two films in the trilogy with a prominent female character. Without Éowyn, the only women with speaking roles who would appear on screen would be Arwen and Galadriel, as in the first film. But after the Fellowship leaves Rivendell and then Lothlorien, neither of these characters is physically present with them, and they appear only in visions or flashbacks.

This was part of the reason for the initially considered idea of having Arwen fight alongside Aragorn at Helm's Deep (see **ARWEN** in **The Fellowship of the Ring**). It was eventually decided that Arwen served the films' purposes far better by remaining a soft and beautiful, ethereal figure, than to turn her into 'Xena, Warrior Princess'. This makes sense – as the elves, and especially Arwen, are presented as ideals, to have her muddy herself by getting involved in physical conflict would diminish her significance. As it is, by keeping her in flashbacks alone, she becomes more closely identified with Aragorn's desires, and with the values for which he is fighting. When he thinks of Arwen, he remembers what it is he has to do, and becomes more resolute (see **ARAGORN AND ARWEN** in **The Two Towers**), just as Frodo's resolve is hardened by his memories of his home (see **THE SHIRE** in **The Fellowship of the Ring**).

Making Éowyn the 'action heroine' of the films is entirely consistent with Tolkien's character; making Arwen the 'love interest' is equally consistent with his version of her. Indeed, in the book, practically the only thing Éowyn does is turn up and kill the Witch King. This may well be an impressive achievement, but it seems to come largely out of the blue, like so many of the unexpected victories in Tolkien's battles (see **THE BATTLE OF THE PELENNOR FIELDS**). The Witch King has also not received much build up before this point.

Thanks to this lack of build up in the book, it seems strange that Jackson and his team did not decide to alter this scene in what must have been a very tempting way – by replacing the Witch King with Sauron on the battlefield. As noted (see **PROLOGUE**), it seems odd to show Sauron in physical form at the very start of the trilogy, especially taking on a vast army almost single-handed, and then not have him return for the final showdown. There is an explanation for this (see **THE RING**), but, in terms of regular film tradition, you do not set up a major villain, showing him right at the start of your story, and then not have him appear again at the end. It would have been utterly unfaithful to the book, but it must have seemed a major temptation to simply have Éowyn kill one of the other Nazgûl (who are also supposedly impossible to kill), and have Sauron himself charging around the battlefield causing chaos, before being forced to withdraw as his army is massacred by the arrival of Aragorn and the Army of the Dead. The fact that Jackson chose not to opt for this obvious Hollywood bastardisation of the original text is only to his credit.

It is also worth noting that Éowyn is far more prominent during Théoden's death scene in the Jackson films. In the book, the king's final words are spoken to Merry, as Éowyn has been knocked unconscious in the act of killing the Witch King. Théoden dies without knowing that she saved him. In the film, the final exchange between the king and his niece is, in a neat parody/homage to Tolkien's habit of making reference to the Anglo-Saxon epics from which his work was descended, taken from the final film of another three-part movie epic that has a similar title to the last part of *The Lord of the Rings*. Éowyn: 'I have to save you.' Théoden: 'You already have.' This is the last exchange between Luke Skywalker and his father, Darth Vader, in *Return of the Jedi* (Richard Marquand, 1983). Besides being a good but subtle in-joke, this also makes for a very satisfying conclusion to Théoden's storyline (see **THÉODEN** in **The Two Towers**) – he has been redeemed.

What is less obviously present in the books, however, is the idea of Éowyn loving Aragorn. The idea is there, certainly (and is explored to some extent in Book VI, Chapter V), but it is embryonic, as with so many of the ideas Tolkien included within his book. The idea is expanded to provide yet more doubt about what the future holds for Aragorn. In a flashback in *The Two Towers*, it is revealed that he has told Arwen that she should be with her people; the introduction of Éowyn's interest in him suggests to an audience unfamiliar with the book that he might have found himself a new love (or perhaps there might be some kind of love triangle to come). But as soon as this plot strand is introduced, Aragorn, as Viggo Mortensen plays him, seems rather to pity her for her interest in him than show any sign of reciprocation. Éowyn's love will get her nowhere.

Strangely, however, despite these expansions of Éowyn's character, the third film then denies her the destiny that she has in the book; she becomes a bigger, more relevant, more noticeable character but without a noticeable endpoint (see **THE STEWARD**).

ÉOMER: In the book, Éomer becomes King of Rohan after his Uncle Théoden's death. This is because he is his uncle's heir following the death of his cousin, Théoden's only child, and

Rohan is, while subservient to Gondor, a separate kingdom with its own succession.

In the early twenty-first century, fewer people are aware of the idea that a king does not need a coronation to become monarch – the concept of 'The King is dead, long live the King' is an especially alien one to those parts of the world which do not have monarchies. In early 1950s Britain, just after the death of King George VI, no one would have needed reminding of this. Legally and constitutionally, the reign of the present Queen, Elizabeth II, began the moment her father died on 6 February 1952, even though her coronation did not take place until 2 June 1953.

In the book, Théoden explicitly names Éomer as his heir and, after Aragorn's coronation as King of Gondor, Éomer returns to Rohan to rule as king there. For Tolkien to make explicit what anyone reading the books in the 1950s would not have needed to be told would suggest that he wanted to maintain the idea that Aragorn was the 'King of Kings' (see **STRIDER** in **The Fellowship of the Ring**). In less religious terms, it is suggested that Aragorn is rather like a feudal overlord to Rohan, but Éomer is still King of Rohan in his own right. On screen, the implication seems to be that Aragorn is the King of all men, including those of Rohan, as Éomer is never named heir.

Therefore, in Jackson's version, the second 'the' in the title seems to mean that Aragorn is *the* King – the *only* King. This seems like a watering-down of the Aragorn as Christ parallels, which had previously been played up with the introduction of the invented death and resurrection sequence in *The Two Towers*. (Although it could be argued that Christ is also *the* King, this is not so powerful a parallel as making Aragorn the 'King of Kings' as he is in the book.) However, this is not the only (and is probably the most minor) example in the films where certain ideas fail to be resolved.

THE STEWARD: It can only be assumed that the limitations of time available for editing the picture, rather than screentime available, played a part in some decisions. Jackson's *The Return of the King* fails to clear up a number of the plot threads left over from the previous two films/the book, but by far the most serious is the failure to provide a satisfactory conclusion to Faramir's story.

On the page, Faramir ends up marrying Éowyn, who falls in love with him while they are both recovering from their wounds in Minas Tirith (Book VI, Chapter V). After fulfilling his duties as Steward (which he becomes thanks to Gondor's principles of heredity – see ÉOMER) and handing over the rule of Gondor at Aragorn's titular return, Faramir is given the title 'Prince of Ithilien' and set to rule the lands to the east of Osgiliath, in which he met Frodo. Though Faramir and Éowyn are standing together at Aragorn's coronation there is little indication of any potential relationship between them on screen.

The lack of this conclusion renders three separate story-arcs largely pointless. By the end of *The Two Towers*, Faramir has fulfilled his basic plot function – he has met Frodo, recognised the urgency of his quest, and sent him on his way – demonstrating that not *all* men are evil, and that it is possible to overcome the Ring's temptation. He has given Frodo a brief bit of hope that he will also manage to overcome temptation, just as his brother earlier gave Frodo the fear that no one could be trusted, making him abandon the rest of the Fellowship (see **BOROMIR** in **The Fellowship of the Ring**).

The introduction of Denethor in both the book and the film gives Faramir some role in the final stages of the story. Denethor is altered here from a ruler who has gone mad due to the malign influence of Sauron, transmitted through the palantir he possesses, to one who is mad due to grief and fear (see **FATHERHOOD**). In the book, Denethor has a purpose within the thematic whole in and of himself – he is another indication of the evil that is being faced, of the lack of will of men, and of the sheer power that the good people of Middle-earth are facing. His corruption by Sauron when, as is made clear, Gandalf once treated him as an equal thanks to his wisdom and strength of will, demonstrates very clearly how even the mighty can be corrupted. It also demonstrates that Gandalf was very sensible to hide the palantir Pippin found at Isengard (through which Sauron saw him, and assumed him to be the halfling Ringbearer that he has been seeking). Furthermore, Denethor's madness underscores the regal strength of will possessed by Aragorn, as in the book he uses the Isengard palantir to directly challenge Sauron, testing his will against the Enemy, and pretending that he, not Frodo, has the Ring in an attempt to keep Sauron's Eye fixed away from Mordor. This in turn makes the distraction of the march on Mordor a more believable one, as Sauron now believes that he will have to kill Aragorn to get his Ring back.

In the Jackson film, however, Denethor exists purely to put Faramir's life at risk, and to provide Gandalf with a reason for taking charge at Minas Tirith. But Gandalf is a well-known and powerful wizard with many lifetimes' experience – he would have been an obvious choice to take charge anyway. Furthermore, with the lack of a conclusion to Faramir's storyline, the reason for Gandalf's decision to take time out to charge all the way across the city in the middle of a major battle in which Gandalf is commander-in-chief seems to have vanished completely.

Yes, Faramir is a good man, and yes, he is worth saving, but Gandalf's energies would arguably be better spent organising the defence of Gondor. On screen, he seems to put one life above many for no real reason or reward, even though he seems to be aware that by going to save Faramir many other lives may be lost. It makes absolutely no sense within the context of the otherwise utilitarian motivations of the members of the Fellowship (see **THE BATTLE OF THE PELENNOR FIELDS**). In the book, Gandalf's decision to save Faramir is justified by his subsequent marriage, and by his ability to hand Gondor over to its new King as ceremony would dictate – it makes the subsequent coronation that much more legitimate than it would be had there not been a Steward to officially recognise the King. Here, Faramir neither hands Gondor to Aragorn nor marries Éowyn. It might be harsh, but Faramir may as well have died – that way Gandalf might have been able to get on to the battlefield and save Théoden, as well as many other men, from the Witch King.

In the Jackson films, both the Denethor and Faramir characters could arguably be jettisoned from the final film without loss. Regardless, the lack of any conclusion to the Faramir story-arc means that, on screen, the expansion of Éowyn's character seems to be entirely so there is a notable female character in *The Two Towers* (see **ÉOWYN**). While this is not an ignoble motivation in itself, it is an odd thing to begin and then not follow through. When the viewer considers that perhaps the marriage between Éowyn and Faramir is also part of the reason for the expansion of both their roles in the Jackson version of *The Two Towers* (Éowyn wants to be loved and Faramir wants to be respected), the decision to remove all references to it looks like one motivated entirely by time constraints. While this is understandable up to a point, it might also be considered odd that a film of this length (which contains many *longeurs* and frequent long-winded whimsical sequences) could not be edited in a way that would make it possible to include information about the eventual fates of all of its leading characters.

THE ROAD GOES EVER ON AND ON: Shooting an adaptation of *The Lord of the Rings* as one long production and then editing it as three separate films has many advantages. Certainly after the success of *The Fellowship of the Ring*, nobody was worried about whether the other two films would be entertaining, well acted, well shot and well made (if slightly scrappily edited). Audiences knew that they would, with more truth than with any series in film history, really be watching another part of one film rather than a sequel with strong continuity and thematic links to an original.

What may be less obvious is that there is one, very real, disadvantage. This is only made greater by the issuing of the Extended Editions on DVD, which were also, after the release of the first one, clearly going to be a great commercial success.

It has been commented on earlier that the Gollum 'Secret Origin' scene was shot for *The Fellowship of the Ring*, then positioned in *The Two Towers*, then cut from that film (Jackson intimates exactly where from in his commentary on the Extended Edition) before being put into the theatrical *The Return of the King*. What this perhaps indicates is a willingness to 'put off' difficult decisions to the third and final film, the last one the co-writers and director would have to deal with. In support of this inference is the cutting of the final Saruman scene from *The Return of the King* – to which there was some considerable public furore. The final Saruman scene now appears only in the DVD extended cut of the film. But it had previously been cut from the theatrical version of *The Two Towers* before being cut again from the extended version of that film. We are talking about a sequence that had been removed for being too difficult to include *on no less than three occasions*.

What this perhaps indicates is that when it got to *The Return of the King* the director and his team began prevaricating again, this time deferring decisions to the final, final version of the last film. It is hard to say for certain. What is certain is that if there was to be no 'Extended Edition' then scenes such as the Saruman/Wormtongue sequence and the final fates of Éomer, Éowyn and Faramir would have been *made* to fit – simply because there would be nowhere else for them to go. Certainly, their absence from the theatrical cut is palpable.

The two authors of this book differ greatly in their opinion of the Extended Editions. It is a very strongly held opinion for one of us that the extended version of *The Fellowship of the Ring* adds nothing in plot or character terms to the theatrical cut. It adds colour and additional elements of world-building, but adds nothing to our understanding of the plot, only to the world in which the plot unfolds. The other of us feels that the extended *Fellowship* is better paced, more affectionate, and full of additional details that bring the audience fully into the world of the films. It is ultimately, for him, a better version of the film.

The extended version of *The Two Towers* is very different to that of its predecessor. The longer version expands upon Faramir, Boromir and Éowyn's characters (among others) considerably, and makes the survival of those at Helm's Deep more plausible in the process but (and this is crucial) it is still fortunate that the absence of these elements from the theatrical cut does not make it seem half-empty. However, one scene in particular – that in which Faramir remembers his close relationship with his brother Boromir – introduces new elements to the mix that are then developed in *The Return of the King*, and that aid the understanding of aspects of that film. Indeed, thanks to the problems with the Denethor/Faramir storyline in the theatrical cut of *The Return of the King*, without this additional scene a lot of the tension between these two characters seems to be even more unjustified than it already is. (One of us is also of the opinion that the additions in the extended version here, though adding character and plot details that aid the understanding of the audience, make the film far slower and the disparate storylines far less clearly interwoven than they are in the theatrical cut.)

With *The Return of the King*, there are things that seem to be absent, even to those unfamiliar with the book. By not telling the audience what happened to Saruman, Éomer, Éowyn and Faramir (let alone Legolas and Gimli, in whom the audience has been encouraged to invest much in but who just disappear – see **THE FELLOWSHIP**), the film-makers deny the audience a full sense of catharsis, and leave them feeling that they are missing some part of the story. The theatrical cut of *The Return of the King* seems to withhold information about characters in whom even the most general, least committed audience member is interested.

The Return of the King is undoubtedly a fine motion picture, but it does seem to have been edited with attention to the wishes of the fans, rather than the need of the general viewer for plot coherence. That the plot-relevant details concerning the above characters should be left until the 'Extended Edition' (which Peter Jackson has repeatedly described as 'For the fans'), rather than swapping them with other material more concerned with world-building than plot, seems an odd decision. After all, as some reviewers did point out at the time, is it really necessary to have a sequence consisting solely of the Fellowship laughing as the hobbits bounce up and down on a bed or dance on a table? Would this screentime not have been better used by showing the audience what happened to Faramir? Arguments that it would have been impossible to present so many complex and interwoven storylines into such a short space of time do not stand up to even vague consideration. For example, *The Godfather* (Francis Ford Coppola, 1972) successfully condenses a novel roughly half the length of *The Lord of the Rings* into a very slow moving and extremely complex 178-minute film. That is less than a third of the running time of the combined Jackson trilogy and the adaptation does not suffer any loss of complexity of character, plot or theme.

The Return of the King not only seems like a sequel to a cut of its predecessor that the majority of its paying audience will not have seen, it also seems to have been cut to theatrically exhibitable length using different criteria. At times *The Return of the King* feels not unlike David Lynch's film version of Frank Herbert's *Dune* (1984), another attempt to film a much-loved book. *Dune* occasionally seems to implicitly ask its audience to fill in the gaps in the plot using their knowledge of the book, or at least assumes that they can do so. There is also, incidentally, an 'Extended Edition' of *Dune*, albeit one which its director later disowned. Lynch did, however, initially plan a five-hour version of the film, but did not shoot enough footage. Pirated rough-cuts, made up with storyboards, voiceovers and studio shots, of what was supposedly Lynch's intention for this 'Extended Extended Edition' do exist, although they are nearly impossible to track down.

Should Peter Jackson ever decide to do an 'Extended Extended Edition' of the *Lord of the Rings* films, he has more than enough footage to make this possible and there are certainly enough people prepared to pay for it. Watch this space.

TOLKIEN AND OSCAR

The 'clean sweep' (to quote presenter Steven Spielberg) that *The Lord of the Rings: The Return of the King* achieved on 29 February 2004 by converting eleven Oscar nominations into eleven statuettes was unparalleled in Hollywood history. In addition to this, the 76th Academy Awards came within days of the announcement that the film had become one of less than half a dozen films in history to take $1 billion at the international box office. This second fact speaks for itself in terms of the movie's colossal success; the first perhaps requires putting more into context.

Only two other films have won eleven Oscars: *Ben-Hur* (William Wyler, 1959) won eleven from twelve nominations; *Titanic* (James Cameron, 1997) won eleven from fourteen. *The Godfather* (Francis Ford Coppola, 1972) was nominated for eleven but won only three. (*Titanic* is, coincidentally, another hugely profitable, very lengthy film made across a protracted shoot outside North America and which provoked – in some of its audience – a reaction more akin to devotion than simple film appreciation.) It is also worth noting that no motion picture has ever won twelve or more Academy Awards. *The Lord of the Rings: The Return of the King* is thus, in Oscar terms at least, officially one of the three 'best' films in cinema history.

There was some considerable acknowledgement throughout the 2004 ceremony, from presenters and nominees alike, that while the awards were ostensibly being given to, and in recognition of, the third and final film in the series, they were also intended to celebrate and highlight the achievement of Peter Jackson and his team in producing the entire trilogy. It had long been assumed by both the series' fans and industry watchers that the relatively small number of (entirely technical) awards handed out to the first two pictures was down to the Academy's members collectively deciding that the third and final film would reap the benefits of the effort put into all three.

This is in spite of, perhaps implicitly in defiance of, the rules of the Academy of Motion Picture Arts and Sciences. These are quite clear that, with the exception of 'Lifetime Achievement' and 'Special' awards (such as the Irving J Thalberg award), Academy Awards are meant to be considered, voted for and presented on the basis of individual achievement in individual films. In practice, of course, actors regularly receive awards late in life either in joint recognition of an individual stellar performance and a whole body of work (notably Walter Huston in *The Treasure of the Sierra Madre*, 1949 or Sean Penn in *Mystic River*, 2003), or sometimes just for a previous body of work, their current nomination seemingly being little more than an excuse (for example, John Wayne for *True Grit*, 1969, Jack Palance for *City Slickers*, 1991, Al Pacino for *Scent of a Woman*, 1992). Key figures as diverse as Randy Newman, Jerry Goldsmith, Akira Kurosawa and Walter Murch have won Oscars due to the fact that it suddenly became obvious that they have never received one before (it is to be hoped the same fate awaits Martin Scorsese). Even some people not intimately involved in the movies, such as Bob Dylan, have won Oscars for their sheer stature in popular culture. Many actors-turned-directors (Ron Howard, Mel Gibson, Robert Redford, Clint Eastwood) have won Best Director at least partially because of their recognition factor over other, faceless, behind-the-camera nominees.

The Academy Awards have often seemed to be voted for by people who are prepared to be flexible with the ostensibly hard and fast specifics of the Academy's own rules; the success of *The Lord of the Rings: the Return of the King* at the 2004 ceremony should be seen in this context. Academy members were not just voting for the final part of the trilogy – they were voting for the entire trilogy.

The Lord of the Rings: The Fellowship of the Ring was, in the 2002 ceremony, nominated for thirteen Academy Awards – the second highest number of nominations ever. These were for Best Picture, Best Director, Actor in a Supporting Role (for Ian McKellen), Screenplay, Art Direction, Cinematography, Costume Design, Film Editing, Make-Up, Music (Score), Music (Song), Sound and Visual Effects. It only converted four of those into actual awards. These were Cinematography for Director of Photography Andrew Lesnie, Visual Effects for WETA Digital, Music (Score) for Howard Shore and Make-Up for Richard Taylor.

This ratio of nominations to Awards compares reasonably favourably with that achieved by the original *Star Wars* (George Lucas, 1977) – easily the most appropriate point of comparison for Jackson's trilogy generally and its first film in particular. *Star Wars* was nominated for ten Oscars. These were Best Picture, Best Director, Screenplay, Actor in a Supporting Role (for Alec Guinness), Costumes, Film Editing, Sound, Visual Effects, Art Direction and Music (Score). It won six – for John Mollo's costumes, John Williams's music, Lucasfilm's editing team, ILM's Special Effects, Don MacDougall's Sound Editing and John Barry's sets. The Academy also invented, on the spot, an Oscar for 'Sound Creation' for Ben Burtt, recognising that no suitable category existed to reward his work. The award would later become as much of a staple of the Oscars as other technical awards.

For both films, the most prestigious categories in which they lost out were Best Picture, Screenplay and Director and a Supporting Actor Award for an ageing knight of the British theatre in a mysterious and avuncular role. *The Fellowship of the Ring* lost out to *A Beautiful Mind* (Ron Howard, 2001), the story of one man's struggle against invincible odds, which will likely soon be forgotten; *Star Wars* at least had the dignity of losing to *Annie Hall* (Woody Allen, 1977), a film still widely revered after more than 25 years.

Where *The Lord of the Rings* films easily trumped the *Star Wars* series was in continuing to be nominated for the more prestigious awards for later instalments. Whereas the later *Star Wars* films would only pick up technical awards, they would also only be *nominated* for technical awards. *The Lord of the Rings: The Two Towers* was nominated (for the 2003 ceremony) for six including, once again, Best Picture. This made it only the second sequel in history to be nominated for Best Picture and the first to be nominated for such when its predecessor did not win the award. (The previous Best Picture-nominated, and winning, sequel was *The Godfather Part II*, arguably the best American film ever made.) *The Two Towers* missed out on Best Picture in what was a strong field but to what was both the least interesting and least original contender, *Chicago* (Rob Marshall, 2002); the Directing gong went to movie veteran Roman Polanski for the excellent *The Pianist*.

The Two Towers won two Oscars: Special Effects for WETA (again) and Sound Editing for Ethan Van Der Ryan and Michael Hopkins. The other nominations were Sound Creation, Film Editing and Art Direction. *The Empire Strikes Back* (Irvin Kershner, 1980) also won Sound Editing and Special Effects but was additionally nominated only for Music (Score) and Art Direction – and the people involved in those two departments had already won on the original *Star Wars*.

The Lord of the Rings series thus seemed to be following the pattern on Best Picture set by not only *Star Wars*, but also other hugely popular, successful and ultimately beloved popcorn-successes-turned-film series. (*Raiders of the Lost Ark* (Steven Spielberg, 1981) was nominated for Best Picture and other prestigious Oscars, while its sequels only got technical nods; the same goes for *Jaws* (Steven Spielberg, 1975) and *Jurassic Park* (Steven Spielberg, 1993). *Psycho* (Alfred Hitchcock, 1960) is another valid comparison.) Its success in February 2004 over-turned this utterly. It would also have overturned *The Godfather Part II*'s record of being the only sequel to win the most prestigious award that it could qualify for had not *The Barbarian Invasions* (Denys Arcand, 2003), the sequel to his own *The Decline of the American Empire* (1986), not done so an hour or so earlier by winning Best Foreign Language Film.

Strangely the single set of awards in which none of the *Lord of the Rings* films won anything is the one that is pretty much universally acknowledged to be consistently above any kind of reproach: the acting. This can, in part, be put down to the ensemble nature of the production's cast (on the end credits of the films, as on many theatre bills, the speaking cast are listed in alphabetical order regardless of the scale of their involvement). In a film with so many characters, who would qualify as the lead? Elijah Wood? Viggo Mortensen? Sean Astin? Andy Serkis? (Following the precedent of the 2003 awards, in which Nicole

Kidman was nominated as Best Actress for *The Hours* despite being onscreen for significantly less time than Julianne Moore, who was nominated as Best Supporting Actress for the same film, such confusion is likely to become increasingly common.)

If *The Lord of the Rings* is a trilogy of movies then it won seventeen Oscars out of a possible thirty, as compared to *The Godfather*'s nine out of twenty-eight and the 'imperial' *Star Wars* trilogy's ten out of twenty. If *The Lord of the Rings* (2001–2003) is one film rather than three (a process only as problematic as looking at it as three films rather than one, as it is arguably both and neither) then arguably only thirteen achieved Oscars should count – still more than any other single movie. (In two categories – Make-Up and Music (Score) – it won twice, and in one category – Visual Effects – it won every time so, for the sake of fairness, the duplicates should be deducted for comparisons.) Whichever way one looks at the numbers, they are impressive and unlikely, in the immediate future, to be overturned.

It is also worth noting that *The Lord of the Rings* is the first unashamedly, and unapologetically, fantastical film to win Best Picture – ending the run noted above that includes *Star Wars*, the first *Indiana Jones* and many others that fell at the final hurdle on Oscar night. In a world of popular cinema increasingly dominated by adaptations, fantasy, science-fiction, comic book films, sequels, series and even movies based on theme park rides, Jackson's success may indicate a significant shift in terms of what kinds of movie can win the top Academy Awards.

THE GREY HAVENS: CONCLUSION

There are some fans of *The Lord of the Rings* who routinely claim, when the numerous adaptations of Tolkien's *magnum opus* deviate from the course of his original narrative, that he would have been 'horrified' by what has been done to his story. To hold this view is to misunderstand his attachment to the antics of Frodo and his fellows. Asked about the reaction of his ardent fans from the United States to his books in the late 1960s, Tolkien stated that he was nowhere near as attached to his work as some of his readers appeared to be: 'Many young Americans are involved in the stories in a way that I am not.'

Tolkien, with his creation of Middle-earth, was attempting, essentially, to synthesise a mythology. So, while it may form the bulk of the general public's understanding of the work of Tolkien, the saga of Frodo Baggins's quest to destroy the Ring was, for its creator, but a part of this vast, millennia-spanning work; the history of a world he had created to help him more fully understand the nature of myth and language.

To demonstrate this at its extreme, Tolkien's myth-creation was so extensive that he even devoted time to explaining the (fictional) origins of his story as if they were fact. Part of Tolkien's world-building exercise was the conceit that *The Lord of the Rings* itself was an adaptation of extant material, lost for millennia, then rediscovered (by a mariner named Aelfwine on the 'Lonely Isle' of Tol Eressëa in the far West, who translated it into Anglo-Saxon) and translated into modern English by the author himself. *The Lord of the Rings* is Tolkien's version of material originally preserved within the (fictional) *Red Book of Westmarch*, a chronicle of the end of the Third Age of Middle-earth and written primarily by Bilbo, Frodo and Sam. Additional material supplied from Bilbo's *Translations from the Elvish* provides much of *The Silmarillion*'s history of the earlier ages of the world. So, *The Lord of the Rings* was a translation of a translation of a multiple-author, multiple-source text, much of which was itself translated from other multiple-source, multiple-author texts. For others to then adapt Tolkien's own adaptation would only be natural, and was certainly not something to which the professor would have objected – it was, after all, Tolkien himself who sold the film rights of his book. Subsequent generations have been far more protective of his work than the author was himself.

As a professional scholar of Anglo-Saxon literature, Tolkien was more than aware that one of the primary characteristics of myth is that it evolves, changing in the telling through a grandiose cultural form of Chinese Whispers. His deep understanding of this is apparent in *The Lord of the Rings* itself: for example, members of the Fellowship fear to enter Lothlorien due to the stories of the sorceress who lives within, and later fear Fangorn Forest thanks to stories of its malevolence. Both tales lack substance, we discover, for the sorceress is the beautiful and helpful Galadriel; Fangorn's malevolence is the benign Treebeard. In classical myth, Zeus becomes Jupiter, Aphrodite becomes Venus, Heracles becomes Hercules; some have argued that Odin of the Norse myths is yet another iteration of Zeus/Jupiter (while others have argued he is Hermes/Mercury). These are in turn traceable to other variants in innumerable other cults and religions, from the Aztecs to the Egyptians to the ancient Chinese. Great floods appear in both the Book of Genesis in the Bible and in the Sumerian Epic of Gilgamesh, as well as (through the Atlantis myth) in Plato's *Republic*; variants on 'the Flood' have been identified in cultures as diverse as those of the Australian aboriginals and the ancient Central American Maya. A variant of the flood myth also crops up in 'Appendix A' of *The Lord of the Rings* with the fall of Númenor.

Dr Joseph Campbell (1904–1987) examined these recurring patterns throughout his career and in his book *The Hero With a Thousand Faces* (1938). He argued that all myths had a common root in the 'vision quest' – a cultural motif which, essentially, dwelled in the collective unconsciousness of the human race and predated even language. In short, all myths are based upon a single original root and hark back to some kind of universally understandable primal truth. Therein lies the perennial appeal and popularity of myths, no matter what form they take – be it Frodo's acceptance of his fate or Christ's. Aspects of Campbell's theory have become accepted, by some, as fact, and his arguments relating to storytelling have become, perhaps more through the work of his acolytes than his own, common cultural currency.

Some of these argued cultural links may seem far-fetched, but the fact remains that these and countless other minor distortions shift the specifics, but not the essence or the purpose, of the stories, fables or parables being told. It is this essence, the moral, human and philosophical content, which is the most important aspect of any mythology – indeed, of any religion.

The French intellectual Claude Levi-Strauss examined the nature of myth in depth in his 1958 book *Structural Anthropology*. He argued that myth, unlike poetry, can be translated, paraphrased, expanded, summarised and otherwise significantly altered without losing its basic shape or structure. What is important with myths is neither the wording nor the detail, but the broad story. Tolkien himself knew this, arguing that 'It is possible, I think, to be moved by the power of myth and yet to misunderstand the sensation, to ascribe it wholly to something else that is also present: to metrical art, style, or verbal skill.' All versions of a myth are equally valid, as long as the central moral of the story remains the same, and all add to the understanding of the whole.

Thomas Malory's fifteenth-century *Le Morte D'Arthur* amalgamated aspects of the myth of King Arthur from the twelfth-century versions of Geoffrey of Monmouth's *Historia Regum Brittaniae*, Wace's *Roman de Brut* and Layamon's *Brut*, the thirteenth-century *Le Roman de Lancelot du Lac* and Cistercian *Vulgate Cycle*, and the fourteenth-century *Morte Arthur*, as well as *Sir Gawain and the Green Knight* and many other variants from all over Europe. Since then, innumerable other versions of Camelot, Arthur, the Round Table and the Grail quest have appeared. These include TH White's semi-comic novels of *The Once and Future King* (the first part of which was turned into an animated movie by Disney, *The Sword in the Stone*, 1963); Susan

Cooper's serious children's novels of *The Dark is Rising* series; the realist comedy *Monty Python and the Holy Grail* (1975); and the muddy and bloody *Excalibur* (John Boorman, 1981). This is not to mention the musical version of Joshua Logan's 1967 film *Camelot* (also loosely based on TH White) and the innumerable adaptations of Mark Twain's 1889 satire *A Connecticut Yankee in King Arthur's Court* (the most extreme of which is perhaps Disney's *The Spaceman and King Arthur* (Russ Mayberry, 1979)). At the opposite end of the interpretative scale is *Arthur of the Britons* (1972), Terence Feely's attempt to create a low-key, historically plausible scenario for an Arthurian TV series. It featured Arthur as an Anglo-Celtic solider fending off attacks from Saxons after the departure of the forces of the Pax Romana from the island of Briton. It was a committed, deliberately small-scale attempt to get away from the excesses of many Arthurian interpretations – much the same intention as producer Jerry Bruckheimer had with his *King Arthur* (Antoine Fuqua, 2004).

Malory's text was the first semi-comprehensive version in English and, as such, has endured better than others. But this was itself altered by his publisher and editor (and England's first printer), William Caxton, for its first edition of 1485. In his preface, Caxton summarised what myth meant to him: 'For herein may be seen noble chivalry, courtesy, humanity, friendliness, hardiness, love, friendship, cowardice, murder, hate, virtue, and sin. Do after the good and leave the evil, and it shall bring you to good fame and renown.' This struck a chord at the time – the newly crowned Henry VII, in an attempt to unify England after the bloody Wars of the Roses, named his first-born son Arthur the year after Malory's book was published in an attempt to associate the house of Tudor with the Arthurian legends. His son, Henry VIII, also played on the legend, proudly displaying an old, painted round table that he'd found in a royal castle and which he claimed to be that of legend. (The table is now in the Great Hall at Winchester where it is regarded as a handsome cultural/historical/ propagandist curiosity as well as, presumably, a superbly well- preserved example of medieval English furniture.)

From his writings it is clear that Tolkien hoped that *his* attempt to write myth might also, if not unite a country, at least present some kind of moral code, so that his readers might learn how to 'do after the good and leave the evil'. His professed 'prime motive was the desire of a tale-teller to try his hand at a really long story that would hold the attention of readers, amuse them, delight them, and at times excite them or deeply move them'. But Tolkien was a committed Anglo-Catholic, and his own conception of morality and the nature of mankind, though never obvious, reverberates subtly throughout (see **THE RING** in **The Return of the King** and **STRIDER** in **The Fellowship of the Ring**).

If later generations decided to alter the detail of the tale he had created, either to broaden its appeal or to better 'hold the attention' of its audience, and in the process perpetuate the myth that he had conceived, Tolkien would most likely have been at first embarrassed, and then secretly pleased. What else could more clearly indicate the success his attempts to replicate the mythologies he had been studying than the adoption of them by popular culture? What else could make as clear that he had succeeded in delivering 'that great Northern spirit', which it was his professed aim to revive, to his inheritors? And it was always the *spirit*, not the detail, that Tolkien hoped to resurrect – why else would he have made up an entirely new set of myths of his own when there were already so many perfectly serviceable ones available?

The important consideration for Tolkien on assessing an adaptation of his work would simply have been whether the message of his book remained intact. Were an adaptation to alter the story so that it is Aragorn, at the head of a large army, who destroys the Ring, or worse still uses it to defeat Sauron, Tolkien would likely have been aghast. Quite what the professor would have thought of the Rankin/Bass version of Aragorn in their take on *The Return of the King* one can only guess at, but his relegation to an irrelevant bit-player, who marches on Mordor not as a distraction but in a serious attempt to storm the Black Gates, is hardly true to Tolkien's conception of the character. The Aragorn of the Jackson, Bakshi and BBC versions remains far truer to the original, despite the numerous variations between these three presentations of the character. Tolkien's shocked reaction to the insensitive alterations present in the aborted 1958 film version prove that it was to the *radical* changes that he was most opposed. His preparedness to accept a 'vulgarised' animated version demonstrates that he did not mind changes *per se*.

In Peter Jackson's version of the tale, the broad message remains, for the most part, intact. The concepts of environment-alism, heroism, friendship, loyalty, good and evil are all there, in largely the same forms as in the book. The one alteration of which Tolkien may not have approved is in fact an omission: the Scouring of the Shire. This sequence, according to its author in the Foreword to the second edition, was something he had meant to have in there from the start, though he adapted it as he developed Saruman; it was essential to the book (see **An Unexpected Party**).

Tolkien himself had altered details of the story for the 1966 second edition, just as he rewrote parts of *The Hobbit* in the early 1950s to fit it thematically to its longer, more 'serious' sequel. Equally, his conceit was that, in 'translating' Aelfwine's translations of *The Red Book of Westmarch*, he had altered certain names and characters to better preserve the underlying tone of the world in which the events took place. The hobbits are the principle reader-identity figures, so they were made more 'English', and given English as their mother tongue. The elves have been around longer than the hobbits, and so speak a language that is based primarily on Welsh, a remnant of the tongue of the Celts who inhabited parts of the British Isles before the coming of the 'English', the Anglo-Saxons. Equally, the hobbits can see similarities between their own culture and that of Rohan, so the Rohirrim are given Anglo-Saxon names, and an approximation of Anglo-Saxon as their language – similar yet different to the hobbits' own.

Tolkien did this to ensure that the 'feel' of Middle-earth was as authentically understandable to a mid-twentieth-century English audience as possible. Had he been Italian, Tolkien would perhaps have chosen Greek or Latin as the basis for the 'older' languages of the elves and Rohirrim, in much the way Italian writer, philologist, and Professor of Semiotics Umberto Eco has done in his novels – notably *Baudolino* and *The Name of the Rose*. Eco has explained that in his invented dialect at the start of *Baudolino* he 'had in mind Western readers who were in some way acquainted with Latin expressions even if they had not studied Latin'. However, this caused severe problems for his Russian translator, who ended up having to render the Latin phrases in old Slavonic to get the same effect.

Had Tolkien been writing at the end of the twentieth century, and for a global rather than primarily British audience, it is possible that he would have taken account of the different cultural background of his readership, much as Eco's Russian translator had to, and made different choices again. The surprise he expressed in interviews of the late 1960s at the popularity of his book in the United States is evidence of Tolkien's Anglo-centric intentions. When creating the *Star Wars* universe for a global audience in the 1970s, George Lucas used the dead Inca language Quechua to represent the speech of one of his alien species, and adopted variations on Sanskrit, Zulu and other tongues to represent the biological and cultural diversity of his creation; the Ewoks, for example, speak gibberish in a proto-Hindi. It is likely that had he been writing for a more multi-cultural setting or audience, Tolkien would have made a similar decision.

This concept of 'translation' is a useful one when it comes to analysing the process of adapting a work for a different medium. Eco explains that 'translation is not only concerned with such matters as "equivalence" in meaning . . . it is also concerned with the more or less indispensable "equivalences" in the substance of expression . . . Translators are in theory bound to identify each of the relevant textual levels . . . to save all of them . . . and to put them in the same relationship with each other as they are in the original text.' This is not always possible, simply because different languages and different media do not always have exact equivalences. There is no novelistic equivalent to the cinematic montage sequence and no true cinematic equivalent of a novel written in first person (although attempts have been made, notably *Dark Passage*, 1947), just as there is not an English equivalent to the German word *Sehnsucht*, or (originally) a word for 'God' in Basque. No matter how good the translation, Mishima's writing rendered in any language other than Japanese loses some of its subtlety and beauty, as does Shakespeare in any language other than English, Tolstoy not in Russian, Goethe not in German, Proust not in French, Cervantes not in Spanish, or even Chaucer in Modern rather than Middle English, and so on.

The trick in translating fiction is to retain as much as possible the feel of the original as well as ensuring that the sense remains, despite the switch to another linguistic and/or cultural system. People who do not have English as their native tongue (and even many who do) may miss the subtleties of Shakespeare's language when they see a performance of *King Lear*, especially if it is performed in a language other than English, but the story and characters will remain the same, and will be as tragically entertaining nonetheless. Even when details of the story are altered, it is rare today to have critics or audiences complain too vocally, as long as the substance of what the play is about remains the same.

In 'translating' a written work of fiction into a film, things do not always work quite the same way. Baz Luhrmann's 1996 film version of *William Shakespeare's Romeo + Juliet* shifts the action to modern America, loads it up with flashy visuals, and replaces swords with guns, but was applauded by many critics as a faithful adaptation because, in almost every sense, it is. Equally, Arthur Laurentis's musical version, *West Side Story* (1961), turns the Montagus and Capulets into 1950s New York street gangs the Jets and the Sharks. *Othello* was originally set in sixteenth-century Venice, but critically lauded versions of the play have relocated the action to the American Civil War, India during Partition, Apartheid-era South Africa, and a Manchester police station in 2002. Verdi's operatic version, *Otello*, has likewise been well-received since its debut in 1887, despite its alterations to Shakespeare's tale (which was in any case itself based on earlier source material). But these adaptations are all from works of fiction that were originally intended for performance – unlike *The Lord of the Rings*.

Adapting a novel for the stage or for film presents all sorts of additional problems. Yet even here, further liberties have been taken with the stories than would have been necessitated through simple 'translation' for the screen. Versions of Dickens's *Great Expectations* have relocated to modern America, a version of *A Christmas Carol* exists where Bob Cratchet is played by Kermit the Frog and Dickens himself by the Great Gonzo. Chaucer's *The Pardoner's Tale* has been very successfully updated to contemporary Edinburgh in *Shallow Grave* (Danny Boyle, 1994). No adaptation of Tolkien's work has yet taken such liberties with setting and style, replacing Aragorn's broken sword with a jammed machine gun, Mordor with Bombay, Arwen with Miss Piggy, or having Frodo pirouette his way into the Cracks of Doom (although apparently there is a musical stage version being prepared as this book is being written). We should perhaps, for now at least, count ourselves lucky.

Ignoring the extreme liberties that can and have been taken with extant literature in its transition to the cinema, one major difference between books and the films they are 'translated' into is simply length. The average novel is several hundred pages long and would take many hours to read, even for fast readers; even the longest of mainstream film releases will rarely top four hours, with three and a half generally being seen as the maximum that an audience is prepared to sit still for. *The Lord of the Rings* is, ignoring the appendices, a little over 1,000 pages in length; this takes Rob Inglis, in his excellent unabridged reading of the book, 52 hours to get through. By contrast, the BBC Radio version clocks in at around 13 hours; Jackson's films, combined, run to around 10 hours (depending on the versions you choose to watch); Bakshi's animated version of the first two-thirds(ish) of the book takes about two hours. In different media, different lengths are acceptable; while one might be willing to spend 52 hours reading a book, there are few cinemagoers that would be prepared to sit through a film that takes a similar length of time to watch.

Film has the advantage over the written word of using sound and images to convey in a matter of seconds a level of detailed information about a scene that would take an author several paragraphs to explain (the process in writing technically referred to as hypotyposis). This explains much of the reduced running-time. In regular translation between languages, the translator's understanding of both the source text and culture and the translation's intended audience is paramount to its success. Here, sensitive alterations are often necessary to retain the essential meaning of the original in its new form: 'In order to make the "deep" story of a chapter or of an entire novel detectable, translators are entitled to change several "surface" stories [or details].' It is a question of deciding which is more important, the actual characteristics of Tom Bombadil (his body-language, choice of words and so on), or the broader concepts of the environmentalist, ancient, harmonious ways of existence he represents. As long as these concepts remain in some form, the most important 'deep' story of that particular section of the book has survived, and this is far more important to the nature of the story than any number of jolly creatures in bright clothes that enjoy singing of a morning.

The major disadvantage of using sound and images rather than descriptive text is that what can, on the page, remain vague and implicit, becomes concrete and explicit on screen. Less room is available for the audience to interpret a scene as they wish, and subtexts that on the page remain subtle can find themselves overemphasised when rendered in a different medium. By the very act of filming a scene from a book, no matter how faithfully it adheres to the original text, the film-makers are compelled to force a particular visual interpretation on the audience. With a book like *The Lord of the Rings*, where descriptions are not so much visual as tonal, and no characters ever find themselves physically described in more than the vaguest of terms, such visual rendering threatens to become even more intrusive than usual. (Tolkien, incidentally, removed several descriptive adjectives from later printings of *The Hobbit* – notably the assertion that Gandalf was short of stature.) For your authors, the Boromir of the Jackson version is far closer to the noble, civilised figure we both (separately) imagined than the fur-clad, bearded demi-Viking of the Bakshi version. Yet from the physical description given of the character in the text (which is non-existent; he is simply described as both proud and tall (Book II, Chapter II)), it is impossible to say which is closer to Tolkien's vision. It is only metatextual knowledge of Tolkien's intentions and interests that makes the Bakshi visualisation seem unlikely to us, not anything revealed in *The Lord of the Rings* itself. Tolkien himself admitted that he did not visualise his characters closely, so this is hardly a surprise: 'I've a very strong visual imagination, but it's not so strong in other points. I doubt if many authors visualise very closely faces and voices.'

No matter how closely described a particular character or place may be, once it is rendered visually, alterations are inevitably going to be identified by those who have perceived that which is being described differently. The decision by Peter Jackson to enlist the aid of respected Tolkien artists Alan Lee and John Howe to produce concept sketches and initial character, costume and set designs, was therefore one of his most sensible moves. By basing the look of his Middle-earth on the style of Lee and Howe, whose illustrations have adorned the pages of innumerable editions of the author's works, in one fell swoop Jackson was able to bring *his* Middle-earth's visual style in line with that of a huge number of fans whose impressions of Tolkien's world had been shaped by the work of those artists. One of the few visual renditions of an aspect of *The Lord of the Rings* that is constant in all the various visual interpretations (including the Tolkien-inspired paintings and drawings by Lee, Howe and others) is the gates at the entrance to the Mines of Moria. Why? Because Tolkien himself provided a sketch of them. Unless he had done the same for every location, character and prop in his story, there could never be a consensus on how a particular thing should look. The combination of the designs of Alan Lee and John Howe is the closest it was possible to get to this consensus – hence the decision to use them.

The same difficulty of rendering a work of fiction in the way the audience imagines it is present with sound. A play, or indeed a reading of a book, can have its significance radically altered by the emphasis the actor chooses to place on particular words and phrases. No matter how expert an author is in the use of punctuation and grammar, it is rarely possible to ensure that every reader reads a particular sentence in the same way. The line 'To be or not to be' from *Hamlet* is a classic case in point. Depending on the actor's interpretation, this can sound mournful, angry, frustrated, hysterical, confused, or have any number of other emotions imposed upon it. The delivery of the surrounding lines can, through the alteration of the context, further change the potential meanings of the line, as precisely why Hamlet is contemplating suicide is never made explicit in the text (although, to be fair, considering the circumstances it is probably any number of reasons).

In the 1981 BBC Radio adaptation of *The Lord of the Rings*, Robert Stephens, a superb and experienced actor, plays Aragorn as an aloof, single-minded, apparently humourless character, with none of the frailty and humanity that is present in Viggo Mortensen's portrayal; the version voiced by John Hurt in the Bakshi film has different emphases again. Ignoring the alterations in the scripts of the three versions, the actors' vocal delivery alone is enough to ensure that they have created different versions of the same character. Yet much of the dialogue they speak is lifted straight from the book. Novels can afford to be ambiguous when it comes to specifics; dramatisations find it a lot harder, simply due to the nature of the medium.

What makes a good adaptation is much the same as what makes a good translation: retaining the essential meaning of the work even while peripheral meanings may be lost in the process of switching between media or language. Thanks to the nature of the change, and the inability to retain every ambiguity of the original text, certain aspects will have to be exaggerated over others. This is a point of which Tolkien was more than aware, as he explained that 'The canons of narrative art in any medium cannot be wholly different; the failure of poor films is often precisely in exaggeration, and in the intrusion of unwarranted matter owing to not perceiving where the core of the original lies.' Let it not be forgotten that Tolkien himself was an accomplished translator of Anglo-Saxon, and had much experience of the difficulties of retaining 'the core of the original' himself.

Deciding precisely what is the essential meaning or 'core' of the original is therefore the central task of anyone attempting any form of adaptation. This is easier with some works than with others. Although a long, structurally complex book, *The Lord of the Rings* is, at its heart, arguably rather simple: it is a tale of good versus evil. Added to this 'core' theme are numerous other important concepts: the nature of free will, temptation, the loss of traditional ways of life, the destructiveness of pride and ambition, friendship, loyalty, mercy, self-sacrifice, destiny, kingship, love, heroism and duty. These themes are universal; they have their echoes and antecedents in every culture; this is partially why *The Lord of the Rings* has been so successful.

Few readers notice, at least at first, the complexities of the different linguistic and cultural systems on display in Tolkien's book, even if this was his professed primary concern. They are drawn to the central stories of individuals up against great odds, struggling to survive and do what is right, even though they know that the chances of success are minimal. If, as with the proposed 1958 film version, the journey of Frodo is reduced in favour of the big battles that crop up in Aragorn's storyline, much of the 'core' of the book is lost. If, as with the Rankin/Bass version of *The Return of the King*, Aragorn acts for his own glory, not to help Frodo, again much of the 'core' of the story is gone.

There are no comparable alterations in Jackson's version, and all the core themes remain more or less intact – even if they are occasionally shifted around to be expressed at different places in the story, or by different characters. In fact, the decision of Jackson, Walsh and Boyens to emphasise the weaknesses, the humanity, of characters such as Aragorn, Gollum and Faramir, who are effectively one-dimensional in the book, actually enhances one of the central themes of the work.

Tolkien largely presents a world of black and white, good and evil, with few shades of grey. This is in part due to the nature of the tale he was trying to tell: there is little room for ambiguity in myth, which by its very nature usually presents a binary choice for living one's life – the right way and the wrong way. Although there is an apparent clear-cut division between good and evil, where elves are good and orcs are bad, Tolkien himself hints at ambiguity within his world of binary choices, and characters occasionally find themselves torn between the two. Even Frodo, the self-sacrificing hero of the piece, succumbs to temptation at the end and takes the Ring for himself – it is only destroyed, and he is only saved, thanks to Gollum biting it from his finger. Does this mean that Frodo is as bad as the orcs? Of course not: the point is that the Ring is so evil that even someone as pure and noble of heart as Frodo can be corrupted by it.

Despite the idea of internal conflict and temptation being one of the 'core' themes of the book, Tolkien rarely mentions it. Reading *The Lord of the Rings* it comes across very clearly, but if one were to note how often the Ring actually causes characters to wrestle with temptation, it is very rare. It has already been noted how Tom Bombadil is unaffected by the Ring, and the same goes (to slightly lesser extents) for Faramir, Aragorn, Elrond, Merry, Pippin, Legolas and Gimli. Gandalf, Galadriel, Bilbo and Sam are all briefly tempted, but resist the urge. As has been mentioned (see **FARAMIR** in **The Two Towers**), this simply serves to make the Ring seem less of a threat, and thus dampens the story's dramatic tension. Boromir, Gollum and Frodo all actually have to directly face up to their desire for the Ring, and all three succumb to the temptation.

In Jackson's version, the Ring is a constant, conscious presence, tempting everyone who sees it. Merry, Pippin, Legolas and Gimli remain unaffected, but they are never shown to come into close contact with the Ring – even Elrond and Aragorn look somewhat disconcerted by its presence when it gets close to them, and Gandalf and Galadriel reject the possibility of getting any closer to it than is necessary. Boromir becomes obsessed and corrupted by the Ring only after he accidentally comes close to touching it by picking it up by its chain on the mountainside; Bilbo is the only character to have actually touched the Ring who is strong enough to reject it. This, apart from Bilbo's response, is not technically a faithful rendition of the story as written. Yet this heightening of the Ring's malevolence is both dramatically more powerful and helps make one of Tolkien's principle themes more clear (see **THE RING** in **The Return of the King**). It is therefore a more than justifiable alteration, and could arguably be claimed as an improvement upon the vagueness of the original.

Tolkien's book is called *The Lord of the Rings*, and it is the Ring that is the principle protagonist and catalyst of the story, but the author himself frequently seems to have forgotten this. For large passages the Ring is forgotten, or becomes of secondary importance – such as during the journey through Bombadil's lands to Bree, the passage through the Mines of Moria, and the whole of Book III as Aragorn and company traipse around Rohan. Another central aspect of the book is the concept of *The Return of the King*, yet this is also frequently understated in the original text. In the book, Aragorn has already accepted his birthright and had Narsil reforged by the time the Fellowship leave Rivendell; it is seemingly only a matter of time before he arrives in Gondor to claim his throne.

One might be forgiven for wondering what all the fuss is about. Why must the quest be Frodo's when Sam and Faramir both show themselves to be equally capable of resisting the Ring's temptations? Why didn't Aragorn have his ancestral sword reforged and go to Minas Tirith to lead the armies of Gondor earlier, while Sauron's forces were still weak?

Jackson's film addresses both these problems with the original more than adequately. The Ring is more evil and corrupting in the New Line Cinema films than it ever was on the page, and the return of the King is far more symbolically significant – but this is not a distortion of Tolkien's aims. The professor intended the Ring to be pure evil, the physical embodiment of temptation, and Aragorn's return was based upon the Christian prophecy of Jesus' return on Judgement Day, but he let his writing run away with him. His book became so long, and he came up with so many subsidiary ideas, that the central themes frequently became submerged, only to surface occasionally – as with Boromir's madness, Sam's brief temptation, and Frodo's final surrender to the Ring's power. From his other writings, it is very apparent that the plot that Tolkien was most concerned with was that of the Ring, yet large sections of his story involve hobbits getting lost in the woods, and a distant country having problems with orcs. Jackson has restored the Ring to its rightful place, while retaining, in essence at least, the majority of the other subplots and concepts.

It is no mean feat to take a 1,000-page book, packed with numerous different cultural and linguistic elements, various subplots and themes, which is also a sequel to another book, and furthermore has a lifetime's worth of additional backstory and explanatory notes on every conceivable aspect of the world in which the tale takes place, and turn it into a coherent series of films. When you add to this the fact that the book had, over the previous fifty years, been read by tens of millions of people, and built up hundreds of thousands of often obsessively loyal fans, all with their own interpretations of the myriad twists and turns of the tale, it becomes clear that the sheer scale of the task facing Jackson and his team as they set out on their attempt to adapt *The Lord of the Rings* back in 1995 was immense.

The New Line Cinema trilogy was not just the most ambitious film project of all time from a technical standpoint; it was arguably also the most ambitious adaptation of all time. When *Gone With the Wind* was adapted for the screen back in 1939, tens of thousands of people had read the original novel. However, it had only been out for three years and had not sunk into the pop-cultural mix to anything like the extent that *The Lord of the Rings* had in the forty years between its publication and Peter Jackson's decision to film it. That's still ignoring the fact that *Gone With the Wind* is a fairly straightforward tale of love and war; Margaret Mitchell's novel, unlike Tolkien's, did not feature such difficult-to-render concepts as wizards, orcs and trolls, and was nowhere near as psychologically or morally complex.

Jackson could easily have faced a massive backlash from fans and critics alike, and it is clear from interviews given shortly after the project was announced that he was more than aware of this. Inevitably, there have been angry complaints from some quarters, and innumerable Internet message boards have been packed out with fans screaming blue murder about changes (both real and imagined) ever since the project was first rumoured. Some of these criticisms have been valid, others have been less so; some have been based on a misreading of the book in the first place. It was also interesting to note how, over the period in which the films were released, some self-proclaimed 'die-hard' Tolkien fans managed to appropriate certain alterations made in the Jackson films and refer to some of the films' interpretations of the story – notably the relationship between Faramir and Denethor – as if they were present in the original text.

What many fans and critics alike have failed to grasp is one simple fact: no film adaptation can ever be the same as the book upon which it is based. All it can ever do is try to retain as much of the book as is possible within the dramatic logic and storytelling techniques that form the medium that it is an example of. Above all, it can try to remain faithful to what the book is about – not just to the plot, but to the 'core' of the material. This Jackson and his team have more than accomplished.

The films are not perfect, but then – if we are honest with ourselves – neither are the books. Tolkien himself admitted that 'there were some frightful mistakes in grammar, which from a Professor of English Language and Lit are rather shocking', and in the Foreword to the second edition he acknowledged that it was not perfect and, even after revision, errors (some bigger than others) remained. Of those criticisms the films did receive from mainstream film critics, the majority stemmed from the original text, not from any innovation of Jackson or his team. Many could be put down to the intellectual snobbery that greeted *The Lord of the Rings* on its initial publication, so well expressed by WH Auden: 'I can only suppose that some people object to Heroic Quests and Imaginary Worlds on principle ... That a man like Mr Tolkien [or, indeed, Mr Jackson] ... should lavish such incredible pains upon a genre which is, for them, trifling by definition, is, therefore, very shocking.'

On a technical level, the praise for Jackson's films was almost unanimous. The special effects were, bar the occasional minor glitch, among the best ever before seen; the locations selected were stunning; the costumes and props were expertly realised, and far more detailed than strictly necessary; the fight choreography was brutal and fast; the editing was always effective and occasionally inspired, especially considering the vast amount of footage; the cinematography was fluid and idiosyncratic, perfectly comple-menting the action on screen; Howard Shore's score improves on each subsequent listening, creating a soundscape that can exist as a symphonic recreation of Middle-earth in its own right. Techni-cally, the films are a masterpiece – a fact that has been reflected in the innumerable awards they have received.

Tolkien used language as a tool to create an impression of a wider world, and more extensive history, than that immediately relevant to his tale. The Jackson films use costumes, set design, special effects, camera movement and music *in addition* to the various languages of Middle-earth – which are, in any case, far more evocative when spoken aloud by actors trained in their pronunciation than when read by a layman, thanks to the addition of dialects and accents within the characters' speech. In the book, only Sam's dialogue among that of the hobbits hints of a different accent, and thus of additional social complexities beneath the surface glimpse that Tolkien affords us of the Shire's way of life; in Jackson's films, all four principle hobbits have distinct styles of speech. Is this idea present in the original text? No. Is it faithful to what Tolkien was setting out to achieve? Entirely.

To some this may sound like sacrilege but, if anything, the New Line Cinema trilogy is better, on a narrative level, than the original book upon which it is based. The films concentrate on the central plots of the original book – Aragorn's journey to reclaim his throne and Frodo's journey to destroy the Ring. In the book, these are often lost for chapter after chapter. In terms of retaining some sense of narrative and temporal coherence on film, Jackson's decision to intercut the disparate storylines is eminently sensible, and demonstrates the interrelationship of the two heroes' separate efforts to defeat Sauron far more clearly than the book.

It is not just in terms of structure that Jackson's films improve the narrative of *The Lord of the Rings*. The cutting of the Tom Bombadil sequences is the most obvious, but others make just as much sense. By removing Prince Imrahil, Beregond, the Dúnedan and the men of the South who come to the aid of Minas Tirith at the Battle of the Pelennor Fields, the Jackson films cut back on the confusion that is rampant throughout Tolkien's multiple-character, multiple-army rendition of the action. The decision to play up the schizophrenic nature of Gollum, only briefly hinted at in the book, and thus turn the character from one with an indeterminate malevolence into a more complex and sympathetic figure, creates far more interest in the Frodo story-line, which in the book often risks seeming flat and predictable. Likewise, Frodo's growing identification with and sympathy for Gollum (and increasing alienation and eventual rejection of Sam) adds psychological complexity to that plot strand, intensifies the impression of the Ring's corruptive powers, makes the conclusion of the quest less certain, and is extrapolated entirely from passages contained within the original.

By delaying Aragorn's acceptance of his fate, that character also becomes more complex, and thus more interesting than the classic heroic archetype he is in the original. The heightening of the varying notions of fatherhood and family displayed by Théoden, Denethor and Elrond likewise adds a more human touch to characters that are, in the book, far more straightforward. Even the greater emphasis on the growing friendly rivalry between Legolas and Gimli, which is again present in the book but not greatly explored, creates an additional focus for audience interest, and thus involvement in the story. The decision to cut the conclusion of the Saruman storyline from the theatrical edition of *The Return of the King* is the only one that risks causing any narrative problems, as the audience is in danger of wondering what has happened to him while the action continues to unfold elsewhere. But the rest of the Saruman storyline in the Jackson films actually improves on what is, in the book, a very sketchily outlined character, whose motives remain unclear, and who keeps almost as much to the periphery of the action as Saruman himself (see **THE ENEMY** in **The Return of the King**). The problems with the alterations to the Farimir storyline have been dealt with elsewhere (see **THE STEWARD** in **The Return of the King**).

In short, the introduction or expansion of emotional, psychological and cultural complexities to Jackson's version of *The Lord of the Rings* that were not wholly present or obvious in the original makes both its characters and its storylines more interesting. The films cut out the less well realised aspects of the story, while retaining a feel for a broader world beyond the on-screen action, and expanding aspects of the book which Tolkien hinted at but then either ignored or failed to develop further. They have rendered visually characters and places which Tolkien failed to describe in detail, based upon pre-existing artwork that has subconsciously helped shape many of Tolkien's readers' visualisations of the book, thus helping to include as many individual ideas of how Middle-earth 'should' look as is surely possible. They have given music to 'songs' that were more poems on the page, and by extension given distinct sounds to places which previously were silent. In the process, the Jackson films have secured themselves a place in the re-creation not just of the look and sound of *The Lord of the Rings*, but also of Middle-earth itself. This fleshing out of the world he had created into dimensions that simply do not exist within the dramatic furniture of prose fiction would surely only have been pleasing to Tolkien.

It was Tolkien's conceit that Middle-earth and *The Lord of the Rings* were somehow real. What Peter Jackson did was to make it more real, for more people, than anyone since Tolkien himself. As well as bridging the divide between Tolkien's apparently irreconcilable notions of 'cash' and 'kudos', Jackson, Walsh and

Boyens kept faith with the book's spirit, retained the 'core' of the work that Tolkien had created along with many of the details, broadened its narrative complexity, and brought it to the attention of more people than ever in the process.

INDEX OF QUOTATIONS

13 'Tolkien's own . . .' Isaacs, Neil D (1968) 'On The Possibilities of Writing Tolkien Criticism', in *Tolkien and the Critics*, Notre Dame, USA, Notre Dame University Press, p. 7.

14 'fantastically badly written' Bayley, John quoted in AN Wilson (2001) 'Tolkien was not a writer', *Daily Telegraph*, 24 November.

14–15 'No fiction . . .' Auden, WH (1954) 'The Hero Is a Hobbit', *The New York Times*, 31 October.

15 'Painful . . . sillification' Carpenter, Humphrey (1981) *The Letters of JRR Tolkien*, London, HarperCollins (Letter No. 198).

THE HOBBIT (1977)

19 'I found . . .' Abrams quoted in Plesset, Ross (2002) 'The Animated Films', *Cinefantastique*, Vol. 34, No. 1 (February).

20 'All Japanese . . .' Abrams quoted in Plesset, Ross (2002) 'The Animated Films', *Cinefantastique*, Vol. 34, No. 1 (February).

21 'a mythology . . .' Carpenter, Humphrey (1977) *JRR Tolkien – A Biography*, London, HarperCollins, p. 126.

30 'how such . . .' Sheridan, Bob (1978) 'The Hobbit or There & Back Again', *Starburst*, Vol. 1, No. 4 (November).

30 'conjured more imagination' Freedman, Jeff (1977) 'The Hobbit', *Hollywood Reporter*, Vol. 249, No. 14 (29 November).

JOURNEY TO THE CROSSROADS: THE STORY OF THE FILM RIGHTS

35 'welcome the idea . . .' Carpenter, Humphrey (1981) *The Letters of JRR Tolkien*, London, HarperCollins (Letter No. 198).

36 'very profitable . . .' Carpenter, Humphrey (1981) *The Letters of JRR Tolkien*, London, HarperCollins (Letter No. 202).

36 'murdered' Carpenter, Humphrey (1981) *The Letters of JRR Tolkien*, London, HarperCollins (Letter No. 210).

36 'I feel . . .' Carpenter, Humphrey (1981) *The Letters of JRR Tolkien*, London, HarperCollins (Letter No. 297).

36   'He has cut . . .' Carpenter, Humphrey (1981) *The Letters of JRR Tolkien*, London, HarperCollins (Letter No. 210).

36   'the irritation . . .' Carpenter, Humphrey (1981) *The Letters of JRR Tolkien*, London, HarperCollins (Letter No. 270).

37   'Can a tale . . .' Carpenter, Humphrey (1981) *The Letters of JRR Tolkien*, London, HarperCollins (Letter No. 194).

37   'without any . . .' Carpenter, Humphrey (1981) *The Letters of JRR Tolkien*, London, HarperCollins (Letter No. 210).

37   'willfully wrong . . .' Carpenter, Humphrey (1981) *The Letters of JRR Tolkien*, London, HarperCollins (Letter No. 297).

37   'quite incapable . . .' Carpenter, Humphrey (1981) *The Letters of JRR Tolkien*, London, HarperCollins (Letter No. 210).

38   'There isn't . . .' Bakshi quoted in Robinson, Tasha (2001) 'Ralph Bakshi', *Onion AV Club*, 6 December.

38   'spine of the story' Jackson quoted in McKinlay, Bob (2003) 'In the Seventh Year The Lord of the Rings rests', *New York Times*, 14 December.

40   'The words . . .' Tolkien quoted in Norman, Philip (1967) 'The Prevalence of Hobbits', *New York Times*, 15 January.

JRR TOLKIEN'S THE LORD OF THE RINGS (1978)

45   'about the . . .' Bakshi quoted in Robinson, Tasha (2001) 'Ralph Bakshi', *Onion AV Club*, 6 December.

45   'heard that . . .' Bakshi quoted in Robinson, Tasha (2001) 'Ralph Bakshi', *Onion AV Club*, 6 December.

45   'like a . . .' Bakshi quoted in Modlin, E Nelson (1978) 'Dateline Spain', *Screen International*, No. 137, 6 May.

46   'nevertheless more . . .' Bakshi quoted in Vito, Steve (1978) 'The Hobbits', *American Film*, Vol. 3, No. 10 (September).

46   'Tolkien asks . . .' Bakshi quoted in Murdoch, Alan (1978) 'The Lord of the Rings', *Starburst*, Vol. 1, No. 9 (March).

46   'So now . . .' Bakshi quoted in Robinson, Tasha (2001) 'Ralph Bakshi', *Onion AV Club*, 6 December.

46   'The evil . . .' Bakshi quoted in Vito, Steve (1978) 'The Hobbits', *American Film*, Vol. 3, No. 10 (September).

47   'about fifteen . . .' Bakshi quoted in Vito, Steve (1978) 'The Hobbits', *American Film*, Vol. 3, No. 10 (September).

55 'designed to . . .' Bakshi quoted in Brune, Scott (1978) 'The Lord of the Rings', *Cinefantastique*, Vol. 8, No. 1 (Winter).

55 'the pressure . . .' Bakshi quoted in Modlin, E Nelson (1978) 'Dateline Spain', *Screen International*, No. 137 (6 May).

55 'Very proud . . .' Bakshi quoted in Murdoch, Alan (1978) 'The Lord of the Rings', *Starburst*, Vol. 1, No. 9 (March).

56 'most devastating . . .' Bakshi quoted in *Empire*, No. 151 (January 2002).

57 'major visual flaws' Stuart, Alexander (1979) 'The Lord of the Rings', *Films and Filming*, Vol. 25, No. 10 (July).

57 'an adaptation . . .' Bilbow, Marjorie (1979) 'The Lord of the Rings', *Screen International*, No. 198 (July).

57 'confusing . . .' 'Har', 'Hobbits? What are Hobbits?' *Variety*, 8 November 1978.

58 'rip up . . .' Canby, Vincent (1978) 'Animated Mythology', *New York Times*, 14 November.

58 'ended just . . .' Atkins, Ian (2002) 'The Lord of the Rings', *Starburst*, No. 282 (February).

58 'It was . . .' Bakshi quoted in Robinson, Tasha (2001) 'Ralph Bakshi', *Onion AV Club*, 6 December.

58 'I told . . .' Bakshi quoted in Robinson, Tasha (2001) 'Ralph Bakshi', *Onion AV Club*, 6 December.

58 'They screwed . . .' Bakshi quoted in *Empire*, No. 151 (January 2002).

59 'People keep . . .' Bakshi quoted in Robinson, Tasha (2001) 'Ralph Bakshi', *Onion AV Club*, 6 December.

JRR TOLKIEN'S THE RETURN OF THE KING – A TALE OF HOBBITS (1980)

65 'we did . . .' Rankin quoted in Plesset, Ross (2002) 'The Animated Films', *Cinefantastique*, Vol. 34, No. 1 (February).

65 'all sequel rights' Bakshi quoted on www.imdb.com, 12 December 2001.

69 'It was . . .' Rankin quoted in Plesset, Ross (2002) 'The Animated Films', *Cinefantastique*, Vol. 34, No. 1 (February).

166 'I couldn't . . .' Sean Astin quoted in Roston, Tom (2003) '4 Hobbits go into a bar . . .' *Premiere* (US), Vol. 17, No. 4 (Winter).

166 'When people . . .' Sean Astin quoted in Roston, Tom (2003) '4 Hobbits go into a bar . . .' *Premiere* (US), Vol. 17, No. 4 (Winter).

THE GREY HAVENS: CONCLUSION

203 'Many young . . .' Tolkien interviewed by Philip Norman in 'The Prevalence of Hobbits', *New York Times*, 15 January 1967.

205 'It is possible . . .' JRR Tolkien, 'Beowulf: The Monsters and the Critics'.

206 'It is possible . . .' William Caxton, 'Preface' in Thomas Mallory, *Le Morte D'Arthur* (Harmondsworth, Penguin, 1969 edition).

206–7 'prime motive . . .'Foreword to the second edition of *The Lord of the Rings*.

208 'had in mind . . .' Eco, Umberto (2003) *Mouse or Rat? Translation as Negotiation*, London, Weidenfeld & Nicolson, pp. 98–9.

209 'translation is . . .' Eco, Umberto (2003) *Mouse or Rat? Translation as Negotiation*, London, Weidenfeld & Nicolson, p. 30.

211 'In order . . .' Eco, Umberto (2003) *Mouse or Rat? Translation as Negotiation*, London, Weidenfeld & Nicolson, p. 72.

212 'I've a very . . .' Tolkien interviewed by Philip Norman, 'The Prevalence of Hobbits', *New York Times*, 15 January 1967.

213 'The canons . . .' Carpenter, Humphrey (1981) *The Letters of JRR Tolkien*, London, HarperCollins (Letter No. 210).

218 'there were . . .' Tolkien interviewed by Dennis Gerrolt on 'Now Read On . . .' BBC Radio Four, January 1971.

218 'I can . . .' WH Auden, 'At the end of the Quest, Victory' in *New York Times*, 22 January, 1956.

INDEX